The Price of Freedom

Greece in World Affairs, 1939-1953

THE PRICE OF FREEDOM

Greece in World Affairs, 1939-1953

Dimitrios G. Kousoulas

Syracuse University Press—1953

To
BARBARA, my mother
and
MARY, my wife

ACKNOWLEDGMENTS

To ALL THOSE who made the publication of this book possible I am deeply grateful. In particular, my everlasting gratitude goes to:

Archbishop Michael and Ambassador Alexis Kyrou for their moral support;
Professor W. W. Kulski for his invaluable guidance and encouragement throughout the preparation of the manuscript;
Dr. William A. Miller for his indispensable help;
and Miss Patricia Mahon for her assistance in editing.

D. G. K.

CONTENTS

INTRODUCTION

THE FOREIGN POLICY of a country can be defined as the endeavor of its appropriate official agencies to fulfill the purposes of the nation within the framework of world society. Consequently, the main factors which determine the foreign policy of a state are: (1) the nation and its objectives; (2) the world society and its complexities. Neither is static, but both are dynamic, changing continually because of new developments in the national structure, the international balance of power, and in science and technology.

The continuous interplay of these two factors imposes certain limitations on the ability of each nation to accomplish its own aspirations without encroaching upon the rights and interests of other nations. Hence, when a nation overrides the interests of others and attempts to accomplish its own objectives, regardless of the consequences, the usual outcome is either immediate subjugation of the weaker nation or war.

* * * * *

In southeast Europe lies a mountainous peninsula amid sunny islands and sparkling seas. It is Greece. For thousands of years it has been the crossroads of destiny; its people standing on the rocky shores as sentinels of Europe's freedom.

Under the bright sky of Greece democracy was born, as were also the ideals of liberty and human dignity, while art and beauty found their best expression in the miracle of the Golden Age. These developments combined to produce what became known as the Greek Ideal.

The Greek ideal was carried forward from generation to generation by warriors, philosophers, and artists. There were the heroes of Marathon and Salamis and the warriors of Alexander the Great, philosophers and artists of ancient Greece and the Byzantine lawmakers and architects. Then on May 29, 1453, the soldiers of Sultan Mohammed II, the Conqueror,* entered Constantinople, the Queen of all Cities.* The Greek people were driven into the darkness of slavery for almost four centuries. But deep in their hearts, they kept the memory of the Greek Ideal and

*This symbol refers to additional information in Appendix I.

dreamed of the day the two-headed eagle* of the Byzantine emperors would again spread its wings over the dome of Agia Sophia.* This dream furnished inspiration and encouragement during the long years of slavery; then in 1828 after seven years of heroic struggle, the Greek nation broke its chains and took its place among the free nations of the world.*

The Greek people spontaneously founded their foreign policy on the "Great Idea," the restoration of the Byzantine Empire which kept their hearts warm during the long cold night of slavery. Literature, press, education, politics—all responded to the Great Idea without political pressure or propaganda influence.

This movement had as its purpose the liberation of the unredeemed brethren—the Greeks who were still under Ottoman rule; it seemed to be a justified and feasible endeavor. But the time came when the Greeks encountered at the north impenetrable national entities that had grown up during the centuries of Ottoman rule. Then the aspirations and objectives of the Greek nation faced the second element of international relations, the interests of other nations. The road to the north seemed to be closed. Of course, there were still unredeemed brethren in Northern Epirus, but, basically, there were no possibilities for expansion to the north. However, in Asia Minor, on the coastal region lapped by the waves of the Aegean Sea, lived hundreds of thousands of Greeks under Ottoman rule. Moreover, to the East was Constantinople, the sacred cradle of national dreams and the seat of the Byzantine Empire.

At the close of the First World War, Greece was one of the victorious powers. Among those who believed that this was the long expected moment when the old dream would materialize, was E. Venizelos, the great Cretan statesman. But when Venizelos brought home the Treaty of Sèvres*—which formally established the Greater Greece—his reward was a crushing political defeat in the elections of 1920.

During the following two years, King Constantine, who returned from exile, failed in his efforts to cope with the emerging power of the New Turkey. Mustafa Kemal, leader of the Neoturks*—an army officer who distinguished himself in the defense of the Dardanelles during World War I—realized that the era of the Ottoman Empire was gone forever. If Turkey was to survive as an independent state, she must be established on national grounds. But the presence of the Greek Army on the fertile Aegean littoral plains of Asia Minor was incompatible with the interests and survival of a Turkish state. True, the existence of more than a million Greeks in this area was sufficient justification for the solution contained in the Treaty of Sèvres according to the principle of nationalities. But in international relations other factors play a more decisive role—interests and power are often more important than right and justice.

In 1921-1922 the situation at the Asia Minor front was projected upon the following international background. On one side was the Greek nation, exhausted by ten years of continuous fighting,* beginning with the Balkan Wars, and the internal political strife—originated during World War I when a grave rift developed between Venizelos and King Constantine on the issue of Greece's participation in the war.*

On the other side was the Turkish nation with its determined leaders and inspired by a new national idealism; an old nation rejuvenated under the impact of defeat and revolution.

A third group of forces were the Allied Powers of World War I: Britain, France, and Italy. Divided in their interests, opposing each other, they paved the way for the collapse of Greater Greece.

Great Britain, under Lloyd George, had favored a strong Greece as a powerful guard of the Straits and the strategic route of the eastern Mediterranean; now she was reluctant to help Greece enforce the Treaty of Sèvres. Insecure political conditions in Greece were undoubtedly among the reasons for Britain's new policy. If Greece were unable to safeguard the Straits, Turkey might be willing to assume this role, although the rapprochment of Turkey and Soviet Russia in 1921 caused the British to question the feasibility of such an arrangement.

France, having special interests in the areas south of Asia Minor, was anxious to establish friendly relations with the new Turkey.

Italy, aspiring to expand eastward in due time, and already in possession of the Dodecanese Islands—occupied by Italy during the Tripolitanian War in 1911—naturally favored a Turkish victory that would result in a weak and crippled Greece.

In March 1921, a Turko-Italian agreement was concluded and a Franco-Turkish protocol was signed, confirmed by the Treaty of Ankara in October. These agreements virtually scrapped the Treaty of Sèvres.

Successful warfare cannot be waged without the will to win it; and in 1922 the will of the Greeks to win the war in Asia Minor was reduced to a minimum. In August 1922, the adventure was brought to an end;* the Greek Army collapsed, and the Turks, in their advance, uprooted the Greek populations of Asia Minor. Hellenism, which had flourished there for over two thousand years, was obliterated in blood and fire. The magnificent dream of a new Byzantine Empire seemed to be gone forever. The two-headed eagle, wounded and bleeding, sought shelter in the ruins of the Parthenon.

The years that followed brought humiliation, confusion, and disillusionment. In the economic field, the world-wide depression rendered it more and more difficult for the Greek government to secure a tolerable standard of living for its people. The concentration of over one million

PART ONE

The Brewing Tempest

THE BREWING TEMPEST

IT IS PROPER to start this work with an account of Albania's occupation by the Fascists on Good Friday of April 7, 1939. This fateful move of Fascist Italy was the first of a series of chain reactions.What followed virtually changed the path of Balkan history, while the consequences still dominate present conditions in Greece and the Balkans, if not a much wider area.

In preparing this first part, the author has drawn upon original sources of information such as the Proceedings and Documents of the International Military Tribunal of Nuremberg, the Diaries and Diplomatic Papers of Count Ciano, the Memoirs of Winston Churchill, publications of the League of Nations and of the United States Department of State, Greek official documents on the war with Italy, the German White Book on the attack against Greece and Yugoslavia, and others.

The first part of this work covers the period between the Italian invasion in Albania and the occupation of Greece by the Germans on May 29, 1941.

CHAPTER ONE

ITALY IN ALBANIA

WHILE THE EFFORTS of Greece to establish an understanding with Turkey and to improve friendly relations with Yugoslavia were advancing successfully and the existing tension slowly changed to limited cooperation within the Balkan Entente, a new source of anxiety emerged on the west coast of the Balkan peninsula.

THE ORIGIN OF THE ALBANIAN STATE

Albania was first established as an independent state by the London Protocol of August 5, 1913, through the initiative of the Italian and Austrian diplomacy. These two powers, had rival interests in the Balkans but were unable to accomplish their objectives because of the opposition of the other powers. Thus, they combined their efforts at the London Conference following the Balkan Wars of 1912-1913 in hindering Greece and Serbia from extending their borders farther on the west coast of the Balkan peninsula and the first Albanian state was established. However, the abortively born child of the London Protocol soon proved to be suffering from grave anemia. An international settlement is unable to overcome economic insufficiency, the absence of spiritual leadership, and the lack of national ideals and history; these elements constitute the necessary foundations for the existence of a country as an independent state.

The Albanian society was largely based on a semi-feudal and semi-tribal system under the omnipotence of the local Bey; consequently, the internal development of the Albanian state was bound to pass through armed conflicts, anarchy, and bankruptcy. Finally, in 1925, Ahmed Zogou Bey succeeded in gaining power. He was a former tribe-leader himself, and soon realized that the only way to preserve his regime was the formation of a strong army capable of suppressing the forces of the Bey. He gathered an armed force which together with the increased gendarmerie absorbed annually more than forty-five percent of the national budget. It soon became clear that the national resources were insufficient to bear such a luxury. A strong army was obviously indispensable for the maintenance of power; but if it could save the regime from subversion, it could not save it from economic collapse. On the contrary, its very

9

existence speeded up bankruptcy. Ahmet Zogou found himself caught in this predicament from the first moment of his ascendancy to power. The only feasible solution was economic assistance from abroad. He first turned to Yugoslavia which had helped him to seize power, but Yugoslavia could not afford to finance such a costly enterprise. He turned next to the League of Nations; but according to its regulations, that organization could not recommend an unsound loan. Thus, the only course of action which remained for Zogou was to appeal to a big power, willing to risk funds in this uncertain enterprise in exchange, of course, for preeminent influence. Austria, together with Italy one of the godfathers of Albania, had been defeated in World War I and was eliminated from the picture. Consequently, the support of Zogou was assumed by the power which for a long time had been waiting for this opportunity; this power was Italy.

ITALIAN POLICIES IN ALBANIA

Italy had pressed for the creation of an Albanian state; but she was not interested in the preservation of Albanian independence. During World War I, while negotiating her entrance into the war on the side of the Allies, Italy proposed the partition of Albania among Greece, Montenegro, Serbia, and Italy. A small part was to be carved out to become an Albanian state under the protectorate of Rome. This solution was accepted by Britain, France, and Imperial Russia as a way to end the unfortunate experiment, begun in 1913, to create an Albanian state; subsequently, a secret treaty was signed in London on August 13, 1915. However, in 1917, Italy adjusted her policies in favor of an Italian protectorate over the whole of Albania. This new drive soon appeared unlikely to meet with success, owing to the objections of the Allied Powers. Italy then gradually switched to the idea of an independent Albania on the condition that Italian pre-eminent interests in this area should be formally recognized by the powers concerned. Finally, the Geneva Declaration (November 3, 1921), signed by the British, French, and Italian governments, formally recognized that ". . . any violation of the Albanian frontiers constitutes a menace to the strategical security of Italy, and . . . any intervention . . . for the purpose of restoring the territorial frontiers of Albania should be delegated to Italian troops. . . ."

Thus, across the Adriatic already existed the power which was ready to take advantage of the awkward situation in which Zogou found himself. In 1925, the Albanian government signed a contract with the Italian Railways granting them exclusive rights to exploit Albanian oilwells. In the following years the Italian government succeeded in spinning, step by step, an economic web over Albania making that country from 1926 to

1939 virtually an Italian dependency. This was not unexpected; on the contrary, in view of the inherent weaknesses of Albania, it is rather surprising that she was able to maintain even a nominal independence until 1939. Probably it was due to the strategic importance attached to Albania by Greece, Yugoslavia and other, non-Balkan, powers.

As Italy gradually but firmly extended her hold over Albania like a giant octopus, the Balkan states and especially Greece and Yugoslavia realized that a new threat was brewing over the Balkans. They had no illusions concerning the expansionistic tendencies of Mussolini's regime, while the formation of the Berlin-Rome Axis in the fall of 1936 made the menace more and more formidable. But the international climate of appeasement had a disintegrating impact on the policies of the Balkan states. Both Yugoslavia and Greece followed a policy of non-provocation and appeasement of Italy hoping that the burden of Italian expansionism would fall on the other's shoulders. As a result the Balkan Entente specifically excluded any obligation for mutual assistance among the partners in case of an external, non-Balkan, aggression.

PREPARING FOR OCCUPATION

At the beginning of 1939, Mussolini clearly realized that the moment for the ultimate trial of strength drew close; as a result he decided to tighten his grip upon Albania. As Ciano reveals in his *Diaries* (p. 23),[1] the decision for the occupation of Albania was taken before February 6, 1939, and the zero day for the operation was to be some time during the Easter Week. However, several political events during February and March temporarily slowed down the preparations. The dismissal of Stoyadinovich, Premier of Yugoslavia, in Febraury 1939, was one of these events. This incident was interpreted by Mussolini as "a veritable coup d'état on the part of the Yugoslavian Regent who wanted to prevent the strengthening of the Fascist dictatorship in Yugoslavia." Stoyadinovich recognized the existing ties within the Balkan Entente, but he advocated each member should be free to establish "an understanding" with other neighboring countries, Italy, of course being one of them. This policy was actually a powder keg under the edifice of the Balkan Entente, already weakened by the half-hearted support of its partners. It was evident that Bulgaria, the expansionism of which the Balkan Entente was primarily aimed to check, could not attempt an aggressive act without the cooperation of a big power, Italy, for instance. If a member of the Balkan Entente had committed itself in an agreement of non-aggression with the big power in question, how would it assist a member of the Entente attacked by Bulgaria? Mussolini, of course, favored such a policy which opened the gates to his intrigues.

After the dismissal of Stoyadinovich, Ciano argued that since the operation in Albania should be undertaken without the cooperation or forbearance of Yugoslavia, Italy should act as fast as possible before Yugoslavia had time to strengthen her contacts with France and Britain on political, diplomatic, and military grounds.

However, the operation was not so simple. The German troops were then in Bohemia and Moravia; after the events of March 1939, Germany occupied the remainder of Czechoslovakia and the German agitation in Croatia was intensified. Under these circumstances it was unwise to attempt anything in Albania that might disturb the unity of Yugoslavia. Such an action might give Hitler a pretext to create an *independent* Croatia under German patronage, thus advancing the German positions in the Balkans. Mussolini, impressed by the German successes in Czechoslovakia and the intensification of Hitler's agitation in the Balkans, became temporarilly doubtful about the merits of Italo-German cooperation. In a conversation with Count Ciano on March 19, 1939, they even "worked for the possibility of an understanding with the Western Powers." However, well-timed assurances by Von Mackensen, the German Ambassador in Rome, that Germany "is not at all interested in the Mediterranean and in the fate of Croatia" and that "it recognizes the pre-eminence of Italian interests" led Mussolini to reverse his pro-Western attitude. He stated, according to Ciano's *Diaries* (p. 49), that the communication was quite interesting, although he commented privately, "provided we can believe in it."

Only four days after receiving this communication, Mussolini decided to move more rapidly. He then considered the time for the operation in Albania politically ripe. It was obvious that Germany needed the cooperation of Italy. In Yugoslavia, the successors of Stoyadinovich followed the policies of their predecessor; Greece was virtually isolated, as the Balkan Entente, ironically enough because of the insistence of Greece excluded any obligation for common action in case of aggression by a non-Balkan Power. Moreover, the Italian people, "humiliated by the German successes in Central Europe," as Mussolini believed, should be given for reasons of prestige "satisfaction and compensation: Albania."

Under the supervision of Ciano and the personal direction of Jacomoni, the Italian envoy in Tirana, preparations for the operation were soon well under way. King Zog[2] was presented with new terms, the acceptance of which would bring about the complete subjugation of the country to Italy. Zog, although an able negotiator, vainly attempted to engage the Italians in prolonged negotiations; the Duce was impatient. He insisted that they should strike quickly before any change in the policies of Yugoslavia might occur, and before the Western Powers had time to react effectively.

On April 1, 1939, Sereggi, the new Albanian minister to Rome, called upon Count Ciano. After a thorough examination of the situation, it was decided that Sereggi together with Jacomoni should fly back to Tirana in order to persuade King Zog to accept the Italian terms. "Then, on the pretext that he (Sereggi) was not able to exchange his Albanian money, he had Jacomoni lend him 15,000 lire, a first installment on a bribe." (Ciano p. 57) This is an interesting example of Albanian diplomatic standards and Fascist methods.

One week later, on April 8, the operation was over. King Zog fled overnight to Greece, while the Italian troops entered Tirana. On April 16, 1939, the ceremony of offering the Albanian crown to the King of Italy took place in the Quirinal Palace.

FOOTNOTES

1. *The Ciano Diaries*, (ed. H. Gibson, New York: 1946.) For the convenience of the reader the number of footnotes has been kept to a minimum. The source of quotations or other information is identified by putting the name of the author and the page in parenthesis. If the source is a document or other publication, an abbreviation of the title of the source is used. In both cases, the reader will find complete identification of the source in the Bibliography.

2. Ahmed Bey Zogou was proclaimed King of the Albanians on September 1, 1928, as Zog I, by unanimous vote of a Constituent Assembly.

CHAPTER TWO

THE NEW SITUATION

THE ITALIAN CONQUEST of Albania created extreme anxiety in Yugoslavia and Greece. Yugoslavia faced now Italian troops on both her Albanian and Istrian frontiers with Italy. Both sides of the entrance to the Adriatic were controlled by Italy, while the communications between Yugoslavia and Greece through the Nestos (Vardar) Valley were directly threatened. Greece feared a further Italian coup on the Island of Corfu, while the distance from the Albanian frontier to the port of Salonika is only about 100 miles. The presence of Mussolini's "glorious legions" on the Albanian frontiers was a painful awakening for the Balkan illusionists. The policies of non-provocation and neutrality were bearing their bitter fruits.

POLITICS IN GREECE

Since 1923, Greece had faithfully followed a policy of irreproachable conduct toward Italy. No opportunity to improve the relations between the two nations was overlooked by the successive Greek governments. So strong was the desire of the Greek leaders to avoid any action that might be interpreted by Italy as unfriendly, that Greece expressed specific reservations when she joined the Balkan Entente in 1934. The Greco-Italian Treaty of Friendship, Conciliation and Judicial Settlement signed in Rome on September 23, 1928, was also grounded upon this policy. The sincere hope that, by such tactics, Greece might escape the danger, blurred the appraisal of the international realities by the Greek leaders and replaced the cool-minded approach, which the situation demanded, by wishful thinking. It was forgotten that sentiment plays but a trivial role in international affairs.

With the Fascist armies only one hundred miles from Salonika, the dark cloud of war hung over the Greek nation. But, in those days of agony and distress, the Greeks once again recaptured the forgotten national aim—to defend the national independence at any cost. Beneath the futile partisan dissensions and materialistic cynicism, the deep affection for the beloved fatherland, an affection which was dimly glowing as a spark in the nation's heart, revived and became an immense flame.

In order to comprehend fully the momentous events, which in the winter of 1940-1941 astonished the world, it is necessary to review briefly the political past. Yesterday's and today's actions are always the springboard for tomorrow's events.

The discord, which emanated from the rift between E. Venizelos and King Constantine, during World War I, on the issue of Greece's participation in the war, was aggravated by the defeat in Asia Minor (1922) and by the political unrest and the economic difficulties which followed. The Republic established in 1924, following the abdication of the monarchy, did not operate successfully and proved unable to cope with the pressing national problems facing the country.

The efforts of King George II, King Constantine's son, who returned from exile after a plebiscite in 1935, failed to reconcile the antagonistic political factions. The elections of 1936 produced a political stalemate which enabled the Communist Party (KKE), with only fifteen deputies, to hold the balance between the two main political groups in the Parliament, the Liberals (Venizelists) and the Populists (Monarchists), thus controlling from the backstage the political situation. The deaths of the major political leaders, Venizelos and P. Tsaldaris (Populist), resulted in an unrestrained partisan contention in which each party ignored the interests of the country and intrigued and manuevered for its own immediate political objectives.

On May 1936, *Rizospastis*, the official newspaper of the Greek Communist Party, in acclaiming the success of a general strike in Salonika, where a state of anarchy persisted for twenty-four hours, stated: ". . . From now on the people throughout the country must pour into the streets . . . must seize power. . . ." Greece was driving full speed to repeat the tragic error of Spain. Although the Cabinet tried to gain control of the situation by proposing fixed wages and compulsory arbitration of labor disputes, the uncompromising communist-dominated labor unions reacted by calling a general strike all over the country for August 6, 1936.

At this crucial moment, General Metaxas, who acted as Prime Minister after the death of Premier Demertzis in April, presented to the King for signature decrees dissolving the Parliament, proclaiming martial law and suspending certain articles of the Constitution affecting the personal liberty of the citizens. The King agreed and an autocratic regime was established, the Regime of August Fourth. The proclamation of the dictatorship was a desperate remedy brought about by a desperate situation. The most probable alternative was civil war.[1] Very often sentimental writers have attacked the Metaxas dictatorship. It is not the intent of this writer to express sympathy for authoritarian regimes in any form, but it is a matter of justice to acknowledge that under the firm leadership of King

George and General Metaxas the weak and stricken country was, within four years, regenerated to a degree that enabled it to stand once again among the elite of history. When the world faced the horrible menace of slavery, Greece alone, among the continental states, was able to resist the Italian aggression and delay the Nazi plans to a degree which fatally affected their outcome. Thanks to the resistance of Greece the operation against Russia was postponed by five weeks from the middle of May 1941 to almost the end of June.

In the years that followed the establishment of the August Fourth regime, Metaxas continued the former policies in the international field; that is, reluctant partnership in the Balkan Entente, continuous improvement of relations with Turkey and—to a lesser degree—with Yugoslavia, and a state of equal friendship with the maritime Powers, Britain and Italy and the Continental ones, Germany and France. But it is an old truth that policies directed to please all the parties concerned, eventually please none.

Metaxas embarked on an extensive program of domestic social and economic reforms, and at the same time built up the military forces[2] whose strength and efficiency had reached a dangerously low ebb. However, his regime was not popular. The Greek by nature is a liberal and resents any infringement upon his liberty; he tolerated the Metaxas' regime as an emergency, for a well-developed political sense would not allow him to deceive himself as to the seriousness of the world situation. Still, the Greek people had not yet reached a stage of national unity. But the tremendous shock that swept the country when the news of the Italian invasion of Albania reached Greece, resulted in the emotional unification of the nation and prepared the road for the miracle which astonished the world on that memorable morning of October 28, 1940.

Immediately after the occupation of Albania, the Greek nation as a whole embraced a national policy of tenacity, and rallied to the defense of the country. Metaxas immediately sought assistance from anyone who would provide it, but neither Turkey nor Yugoslavia had any conventional obligation to extend help. The Balkan Entente stopped at the threshold of non-Balkan aggression[3] and all other existing diplomatic arrangements between Greece and these two neighbors had not reached the form of a military alliance. At this point, a brief review of the Greco-Turkish and Greco-Yugoslav relations is necessary.

GRECO-TURKISH RELATIONS IN THE THIRTIES

In 1930, Eleutherios Venizelos, the great Greek statesman, the most devoted soldier of the Great Idea, took the daring step of tearing off the parchment which inspired generations—the parchment of the Great Idea.

For, the age-old hatred between the Greek and the Turkish nations ought to be eradicated. This was the dictum of reason, the policy which emanated from a cool-minded appraisal of the two paramount forces which formulate the foreign policy of any nation at any time—national objectives and international realities. There was no longer justification for Greek aspirations in Asia Minor after the complete uprootal of the Greek population following the exchange of minorities. Greece and Turkey ought to accept their frontiers as permanent for their mutual benefit. Venizelos and Kemal clearly realized that henceforth their common interests were far more powerful than the minor differences dividing the two nations. They had to protect their northern frontiers from Bulgaria and their very existence from Italian imperialism. Their cooperation was also dictated by their historic past; their respective empires, the Byzantine and the Ottoman, established on both sides of the Straits had to retain control of both areas in order to survive; the loss of either foothold had marked the beginning of their decline. This fact has an important bearing upon the relations of these two nations, now living in the same area.

When Venizelos and Ismet Pasha signed the Greco-Turkish Treaty of Friendship, Neutrality, Conciliation, and Arbitration and the accompanying protocol on naval armaments on October 30, 1930, the world received the news with skepticism. In spite of pessimistic predictions, this treaty was strengthened by a Pact of Cordial Friendship on September 14, 1933 in which the parties gave mutual guarantees as to "the inviolability of their common frontiers" (Art. 1), and promised that in all international meetings each would seek "to defend the common and special interests of both Parties" (Art. 3). The Treaty of 1933, valid for ten years, was expanded by an Additional Treaty in April 27, 1938, which was signed in Athens. This latter treaty indicated a more realistic approach to "an unprovoked act of aggression on the part of one or more powers against one of the parties." It bound the other party "to safeguard its neutrality by opposing, if necessary by arms, the use of its territory, by the said power or powers, . . . for the passage of troops, arms or ammunition . . . or the supply of provisions . . . or for the passage of retreating troops or for the purposes of military reconnaissance." (Art. 1) However, even under the terms of this treaty, Turkey had no obligation to give Greece military assistance in case of an external, non-Balkan attack.

GRECO-YUGOSLAV RELATIONS

Since the first quarter of the nineteenth century, when Greece and Serbia regained their independence, a long and undisturbed friendship existed between the two nations. This friendship took the form of a military alliance as early as 1867, when a treaty, signed in Voeslau, near Vienna, provided for common action in case of a Turkish attack. Greece and Serbia also had common interests in Macedonia, where Bulgaria, by propaganda and terrorism, attempted to gain ground among the Christian population of that area, then under Turkish rule. With unusual insight, Greeks and Serbs renounced their claims to respective territories populated by mixed minorities, and chose a solid friendship based on undisputed common frontiers.

Following the end of the First Balkan War (1912-13), during which Greece, Serbia, and Bulgaria combined forces against the Sultan, Bulgaria revealed expansionist tendencies towards certain parts of Macedonia and Thrace, mostly populated by Greeks and Serbs. Although Russia favored the preservation of the Balkan alliance and made efforts to prevent an armed conflict among the allies—Greece, Serbia, and Bulgaria—"Bulgaria, under the influence of Vienna, had already decided upon rupture with Russia and was preparing a surprise attack on the Allies."[4] On June 8-21, 1913, General Savov, the Bulgarian Commander in Chief, telegraphed to the Commander of the Fourth Bulgarian Army:

> . . . Reply with the least possible delay whether the state of the army is such that it can be counted on for successful operations. . . .[5]

On the evening of the 17th, the Bulgarian army attacked the Greco-Serbian positions, but was defeated, and by July 23, King Ferdinand of Bulgaria appealed to the Czar to mediate for an armistice. The aggressive Bulgarian Premier Danev, resigned in despair. Finally, the Peace of Bucharest was signed on August 10, 1913.

While Bulgaria was preparing the attack against her allies, the Greek and Serbian governments, aware of this vicious design, decided to establish the basis for closer cooperation, and on June 1913, signed a new Pact of Alliance. One year later, on May 10, 1914, the two nations settled the issue concerning the use of the Salonika harbor in Northern Greece, by establishing a Free Zone for Serbian trade. This original agreement was modified and extended later in 1923 and again in 1929; thus, this important question was settled on a basis of mutual benefit. This friendship, of course, did not emanate from sheer sentimentalism; it was a realistic policy, based on sound strategic and political considerations.

Greece dominates the Aegean coast, partially controls the entrance to the Adriatic, and holds the keys to both gates of Yugoslavia's maritime communications with the rest of the world. Without the cooperation of Greece, Yugoslavia would be deprived of any protection by the Western Powers, and thus, would not possess an effective counterbalance to the constant pressure, exerted by Central Europe or Russia. In time of war, Yugoslavia, without the assistance of Greece, would not possess the advantage of a last trench defense, and her army would face the eventuality of being destroyed with no possibility of successful retreat. In addition, Salonika, as a port of entry for supplies and external assistance in case of war, is indispensable to Yugoslavia's defense.

On the other hand, Greece possesses only a narrow strip of land at the north, and lacks a sufficient defensive hinderland to protect the country in case of an aggression from the north. Thus she looks upon Yugoslavia as a vital rampart, whose collapse brings the adversary within sixty miles of Salonika. In case of war, without the cooperation of Yugoslavia, the Greek forces would have to fight with their backs against the seacoast —militarily, an extremely adverse condition. Due to her geographical and strategic location, Greece is ideally situated to serve as an advanced post of the western defense system. However, without Yugoslavia's cooperation, Greece could offer only the uncertain stronghold of a mountain chain, inadequate to withstand successfully the tremendous pressure, exerted by gigantic forces setting out from the heart of Central Europe or the breadth of the Russian steppes.

The traditional Greco-Serbian amity was temporarily interrupted in 1915, during the Bulgarian attack against Serbia. Under the influence of King Constantine who favored a policy of neutrality, Greece refused to extend military assistance to Serbia, in spite of the obligations assumed under the terms of the Pact of Alliance of June 1913. Nevertheless, their friendship survived this crisis; later, during the Lausanne Conference of 1923, Yugoslav support was of great value to defeated Greece.

On September 1924, the so-called Kalfoff-Politis Protocol caused a serious rift between the two nations. By this protocol, Greece agreed to accept the intervention of the appropriate authorities of the League of Nations for the protection of Bulgarian minorities in Greece. Bulgaria, on the other hand, agreed to a similar obligation concerning the Greek minorities in Bulgaria. This protocol caused serious commotion in Athens because it was interpreted as an attempt, on the part of Bulgaria, to re-open the gates to interventions in Greek Macedonia by appeals to the League of Nations for the protection of the suppressed minorities. On March 14, 1925, the League of Nations relieved Greece and Bulgaria from the obligations imposed by the Kalfoff-Politis protocol. However, its repercussions were disastrous for the Greek-Yugoslav relations, as the Yugoslavs, not without reason, feared that this protocol would pave the way for Bulgarian interventions in Yugoslav Macedonia as well. A few weeks after this protocol was signed, certain difficulties in the administration of the Salonika Free Zone caused such a deterioration in the relations of these two countries that the Yugoslav government unilaterally repudiated the Greco-Serbian Pact of Alliance of 1913. This breach of old ties was bound to impose a dangerous uncertainty upon their relations during the following years.

In 1928, E. Venizelos, who again became the master of Greek politics as the head of a great majority in the parliament, embarked on a new drive aimed at solving the problems which confronted Greece in her relations with her neighbors. Presumably, he thought it advisable to iron out the existing disputes with Turkey and Yugoslavia by exploiting the Italian ambition to foster an Italo-Greco-Turkish coalition as a counterbalance to French policies in the Balkans and the Little Entente. Venizelos at first turned to Italy and negotiated a Greco-Italian agreement which Agreement of Friendship, Conciliation, and Judicial Settlement provided for "mutual political and diplomatic support in case the interests and security of any of the High Contracting Parties were threatened by external aggression." Yugoslavia interpreted this agreement to mean that Greece, in case of Italo-Yugoslav conflict, would not permit the transit of military supplies through Salonika. Since the use of Salonika as a port of entry for supplies in time of war did and still does constitute a major issue in the Greco-Yugoslav relations, the Yugoslavs justly regarded a renewal of the old ties of alliance with Greece unnecessary. In view of the existing equilibrium among the major powers in the late twenties, Venizelos was not inclined to press for an alliance with Yugoslavia, as he did in 1913. In an effort to restore the balance between Greco-Yugoslav and Greco-Italian relations, he proposed to Yugoslavia the drafting of an agreement, similar to the Greco-Italian agreement of 1928. After long negotiations and the happy solution of the existing minor disputes by the protocols of October 11, 1928 and March 17, 1929, a Pact of Friendship was signed in Belgrade on March 27, 1929. Unfortunately, this pact did not include the important clauses of the Greco-Italian agreement. This left the impression that Greece was standing closer to Italy; the London *Times* stated on May 16, 1929:

. . .The Serbs are not so well satisfied with the bargain. They wished to be assured of Salonika as a port of entry for supplies in time af war. They have had to be content with a promise of benevolent neutrality from Greece, against which must be set a similar Greek promise to Italy, the country which the Serbs much fear. The Yugoslav Government accepted these terms for fear that it might get less if an arrangement were delayed any longer. . . .

Later in the thirties, the difficulties which arose during the negotiations for the Balkan Entente Pact and the associated military agreements did little to improve the Greco-Yugoslav relations. Political leaders of both nations forsook the policy of close cooperation and, thus, paved the way for the tragic events of 1940-41 which resulted in the destruction of both countries by the Axis war machine.

GREECE TURNS TO THE WESTERN POWERS FOR ASSISTANCE

As Turkey and Yugoslavia had no contractual obligation to assist Greece in case of aggression, she found herself standing alone, at this hour of grave danger, politically and diplomatically isolated; and as an irony of fate the menace was the power to which Greece had shown continuous respect. There was no other alternative than to appeal to the Western Democracies; and to them Metaxas turned in spite of his alleged pro-German sympathies. A soldier trained in Germany, familiar with the German strategy, Metaxas early anticipated the dangers which hung not only over middle Europe but also over the Balkans. Speaking at a conference of Greek politicians as early as March 3, 1934, he expressed the view that "Greece must accept it as a political dogma that under no circumstances can she ally herself with the camp opposing the one to which England belongs." Metaxas clearly realized that Greece, a country surrounded by sea, should maintain friendly relations with the maritime powers in order to preserve her independence. Immediately after the Italian invasion of Albania, he ordered Ambassador Simopoulos to approach the British government. On the morning of April 9, 1939, the Ambassador called upon Lord Halifax, the British Foreign Minister, and expressed the fears of the Greek government because of the Italian occupation of Albania. He also informed Lord Halifax of the rumors concerning an impending Italian attack against the island of Corfu. In facing the new situation, brought about by the Italian coup, the Western Powers pledged immediate protection of Greece. They did not base their assistance upon the principle of reciprocity, nor ask for any special privileges. They merely promised that if Greece were attacked, they would come to her assistance. On April 12, 1939, Premier Chamberlain informed the House of Commons that "in the event of any action being taken, which clearly threatened the independence of Greece and Rumania and which the Greek or Rumanian governments, respectively, considered it vital to resist with their national forces, H. M.'s government feel themselves bound at once to lend, according to the circumstances, all the support in their power to the Greek or the Rumanian government." On the same day a similar declaration was made to the French parliament by Prime Minister Daladier. These guarantees were an additional manifestation of the profound change which the Nazi occupation of Czechoslovakia had effected in British foreign policy. The first outward sign of this change was an address by Neville Chamberlain at Birmingham, on March 17, 1939, when he said ". . . no greater mistake could be made

than to suppose that . . . this nation . . . will not take part to the utmost of
its power in resisting such a challenge (aggression) if it ever were made."

There is a lot of difference between a promise of assistance and a mere
promise of non-aggression. The British guarantees given to Greece and
Rumania were patterned on the previous guarantee to Poland and went
further than the guarantee given to Greece by the Italian government
two days after the invasion of Albania. In the Italian guarantee ". . .
Fascist Italy (reaffirmed) her intention to respect absolutely the integrity
of both the Greek mainland and islands." (*Diplomatic Documents*, No.
27).[6] Neither Mussolini nor Hitler received the information of Anglo-
French guarantees to Greece and Rumania with much enthusiasm, and
on several occasions expressed their vexation. On May 12, during an
official banquet in honor of Prince Paul, Regent of Yugoslavia, Mussolini,
"with a somewhat aggrieved air," expressed to the Greek ambassador his
misgivings in regard to the acceptance of the Franco-British guarantee by
Greece. Von Ribbentrop also interpreted this declaration, following the
guarantee to Poland, as the initiation of a systematic British policy to
form alliances in an effort to encircle Germany. (I. M. T., X, p. 215)[7]

Although the new policy of the Western Powers after March 1939,
definitely aimed at checking Axis aggression, the interpretation attached
by Von Ribbentrop to the Anglo-French guarantee to Greece was rather
misleading. This non-mutual guarantee, far from being an alliance, was
merely a unilateral act; it was a promise—but not an obligation—to extend
assistance in case of attack; there was no specification as to the time, the
form or the extent of the aid. This guarantee was not altogether advantageous to Greece, since it exposed her to the animosity of the Axis without
equivalent commitments from the Western Democracies.

Rushing at the last moment to escape from the wilderness of a partially self-imposed diplomatic isolation, Greece was not in a position to
argue these matters. Disregarding their shortcomings, the Greek nation
accepted these guarantees as a relief, a gesture of encouragement and a
promise that, had the Italians struck, Greece would not fight alone on the
ramparts of Epirus and Macedonia.

FOOTNOTES

1. ". . . no alternative to the dictatorship was in sight." *South Eastern Europe* (The Royal Institute of International Affairs, London: 1940) p. 65.

2. In the period between 1922 to 1936, only five million pounds had been appropriated for the army. After 1936 until 1940, more than thirteen million pounds were appropriated by the Metaxas government for the Greek armed forces. See, *Kathimerini*, February 13, 1949, p. 1.

3. See Appendix II, Note A.

4. Balkanicus, *The Aspirations of Bulgaria*, London: 1915, p. 48.

5. *Report of the International Commission to Inquire into the Causes and Conduct of the Balkan Wars*, Washington, D. C., p. 66.

6. *Diplomatic Documents; Italy's Aggression against Greece*, (Royal Ministry for Foreign Affairs, Athens: 1940)

7. *Trial of the Major War Criminals before the International Military Tribunal*, (The International Military Tribunal, Nuremberg: 1947)

CHAPTER THREE

TURKEY AND THE WEST

MUSSOLINI'S INVASION of Albania had far more extensive repercussions than the Italian dictator ever anticipated. On May 12, 1939, Premier Neville Chamberlain addressed the House of Commons and stated that Great Britain and Turkey had jointly decided to draft a long-term reciprocal agreement in the interest of their mutual security. He declared that until such an agreement had been concluded, the two governments mutually pledged to come to the other's assistance if either of them were the victim of an attack resulting in war in the Mediterranean. At the end of the address, he added that the two governments would consult with each other, in order to secure the regional security of the Balkans. This decision of the Turkish government was truly a historic one, considering the foreign policy of New Turkey in the inter-war period.

RUSSO-TURKISH RELATIONS

During the twenties and, to a lesser degree, during the thirties, the foreign policy of the Turkish Republic may be said to have been founded largely on the Moscow Treaty of March 16, 1921, concluded between Turkey and USSR during the Turkish-Greek conflict in Asia Minor. By that historic document, Soviet Russia recognized the Turkish claims to "those territories included in the National Turkish Convention of January 1336 (1920) drawn up and promulgated by the Ottoman Chamber of Deputies in Constantinople, . . ." (*Soviet Documents*, I, p. 23.)[1] Soviet Russia, under the terms of the Peace Treaty of Brest-Litovsk (March 3, 1918) had ceded to Turkey the frontier districts of Batum, Kars, and Ardahan. The new Turko-Soviet Treaty reallocated Kars and Ardahan to Turkey in exchange for Batum, which Turkey ceded to the Soviet Republic of Georgia. In the preamble to this treaty, the two governments jointly declared that they "are taking note of their solidarity in the struggle against imperialism." Soviet Russia thus reversed the centuries-old policy of the Czars, who combatted the Ottoman Empire, and Soviet Russia became New Turkey's first friend in Europe.

For centuries, the Czarist policy towards the Sublime Porte had taken the form of a continuous effort to win by diplomacy or war territorial or

24

other concessions from the Sultan, particularly over the Straits of Dardanelles. Since Catherine the Great won, by the Treaty of Kuchuk Kainarji (1774), the right for Russian merchant ships to enter the Straits, the Russians sought continually to extract further concessions from the Turks. In this contest, France and Britain usually backed the Turks in resisting Russian pressure. The peak of Russian influence was reached in 1833, with the treaty of Unkiar Skelessi, when the Sultan, weakened by the revolt of Mehmet Ali of Egypt, invited the Russians to assist him, and secretly agreed to block the passage of other foreign warships through the Straits. In 1841, the Sultan negotiated a Convention for the Straits with the major powers of that time. This Convention remained the fundamental rule, governing the Straits, until 1914. According to this agreement, which was reaffirmed by the Treaty of Paris (1856) and again at the Conference of London (1870), the Sublime Porte committed itself to hinder the passage of all foreign warships through the Straits in time of peace.

Russia's influence reached its lowest ebb after her defeat in the Crimean War (1856), when the Czar was denied the right to maintain a fleet in the Black Sea and arsenals on its shores—a restriction which was removed at the London Conference of 1870.

During World War I, when Turkey joined the Central Powers, the Czarist government requested, and by a secret treaty obtained, the consent of Britain, France, and Italy to annex Constantinople and the Dardanelles. The Communist Revolution intervened and the Bolsheviks renounced the secret treaty and the Czarist claims; thus, they reversed the traditional Russian policy, hoping to achieve security by closing the Straits to foreign warships. There were several reasons for their decision. Bolshevik Russia, faced with grave internal economic and political problems, was unable to embark upon ambitious expansionist policies; the Soviets hoped that the Turkish nationalistic movement under Mustafa Kemal might be channeled into a proletarian form, and thus, with a friendly Turkey the guardian of the Straits, they might be able to obtain concessions, unobtainable with a hostile policy. Besides, Turkey, defeated in the World War I, was in the eyes of Moscow a victim of the intrigues of the "imperialist powers."

On the other hand, Turkey, being treated by the powers as an ex-enemy state, isolated and struggling for her national survival, welcomed Soviet friendship as desperately needed encouragement.

This unexpected rapprochement brought about the split of the Western powers, for, two of the signatories of the Treaty of Sèvres—France and Italy—signed agreements with the Turks, virtually scrapping the Treaty of Sèvres. Of course, there were many reasons for their new policy; one of them was their desire to counter the growing Soviet influence in New Turkey.

During the war between Greece and Turkey (1921-22), Soviet Russia extended to Kemal all possible assistance;[2] at the same time, it undermined the morale of the Greek army, through the activities of the Greek communists. At the Lausanne Conference, which convened following the termination of the Greco-Turkish war, Soviet Russia supported Turkey in her efforts to maintain sovereignty over the Straits, but Great Britain, who traditionally had sought to block Russia in the Black Sea, reversed her policy and advocated the opening of the Straits not only to merchant vessels but also to warships at all times. Since Soviet Russia, weakened by the revolution and the civil war—and still striving to recover—did not constitute an immediate threat against the British positions in the Mediterranean, such policy was consistent with British interests. Moreover, Britain had not forgotten the unfortunate adventure of Gallipolis; consequently, she insisted upon the opening of the Straits, and, finally, a Convention was signed at Lausanne on July 24, 1923 by the British Empire, France, Italy, Japan, Greece, Rumania, the Serbo-Croat-Slovene State, and Turkey. Art. 2, Par. 1, provided for complete freedom of navigation for merchant vessels in time of peace. It also provided for free navigation of warships under the limitation that "the maximum force which any one power may send through the Straits into the Black Sea is not to be greater than that of the most powerful fleet of the littoral powers of the Black Sea. . . ." (Art. 2, Par. 2(a).)

Article 4, Par. 1, 2, and 3, provided for the demilitarization of the Straits Zone, while Article 5 established a four member Commission—France, Great Britain, Italy, and Turkey—for the enforcement of the Convention.

The Soviet Union was dissatisfied with the provisions of the Convention, she accepted it under protest, and never ratified it. Moreover, the alleged willingness of Turkey to fall in with the demands of the Western Powers resulted in a cooling off of the intimate Soviet-Turkish relations.

This cooling-off period proved to be only temporary and the isolation which was imposed upon USSR and, to some extent, upon Turkey by the other powers drew the two countries together again. Two years later, the Russo-Turkish treaty of Neutrality and Non-Aggression was signed by the two governments on December 17, 1925, but this treaty did not completely end all friction between Soviet Russia and Kemalist Turkey, especially on ideological and social grounds. The differences between Turkey and the Western Powers remained greater than those dividing her from the Soviet Union. During the twenties, Turkey remained outside the League of Nations, while maintaining close relations with the

Soviet Union.[3] Turkey's decision to join the League of Nations in September 1932, was obviously a prelude to a new orientation of Turkish foreign policy.

THE MONTREUX CONVENTION

As the star of Adolf Hitler ascended in Europe, France, in an effort to prepare for eventual cooperation with the Soviet Union, negotiated the Franco-Soviet Treaty of Mutual Assistance which was signed on May 2, 1935. As the Soviets regarded the regime of the Straits as established by the Lausanne Convention a menace to Russia's security, France agreed to the discontinuation of the Lausanne arrangements.

The Turks, also resented the infringement on their sovereignty over the Straits imposed by the Lausanne Convention, so they took advantage of the opportunity offered by the new French policy, and pressed for the drafting of a new Convention of the Straits.

Great Britain was anxious at that time to conciliate Germany and build a broader balance of power. On the other hand, she was unwilling to accommodate Russia, who had been recuperating her strength through two Five Year Plans; therefore, she hesitated to consent to any change of the Lausanne Convention. But Mussolini's violation of the League Covenant with the Abyssinian campaign, his ever-growing imperialist tendencies in the Eastern Mediterranean, and Germany's all too successful flouting of both the Versailles and the Locarno treaties, rendered the situation ripe for a revision of the Convention.

At the Montreaux Conference in June-July 1936, all the powers concerned were ready to assent to the proposals for the restoration of Turkey's sovereign rights over the Straits. Britain, faced the eventuality of fostering anti-British feelings in Turkey by opposing the revision of the Convention; so she supported the drafting of a new instrument for the Straits in the hope that she would attract Turkey into her own orbit. The Russian point of view was presented, on June 25, 1936, by M. Litvinov. He argued that the Black Sea was "a closed sea, leading nowhere." The Mediterranean powers had no reason for wishing to enter it except for "courtesy visits." Russia could not be expected to stay "shut up in the Black Sea, cut off from sea communications with her other ports on the Pacific and in the Baltic." (*South Eastern Europe*, p. 14.) After the negotiations were prolonged by the effort of the Western Powers to avoid "any draft highly favorable to the USSR," (Belloff p. 45.) the Montreux, Convention was eventually signed by the United Kingdom, Australia, Bulgaria, France, Greece, Rumania, Turkey, USSR, Yugoslavia, and Japan on July 20, 1936. It authorized Turkey to remilitarize the Straits zone and abolished the International Commission by transferring its functions to Turkey. (Sec. IV. Art. 24) The USSR was granted the right to pass surface naval forces through the Straits in time of peace, and, in time of war, as long as Turkey remained neutral and the USSR was a non-belligerent. In either case, the Turkish Government should be notified in advance through the diplomatic channels. Submarines belonging to the Black Sea Powers, constructed or purchased outside the Black Sea area, would be allowed passage through the Straits for the purpose of rejoining their bases, provided that adequate notice should be given to Turkey. Also the said submarines would be allowed passage for the purpose of being repaired in dockyards outside the Black Sea. In either case, these submarines were to travel by day and on the surface, and should pass through the Straits singly. (Sec. II, Arts. 11, 12, 13.) Limitations were imposed upon the aggregate tonnage of non-Black Sea warships which could in time of peace be allowed free passage through the Straits. (Sec. II, Art. 18.) In time of war, if Turkey remained neutral, peace-time conditions applied to non-belligerent powers, but belligerent ships are excluded, except in case of collective action under Art. 25 of the League Covenant or if the said ships were acting to enforce a treaty of mutual assistance, concluded within the framework of the League of Nations, and to which Turkey was one of the contracting parties. (Sec. II, Art. 19.)

Although these arrangements greatly increased the naval security of the Soviet Union, nevertheless, the USSR was dissatisfied. With her strength now increased, Russia desired more extensive concessions, and complained that Turkey was "yielding to the pressure of the imperialist Powers." Turkey accepted these arrangements with satisfaction as it was clear that Turkish friendship was likely to be an important factor in case of war or threat of war, a condition which highly improved her bargaining position.

The emergence of Germany as a predominant power in the Continent, further complicated the already involved situation. Turkey clearly felt that the existing constellation of powers provided the fullest utilization of the bargaining advantages of her position. The leaders of Turkey visualized the role of their country now as a link in a defensive system connecting the Western Democracies with the Soviet Union. In addition, Turkey, by her adherence to the Balkan Entente in 1934 and to the Middle Eastern Pact of July 8, 1937, including Turkey, Iran, Iraq, and Afghanistan, became "the pivot of an embryonic security system spreading from the Danube to the frontiers of India." (Ward, p. 103.)

TURKEY SHIFTS TO THE WESTERN CAMP

The way was now paved for further rapprochement, as the Montreux Convention had removed most of the major obstacles which heretofore hindered the cooperation of Turkey with the Western Democracies. On July 3, 1938, an old dispute between France and Turkey concerning the

Sandjak of Alexandretta (Iskenderon) was partly settled, and the following day a Franco-Turkish Pact of Friendship was initiated in Ankara, in anticipation of the final settlement of the Alexandretta dispute. Article 3 of this Pact provided for the mutual consultation for the maintenance "de la paix gènèrale et de la sècuritè en Mediterranèe orientale." During the spring, Britain had extended a loan of sixteen million pounds to Turkey for facilitating her military preparations. Shortly afterwards, the Turk ambassador to London stated to a New York *Times* correspondent that "whatever may happen, we will never enter a camp opposing Great Britain." True, the Turks, simultaneously, made efforts to cultivate friendly relations with the Axis, but the Axis Powers were not inclined to disregard the growing friendship between Turkey and the West.

On June 1939, with preparations for closer cooperation with the Western Powers already well under way, Turkey, acting under the stimulus of Albania's annexation by Italy and the German-Italian Pact of May 22, 1939, sped up the settlement of the Alexandretta dispute. On June 23, the final agreement was signed in Ankara; by this agreement Turkey annexed Alexandretta. A statement was attached to this agreement, similar to the joint Declaration which was issued in London and Ankara on May 12. By its terms the British and Turkish governments mutually agreed that, pending the conclusion of a definite and permanent agreement, the two governments, in the event of an act of aggression leading to war in the Mediterranean, would cooperate and lend each other all the aid in their power.

The Turk President announced this important turn in Turkey's foreign policy, while addressing the Fifth Great Convention of the People's Party in Ankara, on May 29th. He stressed the point that "as we clearly realize that the blow may fall upon our neighbors today and upon us tomorrow, we are taking precautions in time, in order to cope with the dangers facing us." (Pipinellis, p. 271.)

Intensive negotiations concerning the conclusion of an alliance between Turkey and the Western Powers, continued throughout the summer of 1939, but unforeseen events interrupted the development of the discussions. On August 23, the German-Soviet Pact was signed and, one week later, Germany invaded Poland; the world had not avoided the long-feared conflagration. September 17, 1939, is a date which marks a turning point in Soviet foreign policy. On that day, Soviet troops crossed the Polish border, and the Red Army was ordered to approach the frontiers of Latvia and Estonia. On the same day, the Kremlin requested the Turkish government to send their Minister of Foreign Affairs to Moscow for opening discussions. Turkey, immediately responded to the invitation. During the negotiations, the Soviet government proposed that Turkey close the Straits to all ships belonging to non-Black Sea Powers, obviously in violation of the Montreux Convention. The Soviet Union also proposed an agreement for mutual assistance, under the condition that it should be accompanied by a closer collaboration among the Balkan States to form " a block of neutral Balkan States." Although Turkey favored closer cooperation among the Balkan States, the negotiations failed because of the Soviet demands concerning the Straits and also because a united West-Balkan-Soviet front against the Axis was unobtainable after the German-Soviet Pact. Probably, Von Ribbentrop, then at Moscow, induced the Soviet government to propose new conditions, incompatible with the obligations undertaken by Turkey to the Western Powers. Turkey was not willing to sacrifice Franco-British assistance on the alter of Soviet amity, as it now was a question of naval strength in the Mediterranean. Immediately following Saracoglou's return to Ankara from Moscow, Turkey signed the Pact of Alliance with Britain and France, on October 19, 1939. To this pact, two protocols were attached. The first concerned the date, the second explained "the obligations undertaken by Turkey in virtue of the . . . Treaty cannot compel that country to take action having as its effect . . . entry into armed conflict with the Soviet Union." Thus, the door was left open to future cooperation with the Soviet Union. The pact contained also the provision that "as long as the guarantees given by France and the United Kingdom to Greece and Rumania . . . remain in force, Turkey will cooperate effectively with (them) and will lend them all aid and assistance in her power in the event of France and the United Kingdom being engaged in hostilities in virtue of either of the said guarantees." (Art. 3) A secret protocol defined in detail the form and the extent of the aid in war materiel to be given to Turkey.

Thus Turkey, by a policy far more constructive than that of Greece and the other Balkan States, substantially helped build the desperately needed dam against the oncoming Axis flood. From then on, the main task of all the parties concerned should be to honestly and faithfully fulfill the provisions of these agreements and also to seek their expansion and strengthening by attaching stronger links to those existing with Greece, Yugoslavia, and Rumania, and possibly by gaining Bulgaria's cooperation. The failure to accomplish these tasks resulted in the collapse of the Balkan front and "the liquidation of the Balkan States one by one."

FOOTNOTES

1. *Soviet Documents on Foreign Policy*, (ed. Jane Decras, London: 1951)

2. ". . . with much cannon, money, arms, and military advice. . . ." Louis Fischer, *The Soviets in World Affairs*, Princeton: 1951 2nd Ed.; Vol. 1, p. 391.

3. The assertion of Max Belloff, *Foreign Policy of Soviet Russia, 1929-41*, New York: 1949, Vol. II, p. 41, that Turkey was "adhering more and more closely to the Soviet orbit," is apparently an overstatement.

CHAPTER FOUR

AFTER ALBANIA'S ANNEXATION

ALBANIA'S OFFICIAL ANNEXATION took the form of a fancy ceremony at the Quirinal Palace on April 16, 1939. The pauper crown of Albania was offered to the King of Italy by the representatives of a lavishly bribed Constituent Assembly. Although Mussolini formally promised the aggrandizement of Albania—a promise which was repeated by Italian officials on several occasions—he deemed it necessary to consolidate his gains before undertaking any further enterprises.

THE DUCE REFUSES TO ENTER THE WAR

The reaction of the Western Powers, made it clear that his way to the "espansione del' Impero" would not be paved with roses; so Mussolini decided to link Fascist Italy with Nazi Germany more firmly. Apparently he did not share the opinion of that cynical Roman who once said, "if England wins the war we'll lose, but if Germany wins we will be lost!" Mussolini believed that in case of a general conflict, only an Axis victory would bring about the realization of the Italian imperialist aspirations. Therefore, he should be the partner of Germany with a decisive voice in the future Peace Conference.

Ribbentrop, in his testimony before the International Military Tribunal, asserted that the existing friendly relations between Germany and Italy, "were, at Mussolini's suggestion, intensified and a pact of alliance, which was discussed first by Count Ciano and me in Milan, was drawn up and provisionally signed on the order of the government heads." (I. M. T., X., p. 373.) This Pact of Friendship and Alliance was finally signed on May 22, 1939.

Although Mussolini in Milan conveyed to his partner that Italy was not ready to wage a total war, he commented—probably aiming to prove his strategic abilities—that:

One must take the whole Danube and Balkan area immediately after the very first hours of the war. One shall not be satisfied with declarations of neutrality but must occupy the territories and use them for the procurement of necessary food and industrial war supplies.[1]

31

This aggressive spirit did not last long. On August 9, 1939, Mussolini sent Count Ciano to Obersalzberg with definite orders to beg the Führer to postpone the conflict, as Italy was unable to enter the war because of "economic and strategic considerations." Ciano informed Hitler that Mussolini was willing to propose an international conference for the solution of the existing international problems; he also alluded to the concurrence of France in taking this step. Unfortunately, this proposal was rejected by the Germans as impractical. To his surprise, Ciano discovered that "even if the Germans were given more than they ask for, they would attack just the same, because they are possessed by the demon of destruction." The Führer, in a long monologue as usual, unreeled his shrewd plans for a swift victory, and, among other things, he said:

> Generally speaking, the best thing to happen would be for the false neutrals to be liquidated one by one. This process could be carried out more easily if, on every occasion, one partner of the Axis covered the other while it was dealing with the uncertain neutral. (I. M. T., III, p. 310.)

As an example of this process, he mentioned Yugoslavia, a country to which he had personally given concrete assurances.[2] Ciano replied to this point that, although the Duce was in agreement with the Führer as to the desirability of liquidating Yugoslavia, and Ciano himself was highly interested in seizing Salonika, nevertheless, Italy, for the time being, was in no position to wage war. Mussolini's answer, although given with sorrow and humiliation, was definite; Italy would not move to join Germany in the big adventure, at least at that time. Hitler's majestic eloquence and magnetic personality were not convincing enough to dissipate Mussolini's apprehensions.

TEMPORARY IMPROVEMENT OF GRECO-ITALIAN RELATIONS

General Metaxas knew little, if at all, about Mussolini's decision to abstain from a general conflict. However, he took advantage of a visit paid to him on August 21, 1939, by Count Grazzi, the Italian Ambassador, and made an effort to clarify "a certain question touching (Greece's) relations with Italy." (*Dipl. Doc.*, No. 45.) During this conversation, Metaxas repudiated the Italian allegations against Greece and tried to convince his visitor that Greece had done everything in her power to comply absolutely with her status of neutrality. He stressed the point that although Greece had no intention of interfering in the internal affairs of the Dodecanese Islands, nevertheless, an improvement in the treatment of the inhabitants would go far to influence public opinion in Greece, already disturbed by the presence of ten thousand Dodecanesian refugees at Piraeus. After other points at issue between the two countries had been mentioned, General Metaxas brought up the crucial question, the Anglo-

French guarantee to Greece. He expressed his surprise that Greece was criticized by Italy "for having accepted the guarantee of Great Britain and France, although this unilateral and spontaneously given guarantee applied generally to all cases of aggression against Greece. And yet the Rome Government had given a most warm and friendly reception to the Roumanian Minister for Foreign Affairs, whose country was exactly in the same position as ours." At this point Signor Grazzi bluntly said the guarantee was directed against Italy, as "nobody else was likely to attack" Greece. To this, Metaxas replied that Grazzi was mistaken; Bulgaria might also attack Greece, "in which case Great Britain and France would be under just the same obligation." And he added:

But, how do you expect us to persuade the Greek people to believe that they are in no danger from Italy, when the soldiers you send to the Dodecanese sing a special song: 'Sbarcheremo al Pireo e conquisteremo tutto l'Egeo, etc.'; when your officers and men every day talk openly of invading Greece; when General Badoglio makes a public speech in Albania about the extension of Albania's frontiers; when, on the occasion of Count Ciano's reception at Korytsa, boards were put up bearing, inscribed in black letters, the names of Kossovo and Tsamuria? Kossovo, as we know, belongs to Yugoslavia, with whom you have especially friendly relations, but Tsamuria is Greek.

Count Grazzi apparently disconcerted, attempted to counter these questions with one of his own, and asked how the Anglo-Turkish alliance,— which incidentally was not yet signed—affected Greek policies, seeing that Greece was an ally of Turkey. Metaxas immediately explained that Greece was bound to Turkey only by the Balkan Pact and the special treaties. Grazzi asked, "Should Turkey attack Italy, what will you do?" Metaxas replied that such an eventuality was inconceivable since the Anglo-Turkish cooperation was purely defensive. Even in such a case Greece had no treaty-obligation to follow suit. Then, Grazzi arrived at the question toward which the whole conversation was directed. "Should Great Britain put pressure on you to place your harbors at her disposal, what will you do?"

To this, Metaxas replied, ". . . should we of our own accord place our harbors at the disposal of the British, that would mean the abandonment of our neutrality and consequently war with you. But such a line of action is not in our minds and there is no need for us to consider it." Grazzi asked for the authorization of Metaxas to report to Rome the peaceful intentions of Greece, and Metaxas re-emphasized that "Greece had no intention of acting in a hostile manner towards Italy . . . unless Italy should attack Greece's vital interests and, above all, the integrity of her territory." Before the conversation was over, he expressed the hope that

Grazzi would contribute to the removal of this unjust prejudice against Greece.

"However," he repeated, ". . . should an attack be made on the integrity of our territory, or should our vital interests be assailed, in that case we would fight to defend them."

Count Grazzi replied that Greece would be "quite right in doing so; but there was no question of such a thing happening." Fourteen months later, he himself presented the ultimatum to General Metaxas.

The above lengthy conversation—which better than any analysis illustrates the official Greek attitude and the fears of Italy—revealed to Metaxas Italy's desire for a rapprochement. This desire was, subsequently, fostered by the conclusion of the German-Soviet pact, and the outbreak of the war. Mussolini's indignation had no limits, as he saw Russia, whose aspirations in the Balkans were well known, enter the international arena as a friend of Germany. Italy was not yet ready for a major conflict; and this unexpected development found Mussolini unaware and unprepared. Had he been ready, his best alternative would have been immediate participation in the war so that he would be able to maintain his preeminent position within the aggressive coalition. But, as Ciano reveals in his *Diaries*, (pp. 127, 128, 166.) the Italian army was in no condition to undertake major military assignments. Utterly dispirited, Mussolini on September 1, authorized the Italian Cabinet to include in the official announcement of the outbreak of the war in Europe, a declaration of Italy's determination to abstain from any military operations.

Immediately after the outbreak of war in Europe, Grazzi visited Metaxas and, "in a friendly tone," suggested that inasmuch as the Italian government had officially declared their intention to remain at peace, the concentration of Greek troops opposite Albania was unnecessary. Metaxas expressed his willingness to relax the measures taken, as soon as the Italian forces were removed from the Greek-Albanian frontiers and distributed throughout Albania. On September 9, Grazzi called on Metaxas again to inform him that he had been summoned to Rome. In view of the importance he seemed to attach to this trip to Rome, Metaxas surmised that, on his return, Grazzi would take up "in a more concrete form the suggestion already made." (*Dipl. Doc.*, No. 47.)

When the Italian Minister returned from Rome he handed Metaxas a communication from the Italian government signed by Mussolini himself on September 12, 1939. The main points of this communication were:

I. Italy had already declared on September 1, that she did not intend to initiate any military action.

II. This decision of the Italian Cabinet, which was valid in a general sense, applied more especially to Greece.

III. Even in the event of Italy's intervention in the war, a contingency which she, as a Great Power, could not exclude, Italy would not take the initiative in resorting to any military action against Greece.

IV. In order to manifest in a more concrete form the friendly feelings of the Italian government and particularly of the Duce in regard to Greece, orders would be issued for the withdrawal of the Italian troops from the Greek frontier to a depth of 20 kilometers.

V. Notwithstanding the existing situation, the Duce did not exclude the possibility of resuming and stabilizing the policy of an Italo-Greek entente, which had been previously established by special diplomatic agreements. (*Dipl. Doc.*, No. 49.)

The Greco-Italian treaty of 1928 was expiring at that time; apparently the last paragraph of the above communication suggested the possibility of a renewal. To this, Metaxas replied that, under the present abnormal circumstances, such a renewal should undergo a careful and thorough study. As for the military measures referred to, Metaxas promised that the number of the Greek forces in Epirus, Western Macedonia, and Corfu would be reduced.

Immediately after the Italian démarche, Metaxas turned to the Western Powers and inquired about their views in regard to Mussolini's proposal for a renewal of the Greco-Italian treaty.[3] The British government replied that a new pact was acceptable provided that 1) Greece would preserve her freedom of action in case of a conflict between Italy and Great Britain and 2) Greece would preserve her freedom of action in case of conflict between Italy and any member of the Balkan Entente.

Metaxas realized that such reservations would simply prove to Italy Greece's intention to line up with the Western Powers, should the war be extended in the Mediterranean, and thus produce unnecessary bitterness and distrust between the two countries. The correct line of diplomatic conduct would be to encourage the intention of the Italian government to improve their relations with the Balkan countries. Since such a course was not approved by London and Paris, Metaxas decided to avoid altogether the renewal of the Greco-Italian treaty.

However, the immediate result of Mussolini's communication, was a *communiqué* published simultaneously in Athens and Rome. The two governments respectively declared that the Greco-Italian relations "continue to be sincerely friendly and . . . inspired by a spirit of complete and mutual confidence." A "practical proof of these feelings" was their decision to withdraw their military forces from the Greco-Albanian frontier. (*Dipl. Doc.*, No. 50.) In Rome, Count Ciano received the Greek Minister in a very cordial manner and expressed his satisfaction at the reestablishment of the Greco-Italian relations "on a friendly footing." He also declared that "Italy had no aims of an economic or a political nature directed against Greece. Her only desire was to see complete confidence and friendship prevail in the relations between the two countries." (*Dipl. Doc.*, No. 51.)

On September 30, 1939, Metaxas handed the Italian Minister a memorandum in reply to Duce's communication of September 12th. This memorandum, at Italy's suggestion, was accorded the dignity of a note, which was eventually issued on November 3, although dated September 30, 1939. The last paragraph read:

The Royal Government are fully determined that their policy shall be inspired by the principles [of friendship and cooperation], such as they were proclaimed in the Pact of Friendship, Conciliation and Judicial Settlement between Greece and Italy . . . (*Dipl. Doc.*, No. 54.)

The words "of friendship and cooperation" were added to the original Greek draft at Mussolini's personal suggestion. A similar note was published in Rome on behalf of the Italian government.

REASONS FOR THE GRECO-ITALIAN RAPPROCHEMENT

What was behind this benevolent façade? Was it a plan to lull Greece into security and, thus, attack her suddenly? Although this might seem an obvious conclusion, it was not the case. Mussolini's new policy was prompted by other extremely important reasons.

Following the outbreak of the war, the Soviet invasion of Poland and the subsequent advancement of Soviet positions in Eastern Europe caused grave concern and disquiet to Mussolini. In order to cope with the Soviet advance, he embarked upon a widely-publicized effort to improve relations with Rumania, while the Italian press in fierce editorials exposed the communist plans in the Balkans and visualized for Italy the role of their defender.

As early as October 10, 1939, Grazzi revealed to the Greek Permanent Under-Secretary of State, Mavroudis, "in strict personal confidence that the Italian Government had decided to make public at a very early date and through official channels their intention of definitely remaining neutral." He further gave the Greek diplomat to understand that "the Italian Government had been led to the above decision in consequence of Russia's latest intervention and of her expansion in Eastern Europe . . . Italy could not see with indifferent eyes the interference of Bolshevik Russia in European affairs." (*Dipl. Doc.*, No. 53.)

On December 8, 1939, the Fascist Grand Council issued an official *communiqué* with regard to Italy's position after the outbreak of the war. In this it was stated that "the relations between Germany and Italy continue to be inspired by the Pact of Alliance . . . and the exchange of opinions which took place in Milan, Obersaltzberg, and Berlin." They added, as a warning to both Germany and the USSR, that "Italy is directly interested in anything that happens in the Danube basin and the Balkans, taking into account the common sea and land frontiers which resulted from the union of the Kingdom of Albania with the Kingdom of Italy." The above declaration of the Grand Council appeared only two days after the "*Communist International*," the official journal of the Comintern, had demanded in an article that Rumania should sign a mutual assistance pact with the Soviet Union similar to those between the USSR and the Baltic States. Although this article was quickly disavowed by the Soviet government, it left the impression that the Soviets intended to inaugurate a drive toward the Dardanelles.

On the 16th of the same month, Ciano, in an important speech full of hidden complaints against Germany, declared unequivocally that Italy could not move before the lapse of three years. Then he threw conciliatory hints to Yugoslavia and Greece by stressing the fact that the recent exchange of notes between Rome and Athens provided the basis for further improvement of their relations.

Apparently, Italy, pressed between the Cyanean Rocks of German-Soviet cooperation on one side and Western enmity toward the Italian aspirations on the other, was seeking to establish props of security wherever possible. Her benevolent and conciliatory attitude in the fall of 1939 and the first months of 1940 was not a vicious attempt to lull her prospective victims. As a matter of fact, this was a moment for more decisive policies on the part of the West; policies which might have succeeded in keeping Italy out of the war and probably driving her out of the Axis. The opportunity, however, was overlooked. Mussolini, impressed by the enormous successes of Hitler on the Western Front in May-June 1940, reversed his policies and, lest he might be left out of the partition of the loot, he decided to enter the war.

FOOTNOTES

1. *I. M. Tribunal Proceedings*, Doc. No. 2818-PS, Vol. X, p. 373. Comments by Mussolini, appended to a secret protocol attached to the said Pact.

2. During the conversations between Hitler and Stoyadinovich, the Yugoslav Premier, on January 17, 1938, the following statements were made by Hitler. "As regards Yugoslavia, Germany is highly interested in the existence of a strong Yugoslavia." Somewhat later in the course of the same conversation, he stated, "Whatever may happen there, Yugoslavia's present boundary will remain as inviolable as the border on the Brenner is today." *German Official Documents*, pp. 71-72, Doc. Nr. 28. On June 1, 1939, during an official visit of Prince Paul, Regent of Yugoslavia, Hitler stated, "Germany's friendship with the Yugoslav nation did not spring suddenly. It was deepened and strengthened by the tragic complications of the World War." *ibid.*, p. 78, Doc. Nr. 35.

3. Interesting comments by officials of the French Foreign Ministry are included in Nos. 110 and 111 of *German Official Documents, op. cit.*, pp. 170, 171. See Appendix II, Note B.

CHAPTER FIVE

TILL THE FALL OF FRANCE

NOTWITHSTANDING THE TEMPORARY re-establishment of friendly relations between Greece and Italy, the anxiety and distress, which for a long time prevailed in the Balkan capitals, was intensified following the outbreak of World War II. The reason was the concentration of a formidable military force by Germany, able to inflict irresistible blows upon the smaller nations. Their agony was aggravated as they became aware of the quantitative and qualitative weakness of the Western military forces in the Middle East, where the widely-celebrated Weygand Army was yet in the realm of planning rather than reality.

NEUTRALITY AND ISOLATIONISM

The collaboration of the Soviet Union with Germany dissipated any hope for the building of a West-Balkan-Soviet system of defense and, thus, minimized the possibilities for Balkan cooperation, since the establishment of such a powerful system was generally considered as prerequisite for a Balkan defensive block.

With Germany's military machine able to concentrate its crushing force on the frontiers of the Balkans at any moment; without the counterbalance of an equivalent Western force in the Middle East; with the unexpected Soviet-German rapprochement, there was only one course left open for the Balkan countries: neutrality. But neutrality is not a legalistic conception; it is a matter of political reality. Its successful maintenance and preservation depend entirely on the existence of several factors. Either the neutral state must possess military power, sufficient to discourage the aggressor; or the neutral state's strategic, economic, or political unimportance renders the cost of aggression unequal to the prospective meager benefits, or, finally, the preservation of its neutrality is—for certain particular reasons—of common interest to all the adversaries. Otherwise, the preservation of neutrality depends on the good will and the strategic plans of the aggressor.

Under the circumstances, neutrality was the best policy the Balkan countries could adopt. But their neutrality could have been preserved only if it were a Balkan neutrality, not an individual neutrality; in other words if the Balkan states had formed a solid block of neutral Balkan states.

Important considerations supported the establishment of such a solidified neutral block. The equilibrium which was temporarily established between the German and the Russian influences in the Balkans, following the Soviet-German agreements of August 1939, should have been an important motive for the formation of such a defensive coalition. As a matter of fact, the Soviet Union, during Saracoglou's visit to Moscow in the fall of 1939, had suggested the formation of a "block of neutral Balkan States." The Western Powers would also have welcomed a neutral Balkan block, which would preserve the *status quo* in the Balkans and would bar the way of both Germany and USSR toward the Eastern Mediterranean. Even Italy would have accepted, by necessity, such a coalition, since, in view of her military weakness, she would prefer the maintenance of the Balkan *status quo*, at least temporarily, rather than the successful promotion of the Soviet and German positions in the Balkans. In brief, all the powers, with the possible exception of Germany and USSR, had at that time a common interest in the preservation of Balkan neutrality—although for quite different motives and for quite different reasons.

The formation of a solid block of neutral countries in the Balkans actually would have had far more extensive consequences than the mere preservation of their neutrality. Should their military forces—amounting to about a hundred divisions—been able to act as a unified army, they would have been formidable enough to discourage any aggressor. Evidence in support of this argument was furnished later by Hitler himself. He said to Mussolini in the spring of 1941, while preparing the German blow against Greece, "Yugoslavia is the most dangerous factor (gefärlichsten Faktor) in the controversy with Greece and should become disinterested if possible; however, from our point of view, [she should become] interested in cooperating in the liquidation of the Greek question. Without assurances from Yugoslavia, it is useless to risk any successful operation in the Balkans." (I. M. T., XXVIII, p. 565.) In other words, Hitler regarded the operation against Greece dangerous—even with Rumania and Bulgaria behind his gray curtain at that time—if Yugoslavia's attitude were uncertain. How different the situation would have been, had the Balkan countries formed this solid block in 1940. Instead, the policy of isolationism and individual neutrality was intensified and the responsible leaders of the Balkan nations, impressed by the massive power of the Axis and the unexpected turn of the Soviet Union, followed an entirely unfortunate course of action. As a result, Hitler was able to apply successfully his formula of "liquidating the neutrals one by one."

FAILURE OF THE BALKAN ENTENTE

At the beginning of 1940, the Balkan Pact was due to be renewed. But, at the time of danger when unity was their only hope, the Balkan countries did not have the courage to make a brave decision. The Yugoslav government, continuing the policies of Stoyadinovich, even asked for the cancellation of the Balkan Council's conference on February 1940, in order to avoid any misunderstanding. Only through the persistence of the other members of the Balkan Entente did the Council convene. However, Cincar Marcovic, the Yugoslav Foreign Minister, took care to discourage the optimistic expectations by stating, the day before the opening of the meetings, "the conference is not convoked in face of any immediate danger and, therefore, will not seek the adoption of any defensive measures. The Balkan Entente does not wish to disturb the position of any member by establishing a defensive formation which might be interpreted as aimed against any third party." (Pipinellis p. 303.) Nevertheless, the Pact was finally renewed for another seven years.

This renewal, celebrated as a great success, was in reality a failure. The Conference overlooked the wise suggestion of General Papagos, the Greek Chief of Staff, who vigorously supported the extension of the Balkan Entente provisions that it become a defensive coalition against any aggressor. This suggestion was discussed in Belgrade, but the Council decided that "although the commitments of the members should override the narrow limitations of the Pact's text," nevertheless, in order to avoid any misunderstanding, such an extension should not take the form of a written agreement. Instead, a secret clause was added which provided for "noiseless but direct contact among the four General Staffs in order to study certain problems of defense of interest to the four nations." The four countries decided also that in case of international complications, they would keep close contact and possibly "may convene for consultation at a convenient place which will be designated by common decision." Under the façade of this encouraging wording of the text, the failure to transform the Entente from an obsolete diplomatic makeshift to a solid, active organization was carefully concealed. The interested outside parties—Hitler, Stalin, and Mussolini—did not fail to interpret correctly these agreements, and before the year was over they all took advantage of this ill-concealed disintegration.

BULGARIAN POLICIES AND THE BALKANS

In this unfortunate course of continual blunders, Bulgaria played an invisible although disastrous part. As it has been previously mentioned, she had followed continuously a policy of estrangement, and, in every possible way, attempted to undermine the work of the Balkan Entente. Defeated in the Second Balkan War (1913) and in World War I, the Bulgarians never truly accepted the terms of the Peace Treaty of Neuilly (1919). In the interwar period, the Bulgarian people, united in their nationalistic aspirations, patiently waited for the day when the map of Europe would again undergo a change. As this fatal hour seemed to draw closer than ever following the outbreak of World War II, the Bulgarians intensified their policy of isolationism and of disintegration of the Balkan Entente. Their policy, although simple and old-fashioned, was at the same time very effective. They preserved carefully their freedom of action by avoiding any commitment. They cunningly undermined the unity of the members of the Balkan Entente by ostensibly cultivating friendly relations with some members while maintaining enmity against others and, in general, sowing seeds of discord among all of them. For example, notwithstanding its aspirations to a part of Yugoslav Macedonia, the Bulgarian government repeatedly manifested its friendly feelings toward Yugoslavia. A similar policy was followed in Turko-Bulgarian relations. On November 20, 1938, Kiosseivanoff, the Bulgarian Premier, addressing the Parliament, affirmed that his government would endeavor "without rest, to improve the friendly relations with Yugoslavia and Turkey, while (they) would continue (their) efforts to accomplish the satisfactory solution of the pending issues with the other two neighbors, Rumania and Greece." In this sentence was echoed the whole Bulgarian policy.

On May 1939, Potemkin, the Soviet Vice-Commissar for Foreign Affairs visited the Balkan capitals and advised the governments to cement the Balkan Entente and to try to win the cooperation of Bulgaria. Although the replacement of Litvinov by Molotov was a symptom of a serious change in Soviet foreign policy, Gafenco, the Rumanian Foreign Minister, still under the impression of the Soviet suggestions, undertook in September 1939 an effort to attract Bulgaria to the Balkan Entente. On September 19, he met Marcovic at Gebel and drafted a set of proposals to Bulgaria. According to these proposals, Bulgaria would enter the Entente and assume the relevant responsibilities. In exchange, "as a contribution of the Balkan Entente to the Balkan family," Rumania would cede to Bulgaria South Dobrudja, Yugoslavia the area of Charibrod, and Greece would establish a corridor for Bulgarian trade through Western Thrace. This effort was doomed to failure. After the German-Soviet agreements of the previous August (1939) the diplomatic framework for the formulation of a Balkan block against the Axis no longer existed. Thus, no territorial concession whatsoever could attract Bulgaria to the Balkan Entente.

Notwithstanding this adversity, negotiations among the Balkan governments to attract Bulgaria to the Balkan Pact, continued in the months following the outbreak of the war, with the full support of Greece and

Turkey and the approval of the Western Powers. On January 1940, Menemencioglou, Permanent Under-Secretary of the Turkish Ministry for Foreign Affairs stopped at Sofia on his way home from London. Once again, he tried to convince the Bulgarian Premier that the only way to preserve peace in the Balkans was to form a solid coalition of all the Balkan nations. Kiosseivanoff, who was very little, if at all, interested in the preservation of peace, agreed halfheartedly with Menemencioglou's suggestions. Nevertheless, when Menemencioglou asked him about Bulgaria's reaction in case of aggression against any Balkan country, he assured his visitor that in such an eventuality Bulgaria would maintain her neutrality. The Turk diplomat, as well as his Balkan colleagues, accepted this statement with great satisfaction as an indication that their efforts to win Bulgaria's cooperation had made considerable progress. This optimism was unduly excessive. Ambassador Pipinellis, then Greek representative to Sofia, in a conversation with King Boris was given the impression that the actual Bulgarian intentions did not justify at all such an optimistic interpretation of Kiosseivanoff's statement. The Turkish government continued its efforts and without delay attempted to capitalize upon the hope of cooperation which existed because of this statement. Shortly thereafter, Saracoglou, on his way to Belgrade for the Balkan Conference, met Kiosseivanoff at the railway station in Sofia. Kiosseivanoff repeated to the Turk Foreign Minister the assurances previously given to Menemencioglou in regard to Bulgarian neutrality. At the Conference the question of Bulgaria's adherence to the Entente in exchange for certain territorial concessions was discussed and the parties concerned agreed in principle to such a solution.

Temporarily optimism seemed to be substantiated by facts. But the Bulgarians were not willing to sacrifice their freedom of action even in exchange for long-coveted territories. In the opinion of King Boris and the extreme nationalists who manipulated Bulgarian foreign policy, Kiosseivanoff had gone too far in the way of Balkan cooperation. In February 1940, after his triumphant re-election, Kiosseivanoff was compelled to resign and immediately was replaced in the premiership by the more docile Filoff. The assurances of neutrality given by Kiosseivanoff, were gradually forgotten by the new managers of Bulgarian foreign policy. Bulgaria, of course, was not able at that time to disturb the peace in the Balkans without the cooperation of a great power. Her purpose in resuming the policy of estrangement was obviously to stand by and wait for the hour when she would be able to exploit the European conflict.

BACKGROUND OF BULGARIAN FOREIGN POLICY

In order to comprehend fully Bulgaria's policies, it is necessary to trace briefly their background. Bulgaria was first established as a state by the treaty of San Stefano (March 3, 1878), imposed upon the Sultan by Czarist Russia, under the direct threat of entering Constantinople.[1] At that time, Russia faced Austria's rivalry in the Balkans and attempted to create a bridgehead of her own, close to the Straits, by establishing a satellite state. The Treaty of San Stefano, however, was soon annuled under the pressure of European diplomacy and the Czarist government was compelled by the other powers to admit that, in drafting the frontiers of Bulgaria, they had entirely neglected the ethnologic composition of Balkan nationalities.[2] By the Shuvalov-Salisbury agreement of May 30, 1878, which prepared the way for the Congress of Berlin, it was established that "les frontiers occidentale de la Bulgarie seraient rectifièes sur la base des nationalitès, de manière à exclure de cette province des populations non Bulgares." Beaconsfield, in his speech of April 8, 1878, criticized the Treaty of San Stefano as creating "a large state which, under the name of Bulgaria, is inhabited by many races non-Bulgarian." Salisbury wrote on April 1, that Bulgaria was so constituted, under the terms of the San Stefano Treaty, that the general effect "will be to increase the power of the Russian Empire in the countries and on the shores where a Greek population predominates."

The Congress of Berlin which annulled the San Stefano Treaty and rectified the frontiers of Bulgaria,[3] created "an autonomous principality under the suzerainty of H. I. M. the Sultan" (Article I). This Bulgaria was a small part of "the large state . . . , under the name of Bulgaria" of the San Stefano Treaty. But the Bulgarians never forgot this short-lived treaty. Like the dreams of one's childhood, the San Stefano Treaty was deeply impressed upon the Bulgarian national soul, and since that time it has formed the nostalgic nucleus of Bulgaria's national policy; "it was a holy ideal, no Bulgarian leader has dared renounce." (J. Swine, p. 15.) For the Bulgarians, Bulgaria was not created by the Congress of Berlin; rather, she was dismembered by it. The Bulgarians sincerely believed and still believe that the areas they claim are really Bulgarian territories. For seven decades now, education, press, politics, history, all have been motivated by the enchanting legend of San Stefano.

The Greeks for generations had been inspired by the Great Idea, the restoration of the Byzantine Empire. In view of international realities, they abandoned their aspirations in 1930 and established friendly relations with the Turks, their former enemies. Unfortunately, the Bulgarians did not follow a similar course of action, and even today they are aroused by the memories of San Stefano. This might have been an issue of limited significance, if Bulgaria were a small state at some far corner of the earth. But Bulgaria lies in a strategic location where the threads of international politics cross and the spasms of gigantic geopolitic masses often stir up the area. In consequence, all the Balkan conflicts of the past decades, although directly associated with Bulgarian agitation, have always been connected with much wider international upheavals. Bulgaria, because of her geographic and strategic location, has constantly played the role of an outpost for the Continental Powers, Slavic or Germanic.

Soon the realization of territorial aspirations as they were defined by the fabulous Treaty of San Stefano, became the basic motive of Bulgaria's foreign policy. As this treaty was of Russian conception, Russian influence has always been very strong in Bulgaria. Due to the proximity of the Germanic peoples, however, Bulgaria, twice since her establishment as an independent state in 1908, was compelled by inevitable strategic and political considerations to line up with the Germanic giant. As a result, the Germano-Slavic rivalry in the Balkans has been reflected for many decades in the fluctuations of the Bulgarian foreign policy. This does not imply that the Bulgarian people are divided in their sympathies; on the contrary they are united by the dream of San Stefano. Premier Filoff, in a speech on January 12, 1941, stressed that Bulgaria should not be influenced by any sympathies, but that its policy should be guided by "Bulgaria first policies, working only for Bulgaria and never sacrificing anything for allegedly foreign interests." This remarkable realism has failed so far to substantiate their aspirations.

Germany and Russia are not the only political units which exercise considerable influence on Bulgaria's foreign policy. Great Britain also has constantly tried to cultivate friendly relations with Bulgaria, even to the detriment of Yugoslavia and Greece, Britain's more reliable friends. British diplomatic efforts have been continually subjected to many limitations because of a serious disadvantage; Britain lacks military forces on the spot, ready to support by their presence her diplomatic undertakings. Her forces must be transported a considerable distance, whereas the Slavic and, to a larger extent, the Germanic forces enjoy the strategic advantage of internal lines of communication and attack, and have their military bases and industrial machinery near the front lines. This strategic reality swept away any counter-influence in 1915 and in 1941, when, at both crucial moments, Bulgaria decided to open the gates to the German armies.

In addition to the strategic reasoning of Bulgarian foreign policy, nationalistic ends drove her to join the Central European Powers in both wars.[4] When, during the First World War, Sir Edward Grey, British Secretary of State, spoke about Kavala (Greek) and Monastir (Serbian) as prospective cessions to Bulgaria in exchange for her participation in the Allied front, the Germans presented Bulgaria with the map of San Stefano. In this auction Germany was the highest bidder, while Britain, leaning mainly on Greek and Serbian cooperation, could not offer Bulgaria any substantial bait out of Greek or Serbian territory.

Strategic and nationalistic considerations, as powerful as the laws of nature, thus dictate the course of Bulgaria's foreign policy. Henceforth, it was merely a matter of course that the efforts of the Balkan diplomats to attract Bulgaria to the Entente during the winter of 1939-40 should evenually fail. Docile Filoff, elevated to the premiership by King Boris, was instructed to avoid any commitment that might imperil their precious freedom of action at this moment when fate, moving with gigantic steps, was changing the destiny of mankind. Shortly after the displacement of Kiosseivanoff in February 1940, Popov, the new Foreign Minister, was asked by Balkan diplomats in Sofia, whether the new government would honor the assurances given by Kiosseivanoff the previous month. He replied that he was not yet familiar with the relevant file; a little later he bluntly asserted that Kiosseivanoff had never stated what was attributed to him and he ascribed it to a misinterpretation.

ITALY ENTERS THE WAR

While these discouraging developments were taking place in the Balkans, far to the north the torch of war was setting another country aflame. Soviet Russia, improving her position for the ultimate trial, attacked Finland. Mussolini found in this incident an opportunity to show in a practical way his displeasure with the German-Soviet rapprochement. While Germany remained officially neutral in the Soviet-Finnish conflict, Italy forwarded four large consignments of arms to Finland in December of 1939 and early January of 1940. The Italian government through a controlled press, in continuous attacks against Soviet aggressiveness, stressed the pending danger to the Balkans and called them to rally in defense of their freedom with Italian assistance. "Italy's policy in the Balkans has for its objective the blocking of Russia's drive to the Mediterranean. . . ." *Corriere Padamo* wrote on February 3, 1940. The Soviet-Italian tension was also extended to the diplomatic field. Gorelkin, newly appointed Soviet Ambassador to Italy, left Rome on December 13, 1939, without having succeeded in presenting his credentials to the King during the three weeks he stayed in Rome. A few weeks later, on January 9, 1940, Agusto Rosso, the Italian Ambassador to Moscow, returned home. In the following months, the relations of the two countries remained cold if not hostile.

As the intelligence reports on German military concentrations along the Western Front poured in, USSR decided to test German reaction to any expression of Soviet interest in the Danube basin and the Balkans. On March 29, 1940, Molotov, while reviewing Russia's foreign policy in a speech to the Supreme Council of the USSR, indirectly touched upon the

Balkans by referring to the question of Bessarabia "whose seizure by Rumania, the Soviet Union has never recognized. . . ." This remark did not surprise Berlin since the question of Bessarabia had been settled by the Secret Additional Protocol to the Treaty of Non-Aggression between Germany and USSR in August 1939. Paragraph 3 of the said protocol provided:

> With regard to Southeastern Europe, attention is called by the Soviet side to its interest in Bessarabia. The German side declares its complete disinterestedness in these areas. (*Nazi-Soviet Rel.* p. 124.)[5]

Molotov's speech, however, coupled with the Soviet-Yugoslav negotiations and the re-established contact between Maisky, the Soviet Ambassador to London, and Lord Halifax, caused grave concern in Berlin. Hitler, ready to start his *Drag nach Westen*, desperately needed Russia's benevolent neutrality; hence, he was willing to make concessions in order to preserve Russian collaboration.

With remarkable subtlety, Stalin avoided at first any outrageous demand that might have irritated his emotional friend in Berlin. He merely asked for a seat on the European Danube Commission whose members were Italy, France, Britain and, since 1939, Germany. Germany gave her full support to the Soviet request, reportedly on the grounds that Russia's admission would strengthen Germany's position in the Commission. However, the main reason was that Hitler, occupied on the Western Front, was unable to rebuff the Soviet demand.

In the meantime, the tension between Italy and USSR continued. Stalin took advantage of the Italian anti-Sovietism, and disguised his intentions concerning the Balkans by presenting them as aimed only against Italian penetration, without any antagonistic tendency toward Germany. Italy did not sit idle while the world was holding its breath, waiting for Germany's assault on the Western Front. Twenty-five thousand militarized workers were transported to Albania, while Count Ciano made a trip to Tirana in order to test personally the Albanian attitude toward future Italian adventures. As he writes in his *Diaries* (p. 254.), he received a "very warm welcome" and was pleased to discover that "the Albanians are far on the path of intervention. They want Kossovo and Tzamouria. It is easy for us to increase our popularity by becoming the champions of Albanian nationalism." Simultaneously, the Italian propaganda against Greece, which, following the Greco-Italian rapprochement of September 1939, had ceased for many months, was revived and, during the spring of 1940, reached a state of paroxysm. A characteristic passage was contained in a manifesto distributed and posted in Rome by the Nationalist Organization "Opera Azzura":

> In virtue of indisputable historical rights and by right of superior force, Central and Southern France, the Mediterranean basin, the Adriatic, Croatia, Dalmatia, Greece, Cyprus, Albania and Jerusalem belong to Italy. (*Dipl. Doc.*, No. 71.)

In view of these manifestations of aggressiveness, the Soviet Union wasted no time in discouraging the Italian enthusiasts. On June 6, Radio Moscow broadcast an official announcement:

> The Soviet Government has made it unequivocally clear to Italy that it will not remain passive in the face of a threat to the Balkans. The foreign policy of the Soviet Union is based upon a sincere desire to maintain peace, and also upon the fact that the independence of certain states is a vital condition for Soviet security. The Italian Government will do well to take this warning into account. (Dallin, p. 208.)

Mussolini was brought to understand that in view of open Soviet hostility, the time was not ripe to open another front in the Balkans while the German armies were heavily engaged in the gigantic battle on the Western Front. This statement, moreover, contained a paragraph of extreme importance, namely, the paragraph referring to Soviet security. By this, USSR openly declared that there existed a zone of security or, by a different interpretation, a zone of Soviet influence in the Balkans. Today the world knows what Stalin meant in 1940, when he expressed his concern for the independence of certain states vital to Soviet security.

Following the Soviet warning, the intensified Italian propaganda against Greece was gradually eased down. The rumors of an impending Italian landing on Corfu slowly subsided and the insults against the Greek nation disappeared from the pages of Italian newspapers. The frantic posters against Greece, which for weeks decorated the streets of Italian cities, were covered by other equally frenzied proclamations demanding immediate participation in the war.

A few days before the aforementioned Soviet warning, a descriptive account of this war-like excitement was given by J. Politis, the Greek Ambassador to Rome. In one of his reports to Athens, he wrote:

> 3. Government propaganda intended to influence public opinion continues. The latter is artificially represented as being full of war-like enthusiasm and as straining at the leash. Speeches from the leaders to the people, loyal addresses from the people to the chiefs vie with each other in bellicose spirit and pompous phrases announcing that the Italian bomb is about to burst. . . .

> 4. . . . Balbo's paper has started a campaign against Egypt. Signor

Gayda devotes his attention to the Balkans, . . . from Dalmatia to Crete, . . . Count Ciano has undertaken to cultivate Albanian irredentist claims to Tzamuria and Kossovo. Other Fascist manifestoes stake out future claims to Tunis, Gibraltar, and Corfu. In other words, it is proclaimed that the storm is brewing and that all is ready.

But this is merely the façade . . . Public opinion, cowed and timid, fatalistically awaits the Duce's signal like a kind of death-knell. The Duce, on the other hand, perfectly aware of the public's state of mind, is anxiously following the great battle in Flanders and awaiting his opportunity to score an easy victory. If and when the signal will be given, will depend entirely upon the fortunes of the German arms. In which direction he will strike first, is a riddle which still remains unanswered. No declaration, no assurances, no threat of any kind can be regarded as giving a cue to its solution. . . (*Dipl. Doc.*, No. 67.)

Politis was right when he said that the Italian policy was played out upon the battlefield of Flanders. As the German armies penetrated France, Mussolini decided to drive the dagger into the back of France. At six o'clock in the evening of June 10, 1940, Mussolini bellowed from the balcony of Palazzo Venezia:

Now that the die has been cast and that, by our will, the bridges behind us have been burnt, I solemnly declare that Italy has no intention of dragging into the conflict . . . her neighbors by land or by sea. Switzerland, Yugoslavia, Greece, Turkey and Egypt should take note of these words. On them and only on them it depends whether these promises shall be maintained or not. . . .

The Balkans gave a sigh of relief as they saw the war spirit of the Italians channeled in another direction.

FOOTNOTES

1. ". . . Ignatief imposa au Sultan un traitè qui rendait la pèninsule Balkanique vassale de l'empire russe . . ." in, P. P. Guèrin Songeon, *Histoire de la Bulgarie, 458-1913*, Paris: 1913, p. 346.

2. ". . . Bulgaria was to be extended (by the San Stefano Treaty) to the Aegean and might include Salonica—as Ignatief observed, admittedly not Bulgar in population. . . ." in, B. H. Sumner, *Russia and the Balkans, 1870-1880*, Oxford: 1937, p. 403.

3. It is characteristic that even the Sandschak of Sofia, the present capital of Bulgaria, was not originally included within the frontiers of the new state. "Count Shuvalov emphasized to the Czar that it was only through the personal intervention of Bismark at the last moment that the British and Austrian opposition on the question of the *Sandschak von Sofia* was overcome." *Die Diplomatischen Akten des Auswärtigen Amtes, 1871-1914*, Berlin: 1922, Vol. III, p. 4, Doc. No. 440.

4. ". . . These 'vital interests'—the fulfilment of Bulgaria's dream of a great Bulgarian empire within the frontiers of the peace of San Stefano (1878)—aligned Bulgaria openly with the Axis powers in 1941." *Ten Eventful Years*, Encyclopedia Britannica, 1950, Vol. I, p. 459.

5. *Nazi-Soviet Relations 1939-41*, (ed. R. I. Sontag, New York: 1948)

CHAPTER SIX

THE ITALIAN AGGRESSION

ONCE THE ROARING Panzer Divisions of the Führer entered Paris, crushing under their tracks the legend of the French Army, the Duce was able to boast from the Palazzo Venezia balcony about the magnificent Axis victory. At last, he was able to face the Italian people not with embarrassment but with the air of a glorious victor. All doubts, apprehensions, and uncertainties, which had plagued him during the first months of the war vanished, and he regained his familiar braggadocio.

MUSSOLINI TURNS EASTWARD AGAIN

With France totally defeated, Mussolini turned his attention eastward again. Among Yugoslavia, Greece, and Egypt, Greece offered, according to his appraisal, the certainty of an easy victory accompanied by maximum benefits. He based this conclusion on information which presented the Greek people as unsympathetic, if not hostile, to their government, ready to welcome new leadership. A considerable part of the Greek nation was reported to be openly favoring the Axis, while the rest was divided between unrepentant Anglophiles and neutralists or defeatists. Mussolini had no doubts that the operation should be very easy if carefully planned. The rewards of the conquest were truly tempting. By occupying Greece, he would acquire invaluable naval and air bases from which he would be able to challenge successfully the British position in the eastern Mediterranean. Cut off from the Aegean port of Salonika and, consequently, from any possible assistance from Great Britain, Yugoslavia would more easily surrender to the demands of the Axis, while Italian influence upon that country would become unquestionable. After the occupation of Greece, he would be able to undertake the campaign against Egypt with the priceless advantage of using the short route of supply and air attack provided by the Greek naval and air bases.

PREPARATION OF THE ENTERPRISE

In preparing the ground for the operation against Greece, Mussolini resorted to pitiful propagandistic tactics. In this, he followed Führer's formula for starting a war ". . . use propagandistic reasons for starting the war; never mind whether it be plausible or not. The victor shall not be

49

asked later on whether he told the truth or not. In starting and making the war, not the right is what matters, but victory." (I. M. T, X, p. 366.)

On June 18, 1940, J. Politis, Greek Ambassador to Rome, was urgently summoned to the Italian Foreign Ministry. He was informed that the Italian Government "possessed conclusive evidence that a British aircraft carrier, together with several cruisers and destroyers, had remained in Cretan waters longer than the legal twenty-four hour limit." General Metaxas immediately telegraphed to Rome and denied these accusations by stating categorically that "not a single British warship of any description has even been signaled within the range of visibility from the shore." Soon the truth of Metaxas assertion was completely established and Anfuso—the official who represented Count Ciano when he was absent from the Ministry serving every other week as an airman by Mussolini's orders—expressed to the Greek Ambassador his satisfaction and recognized that "no question existed." Politis, however, was not inclined to dismiss the matter and, with exquisite sarcasm, expressed surprise "that such a question should have arisen at all," and he added:

> I could understand . . . a misunderstanding arising, if in lieu of a single ship, the Italian Navy had spotted several, or if a warship had actually touched at one of our ports and there had been a misunderstanding about the length of her stay. But it seemed to me very strange that such an allegation should be made without the smallest foundation and that details should be given indicating the class of vessel, etc., even if one made allowances for the natural nervousness of the military authorities in time of war. (*Dipl. Doc.*, No. 81.)

Anfuso agreed that it was very surprising and in Politis' presence called the admiral who acted as liaison and drew his attention to the matter, adding that their incorrect information had been the cause of bothering Ambassador Politis, while "there was not the shadow of a foundation for the information in question."

The ostensible sorrow of Anfuso because of the "mistake" of the Italian admiralty did not deceive Politis and the Greek Government. They realized that this incident was merely the prelude to a new period of tension; and they were right. During the following months, Fascist ingenuity employed a continuous fabrication of allegations and formal accusations against Greece—unfortunately for their inventors, however, too easily refutable.

DEVELOPMENTS IN THE DANUBE-BALKAN REGION

Mussolini's decision to resume hostile policies against Greece was evidently brought about by the events which took place in the Balkans immediately after the fall of France. In the middle of June, Gigurtu, the pro-German Foreign Minister of Rumania was elevated to the premiership by King Carol, and on June 21, 1940, by decree, the King banned all political parties in Rumania and transferred virtually all power to the Iron Guard, a semi-military, nationalistic organization. Mussolini discerned in this incident that Hitler's attempt to swallow Rumania bloodlessly had made considerable progress. Once again his partner at Berlin had outstripped him.

Mussolini's apprehensions were aggravated also by the fact that Molotov, on June 24, informed the German Government about the decision of the Soviet Union to annex immediately not only Bessarabia but also Bukovina. The Soviet leaders rightly realized that this was the proper time to act, while the German armies were still concentrated in the West.

The Soviet demand concerning Bukovina came to Hitler as a painful surprise, since Bukovina was not included in the German-Soviet agreements of August 1939. By those agreements, Hitler had accepted the Soviet aspirations on Bessarabia. But Bukovina was not included, as it had never been a province of Czarist Russia. Von Ribbentrop, in his reply to Molotov stressed that "the claim of the Soviet Government to Bukovina is something new." (*Nazi-Soviet Rel.* p. 156.) Molotov, however, was not very much disturbed by the surprise of the German Foreign Minister and in the afternoon of the same day, June 25, summoned the German Ambassador to Moscow and declared that "the Soviet Government . . . had decided to limit its demands to the northern part of Bukovina and the city of Czernowitz. . ." Molotov also added that the Soviet Government "expected German support for this Soviet demand." Hitler was as yet unprepared to give the answer which was more suitable to his temperament and, therefore, he decided to yield; the Rumanian Government was advised to accept the Soviet demands. It may be assumed that the campaign against the USSR was born in Hitler's mind that very day when he was so deeply humiliated by Stalin.

At 10:30 the following day, June 26, Molotov, armed with the consent of the Führer, handed the Rumanian Minister in Moscow, an ultimatum demanding, at twenty-four hour notice, the immediate cession of Bessarabia and Northern Bukovina. In vain the Rumanian Government made an effort to open negotiations, in the hope of gaining time or at least saving part of the demanded territory. Their efforts met with no success. On June 28, at two o'clock in the afternoon, Soviet troops crossed the Rumanian border. The whole operation was executed with unusual speed; even airplanes were used by the Russians to drop paratroops and small tanks.

MUSSOLINI IS INDIGNANT

Mussolini was not even asked about this new "rectification" of the European map. He again felt his prestige fading out, while the advancement of the Soviet positions toward the Balkans caused him misgivings and indignation. In his opinion there was no other alternative but the conquest of Greece, which would not only restore his prestige but also block the advance of the Soviets toward the eastern Mediterranean.

As a result of these considerations, he decided to prepare the ground for the operation. Allegations against Greece became the every day motto of the Greco-Italian diplomatic contacts; imaginary accusations against the Greek Minister to Ankara, the Athenian society, complaints about the presence of British warships—which, as it happened, were Greek—in Greek ports; allegations similar to these followed one another unceasingly, as Mussolini attempted both to terrify the Greek Government and to find a pretext for his aggression. (*Dipl. Doc.*, Nos. 84-109.) The Greek government patiently refuted each of these allegations, using the uncontestable power of truth against falsehood, but to no avail. Count Ciano, in rude and angry tones, warned Politis that "the assistance the British Navy was receiving from Greece was sufficient proof unto today, and meant war with Italy and Germany. It was time (for the Greeks) to realize that the Axis had won and that (they) stop living in a fool's paradise and backing both sides."[1] With notable perspicacity, Politis, interpreted these remarks to mean "either with us or against us." Mussolini said to Count Ciano on August 10, that he was now considering as imminent "an act of force (against Greece) because since 1923 he had some accounts to settle, and the Greeks deceive themselves if they think that he has forgotten," Ciano wrote in his *Diaries* (p. 283.) The accounts mentioned by Mussolini in these remarks apparently referred to the bombardment of the Greek island of Corfu by the Italian Navy in 1923. One who is not familiar with Fascist thinking may be surprised that Mussolini found in that incident a cause for complaint against Greece.

According to Ciano's *Diaries*, (p.283) on the next day Mussolini asked for particulars concerning the Greek province of Tzamuria and that same day he prepared a dispatch which would "start agitation on the question (of Tzamuria)." Speedy action may have been the result of Ciano's suggestion that they should work fast because "it is dangerous to give the Greeks time to prepare." The dispatch, which Mussolini himself prepared, appeared in the newspapers of August 11, 1940. It was the story of the assasination of the "Albanian patriot," Daout Hodja, actually an ordinary criminal from Tzamuria who had fled to Albania twenty years previously and who had convictions against him by the Assize-Courts of Jannina and Preveza for murder, brigandage robbery, etc." (*Dipl. Doc.*, No. 114.) The story completely out of proportion with the actual events, was decorated with impressive descriptions. ". . . the murderers were Greek agents who carried the head back into Greek territory . . . his head was paraded about from village to village by order of the Greek local authorities and exposed to public view so as to terrorize the unre-deemed Albanian brethren." In preparing this dispatch, Mussolini delib-erately overlooked the fact that on July 25, the Royal Italian Legation had addressed a note to the Greek Foreign Ministry requesting that Pilo Kotso and Elia Foto, "natives of Moursi (Albania) . . . who had treacher-ously murdered . . . an Albanian forest-guard named Daout Hodja from Tzamuria . . . should be held in temporary custody pending a formal demand for their extradition which will shortly be made by the Albanian Ministry for Justice." (*Dipl. Doc.*, No. 112.) The reply of the Greek Government completely confounded the Italian allegations; however, for Mussolini such facts were minor details, and, undisturbed, he proceeded to the execution of his plan. The Italian press was instructed to intensify the attacks against Greece. In the murder of Hodja, Farinacci and Gayda discovered the most recent chapter of the policy of terrorization directed by the Greek Government against Albania. The headless corpse of Hodja provided inspiration to the *Popolo di Roma*, which declared that in the rectification of the European map, Italian sovereignty should include the whole section between the Adriatic and the Black Sea.

In a telegram to Athens on August 14, Politis explored the inner mean-ing of this frenzied propaganda. Since "in diplomatic circles, it is taken for granted that Germany is opposed to a conflagration in the Balkans . . . ," he was "wondering anxiously whether the Italians contemplate im-mediate action against (Greece), or whether they merely intend to raise the question of Tzamuria . . . and to bully (Greece) into making con-cessions, as has been the case with Rumania." (*Dipl. Doc.*, No. 116.) Actually the latter was the case; two days earlier, according to Ciano's *Diaries* (p.284) the Duce had set "the political and military lines for ac-tion against Greece; if Tzamuria and Corfu are yielded without striking a blow, we shall not ask for anything more. If, on the other hand, any resistance is attempted, we shall go the limit. . . ." With reference to the alleged German opposition to Italian aggressive plans, Politis observed that Greece should not rely too much on these objections; since "the plan for the invasion of England seems to have, for the moment, been put aside," no one can tell "how far this modification in their military programme will affect the views of the Axis Powers . . . more especially their policy in the Balkans . . ." Concluding his telegram, Politis expressed the opinion that the statement of Mavroudis, who declared to Count Grazzi that "in the event of an attack by Italy, the Royal Government's decision to resist remained unshaken" may prove to be "an important factor . . . if it is a case of purely Italian initiative . . ."

The next day was the Feast of the Assumption. This important holiday for the Greeks was defiled by the Italians. The Greek light cruiser *Helle* dressed with bunting from peak to stern in honor of the Feast, and

anchored in the harbor of the island of Tenos was torpedoed by an Italian
submarine. Ciano commented on the incident in his *Diaries* (p. 284) and
attributed it to "the intemperance of De Vecci," the Italian Governor of
the Dodecanese. Mussolini, who aimed at taking Greece by surprise when
the time was ripe, apparently disapproved this incident, because he feared
it might precipitate British intervention in protection of Greece; therefore, he advised Ciano to settle the matter peacefully. However, such a
settlement became unnecessary as the Greek Government preferred to
dismiss the matter altogether, in the hope that the danger of war would
thus be averted. Although the identity of the submarine was positively
established by an examination of the fragments of the torpedo, Metaxas
issued an order to the press censors forbidding "all mention in the press
concerning the nationality of the submarine . . . and generally all news
relative to the torpedoing of the vessel." In issuing this order, the position
of the Greek Government was quite clear. Had Greece divulged the
truth, she would have been compelled either to declare war or to have
war declared against her. But Greece never wanted war with Italy, either
with or without allies, since it was evident that whatever the outcome of
the first battles with the Italians, the conflict would be resolved eventually
by the German armies.

As the incident of *Helle*, followed as it was by the air attack against
the passenger ship *Frinton* on the afternoon of the same day, revealed
that Italy was resolved to employ extreme measures, Metaxas turned to
Hitler.[2] Since all the indications supported the assumption that Germany
disliked the idea of a new theater of war in the Balkans, Metaxas hoped
that Hitler's timely intervention might prevent the Italian aggression.
Hitler, however, replied that Greece had nothing to fear from Italy, provided she would not offer any pretexts to Italy, that is to say, provided
she would not mobilize.[3] Apparently on Hitler's order, Von Ribbentrop
had a conference with the Italian Ambassador, Alfieri, and informed him
that the German Government would not welcome a too close Soviet-
Italian rapprochement. According to Ciano's *Diaries* (p.285) he also
suggested the abandonment of any plan of attack against Yugoslavia and
also of any action against Greece. The first of Ribbentrop's suggestions,
concerning the Soviet-Italian relations, clearly shows that the Barbarossa
Plan had already started to ripen in Hitler's mind. Indeed, as General
Keitel revealed during his testimony at the International Military Tribunal at Nüremberg, the first time the possibility of an armed conflict with
the Soviet Union was brought under consideration, "was at the beginning
of August 1940, on the occasion of a discussion of the situation at Berchtesgaden, or rather at his (Hitler's) house, the Berghof." (I. M. T., X,
p. 524.)

On August 22, apparently as a result of the German *demarchè*, the Duce gave to Ciano "a copy of certain military directives he had formulated, in which the action against Greece and Yugoslavia (were) indefinitely postponed, as a result of German pressure. Germany (wishes) to avoid a crisis in the Balkans at all costs." Within one week, the press war against Greece, which had been conducted, for months, by the Italian newsmen with remarkable consistency, subsided entirely. In a long telegram to Athens, Politis, obviously unaware of the "German pressure," concluded: ". . . The campaign stops at this point for the time being. It has ceased as suddenly as it has begun." (*Dipl. Doc.*, No. 140.)

AXIS-SOVIET ANTAGONISM OVER THE BALKANS

Count Ciano did not fail to comprehend the exact meaning of Ribbentrop's advice with reference to the Soviet-Italian relations. He realized that the strange Soviet-German honeymoon had lasted too long and that Germany would soon turn to Italy as her only significant ally in Europe. As Russia's interest in the Balkans would not be satisfied merely by the annexation of Bessarabia and Northern Bukovina, the German-Soviet relations could not remain friendly. The USSR anxiously watched the penetration of the Balkans by Germany. As she desired to establish direct contact with Bulgaria, Rumania was an undesirable obstacle in the way. On August 19, the Kremlin protested to the Rumanian Government on a series of frontier incidents while, a few days earlier, both *Izvestiya* and *Pravda* lent vigorous support to Bulgaria's claims on South Dobrutza. Apparently the USSR disliked the possibility that the Dobrutza question might be settled through the offices of Germany and Italy. In the meantime, the direct negotiations between Rumania and Hungary on the question of Transylvania virtually broke down, and a series of frontier incidents threatened to precipitate war. Such an eventuality might have given the Russians a pretext to intervene and seize additional Rumanian territory. Germany, of course, was unwilling to tolerate an open conflict between Rumania and Hungary, which in addition to the foregoing, would jeojardize Germany's supplies of petroleum and foodstuff. But this time Hitler did not act alone, as he did in the case of the cession of Bessarabia and Northern Bukovina. By this time it was evident that the battle against Britain would be a very difficult and uncertain enterprise, while the Soviet policies caused grave concern in Berlin; therefore, the bonds between Italy and Germany should be strengthened. As a result, Ciano was invited by Hitler to participate in the settlement of the Rumano-Hungarian dispute. Moscow was aware of the Axis intentions to settle this dispute unilaterally. Determined to emphasize the Soviet interest in Rumanian affairs, the Soviet government handed another note of protest to the Rumanian Government on August 29. In response, Germany and Italy solemnly guaranteed the frontiers of Rumania. Apparently this guarantee—which, incidentally, was a recognition of Italy's influence in the Danubian-Balkan affairs—was primarily aimed at Russia. On August 30, Von Ribbentrop and Count Ciano handed down their "arbitrary award" to the Rumanian and Hungarian delegates in Vienna. By the terms of this instrument, Rumania ceded the northern half of Transylvania to Hungary. One week later, Rumania pressed by Berlin signed the Craiova Agreement by which she ceded South Dobrutza to Bulgaria.

These "rectifications" of the Danubian-Balkan frontiers, carried out without the participation of the Soviet Union, constituted an open violation of the German-Soviet agreements which specifically provided for mutual consultation on matters concerning "their common interests." (Art. III.) They were also a clear warning to Greece and Yugoslavia who had not shown as yet any indication of their willingness to abide by the Axis dictates.

Although Bulgaria expressed to Germany her everlasting gratitude for the solution of the South Dobrutza question, she was still reluctant to abandon her status of neutrality and join the Axis. As long as the German and Soviet armies were away from her own borders, Bulgaria could not afford a policy openly favoring either one of the two continental giants. It was apparent that she did not need to solve the problem herself since it would be finally solved by the fate of Rumania. King Boris and his government knew that eventually Bulgaria must ally herself with the power that would acquire unquestionable domain over Rumania. Soon they were given the answer.

Hitler's plans for a *blitzkrieg* were shattered by the resistance of Britain, and he began to think in terms of a long and costly war. It is now known that the lack of adequate means of transportation for his troops over the Channel, and the failure of the *Luftwaffe* to secure undisputed domain over the British sky, compelled Hitler to revise his plans for an assault on Britain in the fall of 1940.[4] He then considered the war on a global scale, and since he was unable to crush Britain herself he decided to dismantle the British Commonwealth.[5] The outcome of these considerations was the signing of the *Dreimächtepact*. This pact, hereinafter cited as the Tripartite, was signed by Germany, Italy, and Japan on September 27, 1940. It was a ten-year military and economic alliance, in which the three governments pledged "to stand by and cooperate with one another in regard to their efforts in Greater East Asia and regions of Europe respectively wherein it is their prime purpose to establish and maintain a new order of things (Neue Ordnung) . . ." (I. M. T., XXXI, p. 56.)

Although the Tripartite provided for the cooperation of the two European partners, Hitler soon violated this provision by instigating in Rumania—without consulting or even informing his partner in Rome—a military coup d'etat. On October 6, General Antonescu, with German support took over the reins of government, expelled King Carol and on the same day, upon his invitation, German troops crossed the Rumanian border in order "to protect the country from British intervention." This explanation, of course, was too transparent to conceal the true purpose, which obviously aimed to forestall further Soviet intervention in Rumanian affairs. Hitler was now considering the feasibility of "an Eastern campaign . . . prior to victory in the West . . . with the object of first eliminating (Germany's) last serious opponent on the Continent (USSR)." (I. M. T., III, p. 141.) As a result, Rumania and the Balkans, in general, came to the foreground of Hitler's concern. However, his lightning-like operation in Rumania surprised and displeased not only the Kremlin but also the Duce.

MUSSOLINI IS DETERMINED TO ATTACK GREECE

Ciano in his *Diaries* (p. 300) writes that Mussolini "above all is indignant at the German occupation of Rumania. He says that this has impressed Italian public opinion deeply and badly, because, in view of the decisions taken at Vienna, nobody expected this to happen. 'Hitler always faces me with a *fait accompli*. This time I am going to pay him back in his own coin. He will find out from the papers that I have occupied Greece. In this way the equilibrium will be reestablished'. . . ." To this Ciano commented: "In fact I believe that the military operation will be useful and easy." On October 13, the Greek Ambassador in Budapest reported to his government that "in the circles of the Hungarian Ministry for Foreign Affairs an Italian attack on Greece is regarded as imminent." (*Dipl. Doc.*, No. 163.) The accuracy of this information is proved by the entry of October 14 in Ciano's *Diaries* (p. 301) where he reveals that Mussolini had fixed the day of the invasion for October 26. However, the three Chiefs of the Italian General Staff were against the operation and, in a conversation with Ciano, they frankly expressed their misgivings. Ciano openly disagreed with the arguments presented by General Badoglio against the invasion and, with the air of an experienced diplomat, he insisted that "from political point of view the moment is good. Greece is isolated. Turkey will not move, neither will Yugoslavia. If the Bulgarians enter the war it will be on our side . . . " He was correct in his appraisal of the reaction of the Balkan States in case of Italian attack on Greece. Yugoslavia had followed a policy of isolationism and neutrality for a long period. Once, shortly before the Italian attack against France, Pourich, the Yugoslav Minister to Paris, had stated to the French Foreign Minister that, in case of an Italian attack against Greece, Yugoslavia would remain neutral and only "if the Italians entered Salonika would she re-examine the situation." (Pipinellis p. 302.) Ciano was apparently aware of this decision and thus, he was able to assure the Italian generals that Yugoslavia would not move. In view of her well-known aspirations in Macedonia and western Thrace, Bulgaria would not come to Greece's aid. Only Turkey remained, but she was not likely to move. The policy of the Soviet Union at that time was to reconquer all the regions formerly held by the Czarist Empire. Turkey, therefore was afraid that the Kremlin might take advantage of her involvement in war and claim the frontier districts of Kars and Ardahan which Moscow had ceded to the Turks in 1921. Ciano was right when he expressed the opinion that Greece was isolated. In addition documents of the French government, captured by the Germans after the collapse of France, revealed the meager assistance the Allies were able to extend to Greece. (*Ger. Doc.*, Nos. 107, 109.)[6] Ciano, therefore fully supported Mussolini's decision to attack Greece. Mussolini, however, was also considering the possibility of a peaceful solution without the undesirable complications of an open conflict; a settlement resembling the German occupation of Rumania would have been very welcome. In consequence, the rumors which emanated from Rome ranked from "an amicable formulation of claims to a sudden invasion" as Politis phrased it in his telegram of October 15. During the following days, the reports of the Greek diplomatic representatives in Italy, Albania, and other European countries contained concrete information concerning Italian military concentrations in Albania, and the form and date of the imminent Italian action.

This time Mussolini had made the decision to act and nothing would stop him. His partner in Berlin was actually carrying the war on his own initiative, while Mussolini was put in the position of a junior member without a decisive voice, if any voice at all. His displeasure was aggravated by some recent, extremely important developments in Hitler's policies. Hitler, at the end of the summer, adopted a course of rapprochement with Vichy which aimed to achieve a closer cooperation with the Petain government, and gain its support in his struggle with Britain. In order to gain such cooperation, Hitler was inclined to make certain concessions; one of them would be the abandonment of Italian claims to Tunis, Corsica, and Djibouti. The meeting of Hitler and Marshal Petain in October deeply distressed the Duce.[7] Hitler's meeting with Franco, immediately after the conference with Petain and Laval at Montoire, was not at all pleasant to Mussolini who feared that his position in the Axis might be weakened by the admission of new members. In his opinion, the time had come for Italy to act and restore her prestige; otherwise, she might find herself placed even behind defeated France. On October 22, Ciano wrote in his *Diaries* (p. 303).

Mussolini . . . has prepared a letter for Hitler on the general situation. He alludes to our pending action in Greece, but does not make clear either the form or the date because he fears that once again an order might come to halt us. Many indications lead us to believe that in Berlin they are not very enthusiastic about our going to Athens. The day fixed now is the 28th of October . . . I begin to draw up the ultimatum which Grazzi will hand to Metaxas at two o'clock in the morning of the 28th of October. Naturally it is a document that allows no way out for Greece. Either she accepts occupation or she will be attacked.

We may suppose that Mussolini's letter did not reach Hitler in time, probably it was never sent. In any event, Hitler, then in France, received information concerning the Italian operation against Greece, through Göring and the *Auswärtiges Amt;* immediately he rerouted his train, which was on the way from France to Berlin, in order to speak to the Duce in Florence. On October 25, Von Ribbentrop telephoned to Ciano and proposed a conference between Hitler and Mussolini at Florence on Monday the 28th of October. The proposal was accepted, but Ciano did not neglect to comment in his *Diaries* (p.304) that "this rush of the Führer to Italy, so soon after his conference with Petain, is not at all pleasing to me." Apparently Ciano presumed that the purpose of the proposed visit would be to squeeze from Italy concessions in favor of France. He knew that at the time of the meeting the Italian legions would be already marching toward Athens. Göring's contention that the order for the invasion was released 24 or 48 hours before schedule is contradicted by the entry in Ciano's diary, of October 22, in which he notes that the time of the attack was fixed for the early morning of October 28. Ciano was in a better position to know than Göring.

The meeting took place Monday morning at ten o'clock. Hitler expressed his misgivings concerning a new theater of war in the Balkans and stressed his intention to prevent, under all circumstances, an expansion of the conflict in the Balkans and the eastern Mediterranean. He further urged the Duce to forego such unnecessary plans. With a hardly concealed smile of triumph, Mussolini replied that it was too late to prevent the conflict, because "we are on the march," and shortly the Italian troops would be in Athens! This news did not please the Führer at all. Keitel testified at the International Military Tribunal that Hitler became "extremely angry about this development and the dragging of the Balkans into the war, and only the fact that Italy was an ally prevented a break

with Mussolini." (I. M. T., X, p. 522.) Peace in the Balkans was obviously
indispensable to Hitler's plans. Their neutrality not only assured him a
corridor for supplies but also kept Britain away from the Continent. In
case of a conflict with Russia, neutral Balkans would mean a safe flank for
his armies. Now, the attack on Greece would under certain circumstances endanger the relations of Turkey with the Axis Powers; but more
important, it would create another theater of war. Hitler realized that
sooner or later Italy would draw upon her German ally for help. The
unreasonable step of his Italian partner had upset his plans and jeopar-
dized their successful outcome.

THE ULTIMATUM

Shortly before three o'clock on the morning of October 28, Metaxas
was awakened by the ringing of the telephone. When he picked up the
receiver, he heard a voice he did not recognize. "Ici le ministre de France
qui dèsire vous voir immediatement." General Metaxas supposed that the
French Minister had something of extreme urgency to communicate and
asked him to come to his house. A few minutes later, Metaxas went
downstairs in his dressing gown to open the front door and found that his
visitor was the Italian Minister, Count Grazzi. They both went to the
Metaxas small library and there the Italian Minister handed the ultimatum:

. . . The Italian Government has . . . decided to demand from the
Hellenic Government, as a guarantee of the neutrality of Greece and
the security of Italy, the right to occupy with her armed forces, for
the duration of the present conflict with Great Britain, a number of
strategic points in Greek territory. The Italian Government demands
that the Hellenic Government shall not oppose any resistance to this
occupation. . . Should the Italian forces meet with resistance, the
resistance will be crushed by force of arms, and in that case the Hellenic Government will bear the responsibility for whatever may ensue.
(*Dipl. Doc.*, No. 178.)

"What exactly are these strategic points?" Metaxas asked.
"I don't know, your Excellency, my Government has not informed
me." Count Grazzi paused for a moment and then he added, "I only
know that the ultimatum expires at six o'clock this morning."
"Then this communication is in fact a declaration of war.
"No, Excellency, it is an ultimatum.
"It is tantamount to a declaration of war.
"Of course not, as I believe you will give the facilities my Government
requests."
"No," replied Metaxas, and with that word unified the Greek nation
beyond his most ardent hopes, and added to the World's oldest and rich-
est roll of honor another immortal name.

It is worth mentioning a passage from the report of His British Majesty's Minister:

The President of the Council (Metaxas) has assured himself an outstanding place in Greece's history, and whatever the future may bring, his foresight in quietly preparing his country for war, and his courage in resisting the Italian ultimatum when delivered in the small hours of this October morning will surely obtain an honorable mention in the story of European statecraft. He means to fight until Italy is completely defeated, and this reflects the purpose of the whole Greek nation. (I. M. T., III, p. 310.)

Metaxas' foresight "in quietly preparing his country for war" was deserving of praise. The iron discipline which he had imposed upon the Greek nation paid its dividends at the crucial hour. The nation's decisiveness was saved from discussions which might have divided the country at this contingency. The suppressed indignation of the Greek people for the continuous insults to their sacred traditions by the Fascists, and the monstrous calamity of the *Helle's* sinking, combined with their national pride and honor, toughened by forced silence, acquired a volcanic force which swept over the Italian legions and turned their "glorious march to Athens" into a miserable flight back into Albania.

FOOTNOTES

1. See also, *The Ciano Diaries*, p. 272.

2. Metaxas more than once appealed to Hitler. See Pipinellis, *op. cit.*, p. 328. Also E. I. Tsouderos, *Diplomatica Paraskinia 1941-1944*, Athens: 1950, pp. 70-75.

3. See also Von Ribbentrop's testimony to the I. M. Tribunal in *I. M. Tribunal, Proceedings*, Vol. X, p. 287.

4. See the letter of Admiral Raeder to Admiral Assman in *I. M. Tribunal, Proceedings*, Vol. III, p. 141.

5. See Directive 18, signed by Hitler, initialed by Jodl, dated November 12, 1940 in, *ibid.*, Exhibit GB 116, Vol. III, p. 311.

6. *(German) Official Documents on the Conflict with Yugoslavia and Greece*, (Auswärtiges Amt/Nr. 7, Berlin: 1941)

7. Laval, during his testimony in the trial of Marshal Petain, stated that Hitler, in their meeting of October 1940 in Montoire, clearly alluded that France could avoid the consequences of defeat by helping Germany in the destruction of the British Empire.

CHAPTER SEVEN

"DIVIDE AND CONQUER"

THE DECISION OF THE Greek Government to reject the Italian ultimatum virtually astonished the world. But even the freedom loving nations were not optimistic in regard to the outcome of this brave but, as they thought, foolish decision. The continuous successes of the Axis during the first year of the war resulted in a widespread psychosis that the Axis was undefeatable. The general prediction was that Greece, by resisting the Italians, would only offer a futile sacrifice on the altar of freedom.

THE ITALIANS FLEE INTO ALBANIA

In spite of these pessimistic prophecies, by the end of November at least four Italian divisions had been shattered, large numbers of prisoners captured, and not a single invader remained on Greek soil. In achieving these startling results, the Greek army fought virtually without any assistance except for British air and naval aid which was far from negligible.

Immediately after the Italian invasion of Greece, diplomatic efforts were made by the German Government to settle the conflict as soon as possible. Hitler desperately needed peace in the Balkans and, an early settlement of the conflict, before it developed into a serious and dangerous situation was necessary. However, if Mussolini had accepted the conciliatory services of the Führer, his prestige would have sunk even lower. Therefore he made it clear that as long as there was hope for a military victory he had "no intention of engaging in *pourparlers* with a view to peace, and that the war machine having been set in motion could not be stopped until the conflict had been decisively settled."

This brought an end to Germany's efforts for a possible settlement. On November 7, 1940, the official German Agency (D.N.B.) announced that "Italian political circles declare that, military operations having been rendered necessary by the rejection of the Italian ultimatum, no change can be effected in the situation except through military developments. . ." Soon the operations effected such a serious change in the situation that by December 4, the Italian commander in Albania was compelled to suggest that "the situation must be settled through political intervention." (Ciano's *Diaries*, p. 318.) Utterly depressed, Mussolini himself admitted that "there is nothing else to do. This is grotesque and absurd, but it is a fact; we have to ask for a truce through Hitler." As there was not the slightest indication that Greece would accept any other solution than the unconditional withdrawal of all the Italian demands, Mussolini decided to request "Germany's military intervention in Thrace through Bulgaria."

More than one month before Mussolini's appeal, Hitler issued his Directive, Nr. 18, dated November 12, 1940, "on the preparatory measures of the OKW (Supreme Headquarters of the German Army) for the prosecution of the war in the near future." In that part of the directive dealing with the Balkans, Hitler gave "the following preliminary instructions in regard to an operation against Greece: . . . Balkans . . . The Commander-in-Chief of the Army will make preparations for occupying the Greek mainland north of the Aegean Sea, in case of need, entering through Bulgaria and thus make possible the use of German Air Force units against targets in the Eastern Mediterranean . . . In order to be able to face all eventualities and keep Turkey in check, the use of an army group of an approximate strength of ten divisions is to be the basis for the planning and the calculations of deployment . . ." (I. M. T., III, p. 311.) Hitler early realized that his intervention would be necessary. Directive 18, and especially the part concerning prosecution of the war in the Balkans was closely related to Hitler's growing inclination to attack the USSR even before the capitulation of Britain. The German campaign against Greece soon became an essential part of Hitler's master-plan for an assault against the Soviet Union. On September 3, 1940, when Hitler gave the first order to General Von Paulus to prepare the tactical and strategic plans for Operation Barbarossa, the Balkans were at peace and Hitler was really anxious to preserve that condition. But following the Italian invasion of Greece, and Hitler's failure to prevent it or, at least, minimize its consequences, a German attack against Greece became an inherent part of Operation Barabarossa.

MOLOTOV VISITS BERLIN

Notwithstanding his assignment to Von Paulus and the preliminary orders for an attack on Greece, Hitler desired to clarify the Russian intentions before any definite decision was made with reference to the future. Therefore, he invited Molotov to Berlin to discuss certain issues bearing upon the relations between the two countries, and to check the possibility of Russia's adherence to the Tripartite. Molotov accepted the invitation and arrived in Berlin on November 12, 1940. During the three-day conversations, it became evident that the main points at issue were their respective relations with the Balkan countries and Finland. Despite their serious disagreements on very important questions, Ribbentrop handed Molotov on November 13, a draft agreement concerning the division of the zones of influence, as a preliminary step in their master-agreement concerning USSR's adherence to the Tripartite. According to this draft, "the focal points in the territorial aspirations of the Soviet Union would presumably be centered south of the territory of the Soviet Union in the direction of the Indian Ocean." In regard to the Straits, Germany proposed that "the Straits Convention of Montreux presently in force, be replaced by another convention which would accord to the Soviet Union the unrestricted right of passage through the Straits for her warships at any time, whereas all other powers except the other Black Sea countries, but including Germany and Italy, would renounce in principle the right of passage through the Straits for their warships." (*Nazi-Soviet Rel.*, pp. 250-258.)

Germany requested for herself a decisive voice in Europe and pre-eminent influence in the Central African region. Italy was assigned North and Northeast Africa. In this draft, Hitler's effort to channel Soviet ex-pansionism toward the Asiatic shores and retain for Germany monopo-listic influence in Europe including the Balkans was quite obvious, in spite of his assurances that Germany had "no territorial interests in the Balkans, but solely economic."

The Soviet answer was given by Molotov on November 25. He for-mally informed the German ambassador in Moscow that the Soviet Gov-ernment was willing to accept Ribbentrop's draft agreement for a Four-Power Pact—Germany, Italy, Japan, and the Soviet Union—subject to the following conditions:

1. Immediate withdrawal of the German troops from Finland "which under the compact of 1939, belongs to the Soviet Union sphere of influence."
2. Signature of a Mutual Assistance Pact between the USSR and Bul-garia "which geographically is situated inside the security zone of the Black Sea boundaries of the Soviet Union."
3. Establishment of a Soviet base for land and naval forces within range of the Bosporus and the Dardanelles, and also a base for light naval and land forces of the USSR on (*am*) the Bosporus and the Dardanelles.
4. An interest in the outlets of the Baltic Sea.
5. Abandonment of Japanese concession rights on coal and oil in Nor-thern Sakhalin.

He added that the foregoing conditions should be incorporated in three more secret protocols. In conclusion, Molotov emphasized that Germany should recognize the Soviet right to expand in the direction of Iran and the Persian Gulf in general, while Turkey should be compelled by joint

Soviet-German pressure to accept the "rectifications" concerning the Straits and comply with the provisions of the future agreements.

OPERATION MARITA AND OPERATION BARBAROSSA

The negotiations between the two governments practically ceased at this point. Finally, on December 18, 1940, Hitler issued Directive No. 21, which began with these words:

The German armed forces must be prepared in order to smash Soviet Russia in a swift operation, (in einem schnellen Feldzug nieder-zuwerfen), even before the end of the war with England . . . . (*Nazi-Soviet Rel.*, p. 260.)

The two-front war, which Hitler himself had condemned in *Mein Kampf* as the chief reason for Germany's defeat in World War I, became a certainty for the second time, in this instance by his own initiative.

As a result of Directive 21, the center of gravity in the continuation of the war was shifted decidedly eastward. Operation Sea Lion against England already had been indefinitely postponed. The amphibious operation against Gibraltar, which during the Hitler-Franco meeting (October 23, 1940) had been fixed for January 10, 1941, was also eventually dropped because Franco, by December, expressed his misgivings to Hitler and asked for the deferment of the operation. The Greek victories and the successful British air raid on Taranto (November 11, 1940) when half the capital strength of the Italian fleet was put out of action, were, of course, largely responsible for Franco's deviation from the original plans.

Hitler was prompted by pressing strategic considerations in taking the fatal step to order the preparation of an attack on Russia. His failure to vanquish Britain, after the fall of France, exposed Germany to the grave danger of facing not only a joint attack by the United States and England, but also an invasion by Soviet Russia, at such time as Soviet leaders regarded the operation safe. As Von Ribbentrop revealed during his trial, Hitler's "great anxiety was that Russia on the one hand and the United States and Britain on the other, might proceed against Germany . . ." (I. M. T., X, p. 294.) Later in 1943, when Hitler was asked by Shevov, the Counselor of the Bulgarian King, whether he should have started the operation against Russia, had he been aware of Russia's military potentialities, he replied: "I would have started earlier!"

The relation of conditions in the Balkan countries to any military operation against Russia through the Ukrainian plains is quite obvious; a stable situation in the Balkans was essential to the successful execution of the Operation Barbarossa. No operation against Russia could be undertaken as long as a serious theater of war existed in Albania. The Italians, however, were unable to settle the military situation; therefore, Hitler decided to prepare an operation against Greece as a prerequisite for his major operation against USSR. It is characteristic that five days before the release of Directive 21, another important document came from Hitler's drafting board; it was top-secret *Weisung No. 20*, for the Operation Marita. In this Directive 20, the Führer outlined as follows the necessary steps for the operation against Greece:

> My plan, therefore, is (a) to form a slowly increasing task force in South Rumania within the next months, (b) after the setting in of favorable weather—probably in March—to send this task force for the occupation of the Aegean north coast by way of Bulgaria and, if necessary to occupy the entire Greek mainland . . . The support of Bulgaria is to be expected (mit der Unterstützung durch Bulgarien ist zu rechnen) . . . (I. M. T., XXVII, p. 336.)

The reasons for the operation, as given by Hitler in this directive, were that "because of a dangerous situation in Albania it is doubly necessary that the British endeavor to create air bases under the protection of a Balkan front—which would be dangerous above all to Italy as well as to the Rumanian oil fields—be foiled." He had expressed the same fears to Ciano in November 18, when he promised the Italian Foreign Minister to march on Greece through Bulgaria by the middle of March.[1] It is significant, however, that in both cases, Hitler carefully avoided any mention of his plans concerning Russia; apparently the circulation of Directive 21 was restricted to a few top officials, directly concerned with Operation Barbarossa.

HITLER'S STRATEGY OF TERROR AND DISINTEGRATION

In his Directive 20, Hitler had asserted that, in carrying out Operation Marita, "the support of Bulgaria is to be expected." Bulgaria was still neutral at that time, at least formally, and King Boris, during his visit to Berlin on November 17, had refused to join the Tripartite and support the New Order in Europe. He had rejected Hitler's offer of an outlet to the Aegean Sea at the expense of Greece, although "many voices were raised in Sofia in favor of this plan." (Dallin p. 281.) As a compromise, King Boris had agreed to fulfill the Axis demands within the Balkan area, while remaining "neutral," particularly in the Soviet-German conflict. In spite of the extremely cautious attitude of King Boris, Hitler was able to count on Bulgaria's cooperation because he knew that Bulgarian policies eventually would be influenced by the successful penetration of Rumania by the Germans.

Hitler's pressure upon Bulgaria was part of his plan to line up the eastern and southeastern European countries in support of his oncoming crusade against Communism. Although this pressure temporarily failed to bring Bulgaria within the Tripartite alignment, Hitler's efforts met with success in the case of Hungary, Rumania, and Slovakia, which countries signed the Tripartite on November 20, 23, and 24 respectively. Similar pressure on Yugoslavia and Turkey did not meet with success. These two countries, encouraged by the Greek and British successes in Albania and North Africa, gave no indication that they would heed repeated German and Italian admonitions to join the Tripartite Agreement. The Turkish Government re-emphasized, on November 22, its determination to resist any attack and, as a precautionary measure, martial law was declared in the Turkish districts adjoining both sides of the Dardanelles and the Bosporus.

Notwithstanding these temporary and in any event minor failures, Hitler persistently continued his efforts to bring about the eventual elimination of Bulgarian, Yugoslav and Turkish opposition to his far-reaching strategic plans. Obviously, since Hitler's strategy was subject to two basic limitations—forces and time—the policies of these countries were of extreme importance. Should these countries cooperate with Germany, or at least not intervene in favor of Greece, Operation Marita would be ended rapidly. Then his forces in the Balkans would be freed in time for their transportation to the Soviet border in order to participate to the launching of Operation Barbarossa. On the contrary, "an ambiguous attitude on the part of Yugoslavia would leave open the flank of the German army for some 350 kilometers and any possible hostile action by Belgrade would have the effect of producing Turkish intervention which might compromise the course of German military operations in the Balkans. . . ." as Hitler himself told Ciano, according to his *Diplomatic Papers* (p. 431). As a result of these considerations, Hitler concentrated his diplomatic efforts in forestalling such eventualities before it would be too late. His plan was as simple as it was effective. First, a stronger hold should be secured upon Rumania. The pretext was given by a revolt which broke out in Bucharest on January 21, 1941. The leader of the rebels, composed of a faction of the Iron Guard, was Horia Sima, Vice-President of the Antonescou government. The revolt was represented as an attempt to overthrow Antonescou, whom the rebels accused of failure to carry out a total social and economic revolution against the capitalists, Jews, and old-time politicians, but it was actually aimed against the German penetration.[2] The revolt was immediately suppressed with the assistance of the German troops which were already within the country; under the pretext of protecting the Antonescou regime from subversion, Hitler acquired unquestionable domination over Rumania.

The second step in Hitler's plan was to convince Bulgaria of the desirability of joining the Axis camp. Filoff had been summoned to Berchtesgaden shortly before the Rumanian incident. There he was presented with concrete demands. Bulgaria should enter the Tripartite and with her army protect the rear of the German divisions from any attack by Yugoslav or Turkish forces, especially during the first days of deployment. The annexation of "Thrace to the Aegean Sea" would be Bulgaria's reward. King Boris, however, was still reluctant. True, he had already agreed to the entrance of German troops under the disguise of "tourists" and "technicians" but he was not yet inclined to proceed to open participation in the Axis alignment. The price was still not high enough, and Soviet intentions were rather disturbing as the Kremlin became more and more aware of the penetration of Bulgaria by German soldiers disguised as tourists or technicians. On January 12, 1941, Moscow released through *Tass* the first public warning:

> If German troops are actually in Bulgaria and if they are continuing to enter the country, this has taken place without the prior knowledge or consent of the USSR.

A few days later, Dekanosov, Soviet Ambassador to Berlin, officially stated to Weizäcker, Under-Secretary of the Auswärtiges Amt that "the Soviet Government . . . considers the territory of Bulgaria and of the Straits as the security zone of the USSR and that it cannot be indifferent to events which threaten the security interests of the USSR." (*Nazi-Soviet Rel.*, p. 268.) Soviet reaction to German penetration of Bulgaria, although quite impressive, was not strong enough to discourage Hitler. In the German reply, given on the 22nd, Berlin asserted that the reason for the German moves in the Balkans was Britain's attempt to regain a foothold on Greek territory, and assured that "Germany does not intend to occupy the Straits; she will respect the territory under Turkish sovereignty unless Turkey on her part commits a hostile act against German troops." The German reply disclosed that "the German army will march through Bulgarian territory . . . to checkmate any English attempt at building up a front in those regions. The Reich Government believes that in so doing it is also serving Soviet interests, which would be opposed to England's gaining a foothold in these regions." (*Nazi-Soviet Rel.*, pp. 271-272.)

Following Rumania's complete subjugation, the presence of strong German forces on the Rumano-Bulgarian frontiers rendered Hitler's arguments fully convincing. Premier Filoff was now in a position to argue effectively that "if we (the Bulgarian Government) don't allow the Germans to cross our country they will treat us as an occupied country. From a British victory we have nothing to expect, because as soon as the Germans have collapsed we'll be all sovietized." Therefore, it was prudent to accept the German terms in exchange for Bulgaria's aggrandizement. Once King Boris was convinced that the time had come, he asked through the Bulgarian Minister to Berlin, for the clarification of the term "Thrace to the Aegean Sea." Ribbentrop explained that he meant the Greek territory between the rivers Evros on the east and Nestos on the west. The price was not yet high enough, but the presence of mighty German armies on the Rumano-Bulgarian borders did not allow any choice. On February 8, 1941, General Boindev, Commander-in-Chief of the Bulgarian Air Force and Marshal List, Commander of the German forces of the Southeast, signed in Bucharest a Protocol defining the form of the Germano-Bulgarian military cooperation. Under the terms of this Protocol, the Bulgarian army was assigned the task of protecting defensively[3] the Turko-Bulgarian borders, thus relieving considerable German forces for Operation Marita. Since the question of saving time and forces was of such fundamental significance for the success of Hitler's plans, it is obvious that the decision of the Bulgarian government to cooperate with Germany, even in a defensive manner, was extremely important.

Mussolini officially requested Germany's military assistance to solve his predicament in Albania. On January 19 and 20, conferences took place between Keitel and the Italian General Guzzoni and also between Hitler and Mussolini in the presence of Ribbentrop, Keitel, and Jodl. According to the minutes of these conferences, as presented to the International Military Tribunal, (I. M. T., III, pp. 313-314.) Hitler's objectives in massing troops in Rumania were: (a) an operation against Greece, (b) protection of Bulgaria against Russia and Turkey, (c) safeguarding the guarantee to Rumania. He further explained that "the tendency will be to cross the Danube at the last possible moment and to line up for attack at the earliest possible moment in order to keep the moves secret. . . ." In brief, Hitler was coming to Mussolini's rescue.

As the imminence of a German attack against Greece became more and more apparent, General Metaxas discussed with General Wavell the course of action to be followed in such an eventuality. On January 15, 1941, Metaxas stated to the British general that the Greek Government would agree to a landing of British troops in Salonika provided these troops were strong enough to act offensively. General Wavell replied that no more than two or three divisions were available to be sent to Greece. Even these forces would be ready for transportation only after two months. The only forces available for immediate transportation were: one artillery regiment, one regiment of anti-aircraft and anti-tank artillery and one unit of 60-65 tanks. The Greek Prime Minister bluntly stated that these forces would be quite insufficient and refused to approve their transportation to Greece. Winston Churchill, in his memoirs, attributes Metaxas' reply to his desire to avoid any action which might have given the Germans a pretext for attack, and asserts that "those grounds were

by no means unreasonable." (Churchill, II, p. 37.) It is questionable, however, that Metaxas really believed that Hitler needed any pretext to
attack Greece; more likely he used this argument to extract effective assistance from the British. It is regrettable that the vague form of the British
guarantee caused unnecessary disagreements which did cast occasionally
a note of distrust and misunderstanding upon the Greco-British relations
at a time when the closest cooperation and mutual confidence were indispensable.

The Germans labored to clarify the Turkish position in regard to the
oncoming operation in the Balkans. The German-Bulgarian protocol of
February 8, did not eliminate the possibility of Turkish intervention. A
serious cause of apprehension to both Germans and Bulgarians was the
concentration of the bulk of about twenty-six Turkish divisions near the
Turko-Bulgarian frontiers. In the opinion of the German General Staff,
the intervention of these forces before the deployment of the German
armies might endanger the whole operation and also adversely affect the
major operation against Russia. In the Directive No. 2099 of the O.K.W.
there was a sentence which reflected their misgivings:

> In case that Turkey would intervene or however adopt a hostile po-
> sition, the relief of our forces in the Balkans in time for carrying out
> the Operation Barbarossa is regarded very uncertain. (Par. 11)

In consequence, before any decisive step was taken in the realization of
the Plan Marita, Turkey should become neutralized.

In diplomatically eliminating Turkey, Germany used as a tool the
prolonged Turko-Bulgarian negotiations concerning the drafting of a
non-aggression agreement. For about one year, Turkey, with the concurrence of Great Britain, had vainly attempted to convince Bulgaria that the
establishment of friendly relations between the two, was necessary for
the preservation of peace in the Balkans. Negotiations between the two
governments had been opened repeatedly, only to reach almost immediately another stalemate. In November 1940, Kyrov, the Bulgarian Minister
to Ankara, was summoned to Sofia and a decision was made to reopen the
negotiations, with a view to reaching an agreement. By that time, however, the situation in the Balkans had changed entirely and the negotiations, originally aimed at the formation of an anti-German block, instead
played into the hands of German diplomacy.

In proceeding to the conclusion of a non-aggression agreement, the Turkish view apparently was that any action leading to the relaxation of the
existing tension in the Balkans was a contribution to the preservation of
peace in this area. Unfortunately this was not the case; a Turko-Bulgarian
agreement, which would have been welcome one year earlier, now was in
effect a dagger blow in the back of Balkan security, because it would

eventually prevent Turkey from intervening in the event of the occupation of Bulgaria by the Germans. The Turks, must have realized the consequences of such an agreement; however, they proceeded to its signature because of pressing strategic and political considerations. Their dilemma was should Turkey intervene and, thus, become involved in the war, or should she maintain her neutrality, even though a very precarious one? What were Turkey's chances of successfully resisting a German attack? The Turkish army was poorly equipped and Britain, Turkey's only ally, was too distant to be an effective aid. The valley of eastern Thrace was an ideal field for the operations of Hitler's Panzer Divisions. And even more disturbing was the uncertainty concerning the attitude of the Soviet Union. Should the Soviets take advantage of Turkey's involvement in the conflict and demand concessions in the Straits or the frontier districts of Kars and Ardahan, Turkey would face a two-front threat with no hope to resist successfully either Germany or the USSR. The only course of action which, under the circumstances, seemed to them expedient was to remain neutral and allow Germany to absorb Bulgaria and Greece. An additional factor contributing to this conclusion was Germany's favorable attitude toward the proposed Turko-Bulgarian agreement. Under the terms of such an agreement, Bulgaria should abstain from any hostile action against Turkey. Since German armies attacking Turkey would necessarily pass through Bulgarian territory, the Turks assumed that Germany had no intention of attacking them, at least in the near future. As a result of these considerations, a Non-Aggression Pact was signed by the two governments on February 17, 1941.

Immediately the Soviet Government expressed its displeasure at the culmination of this pact by issuing a communiquè denying the alleged participation of the USSR in the drafting of the agreement. Viewed from a narrowly Soviet standpoint, this pact might have been interpreted as assuring the inviolability of the Straits, since a German attack on the Straits would necessarily involve the use of Bulgarian territory. The opinion which prevailed in the Soviet capital was that this pact would facilitate the advancement of the German positions toward the Straits. In Athens and London this agreement was interpreted as an advance notification to Germany of Turkey's decision not to oppose in any way the occupation of Bulgaria.

The Turkish Prime Minister, apparently alarmed by these interpretations, officially declared that "Turkey would be unable to remain indifferent to foreign activities that might occur in her security zone." The net result of the said pact was the desertion of Greece on the eve of the oncoming German aggression.

Now that the uncertainty, expressed in Directive Nr. 2099, had been eliminated through the Turko-Bulgarian agreement, Hitler proceeded to the further realization of his plans. On February 19, only two days after the signing of the pact, he set the dates for the first part of the Operation Marita. He ordered the construction of the bridge across the Danube to begin on the 28th of February and the river to be crossed on the 2nd of March; the final orders would be issued on the 26th of February at the latest. (I. M. T., XXXIV, p. 264.)

On February 28, Von Schulenburg, German Ambassador in Moscow, informed Molotov that Bulgaria had subscribed to the Tripartite Pact and would sign a concurring protocol on March 1. Molotov promptly expressed the displeasure of the Soviet Government, and emphasized that the situation which existed on November 25, when the Soviet Union presented her counter-proposals with reference to Soviet participation in a Four Power Pact, had entirely changed because of the recent developments in the Balkans. Because of Hitler's determination to attack the USSR, Molotov's reaction to the German policies was too mild to forestall the completion of Nazi designs in the Balkans. One can venture to say that Stalin was deliberately permitting Hitler to take the initiative in opening the conflict. It was a tremendous risk but Stalin as a shrewd calculating leader, realized that only a German assault against the Russian fatherland could electrify the masses and rally Russia's peoples to the defense of the Soviet state.

EDEN IN ATHENS AND ANKARA

Hitler's approval and support of the conclusion of the Turko-Bulgarian Pact of non-aggression was a further indication that the German attack against Greece was only a question of time. Therefore, a closer contact between the British and the Greek Government was absolutely necessary. On February 22, Anthony Eden, accompanied by General Wavell, Sir John Dill, and other officials, flew to Athens to confer with King George and the Greek Government. Shortly after his arrival, Eden, upon the King's request, met privately with Koryzis, the economist who had been appointed Prime Minister following the death of General Metaxas on January 30th. The purpose of this meeting was to inform the British Foreign Minister that Greece had decided to resist the pending German attack even without British assistance; therefore, if any differences of opinion should arise during the military discussions, they should not be interpreted as an indication of reluctance of Greece to resist German aggression. During this meeting, Koryzis declared "most categorically, that Greece, as a faithful ally, is determined to go on fighting with all her forces until the final victory." He added that "this determination is not limited to the case of Italy but will apply to any German aggression. Greece," he concluded, "whatever the outcome . . . will defend her national territory, even if she can only count on her own forces." (Churchill, II, p. 74.) This sincere and forthright presentation of the intentions of the Greek Government presents a striking contrast to the policies followed by the other Balkan countries during that period. It was not an outstanding example of orthodox diplomatic tactics, an essential element of which is bargaining, but it reflected the heroic spirit which had swept the whole Greek nation, from the front lines in Albania to the King's palace in Athens. During the military discussions which followed, Eden and the other British officials "were all impressed by the frankness and fair dealing of the Greek representatives on all subjects discussed. . . ." (Churchill, II. p. 76.)

The political and military situation that confronted the Greek and British officials during the discussions was rather discouraging. The Greek army had succeeded in checking and throwing back into Albania the attacking Italian forces, but it was not strong enough to end the conflict; the operations had now reached a stage of trench-fighting. The Italians were unable to cope with the situation and their only hope resided in the military intervention of the Germans. No solution was obtainable by diplomatic means since neither the Greek Government would accept a settlement involving infringements of Greek independence and integrity, nor would the Axis agree to any solution short of Greece's subjugation and the expulsion of the British from her territory. Consequently, a German attack against Greece was the next logical step to be taken by the Axis.

The Greeks could not possibly expect to repel a German attack without assistance, since they had only three divisions available to man the Macedonian frontier. But they had decided to fight even in case the British would be unable to contribute enough forces to the defense of Greece, because of their commitments to Egypt and the defense of the Suez Canal.

Eden informed Premier Churchill that the British had "the following forces available for Greece; firstly, one armoured brigade and the New Zealand division, now raised to three infantry brigades, ready to sail; to be followed by a Polish brigade, an Australian division, a second armoured brigade, if required, and a second Australian division, in that order." (Churchill, II, p. 72.) These forces lacked sufficient air protection and anti-tank equipment to decide the outcome in the Balkan campaign, while their presence in Egypt was indispensable to the defense of the Delta region. Their mission in Greece, however, was much broader than the mere assistance of that country; there was still hope that their presence might stir the united action of Turkey, Yugoslavia, and Greece.[4] Should these three countries act together with the British, Hitler would face a military force stronger than he originally expected. He might have to postpone Operation Marita indefinitely; or should he decide to strike, regardless of the power of his adversaries, he would find himself engaged in a prolonged and costly enterprise.

Operation Barbarossa was an unknown factor to the Allies. Had these countries formed a combined military force, Hitler would have faced the dilemma of choosing between the attack in the Balkans and the attack on Russia. True, Operation Marita was the prerequisite of the Operation Barbarossa from the strategic point of view. But had Hitler been faced with the possibility of a prolonged campaign in the Balkans and, consequently, the postponement of Operation Barbarossa to a degree that might endanger the entire operation, then he might have been compelled to give up Operation Marita.

Eden realized that the outcome of the Balkan campaign depended entirely upon the full and timely cooperation of the Turkish and the Yugoslav armies with the allied forces in Greece; so he concentrated his efforts in bringing these two countries within the allied camp. On February 28, he met with the Turkish Prime Minister and the Commander-in-Chief and tried to convince them that the only means of protection lay in facing the Germans at that time before the collapse of Greece would bring the Nazi divisions to the frontiers of Turkey. The Turks admitted such an eventuality was quite undesirable, but they declared unequivocally that their available forces had no offensive power. The common cause, they argued, would be better served if Turkey remained a non-belligerent. They assured their visitor however, that they were determined to fight in the defense of their country in case of German attack. The disastrous policy of individual neutrality still undermined every effort for concerted action.

BULGARIA JOINS THE TRIPARTITE

The adherence of Bulgaria to the Tripartite Agreement was officially announced on March 1, as Eden was leaving Ankara deeply depressed by the results of his mission. Bogdan Filoff, the Bulgarian Prime Minister signed at Vienna the Tripartite in the presence of Hitler, Ribbentrop, and other Nazi officials. On the same day, Von Schulenburg called upon Molotov to inform him that German troops were about to move into Bulgaria. Molotov immediately drafted a note expressing the regret of the Soviet Government because, "despite the caution contained in the démarche of November 25, 1940, the German Government has deemed it possible to take a course that involves injury to the interests of the USSR and has decided to effect the military occupation of Bulgaria." (Nazi-Soviet Rel., p. 278.) A note of regret was not exactly what Hitler needed to revise his plans. The next day, German troops crossed the Danube.

Filoff attempted to appease the Soviet Government by assuring the

Soviet Minister to Sofia, that he had consented to the passage of German troops through Bulgarian territory in an effort to consolidate peace in the Balkans. Two days later the Soviet Government declared that it could not share the opinion of the Bulgarian Government, since such a passage would lead not to the consolidation of peace, but rather to the extension of the scope of the war and to Bulgaria's involvement in it.

British-Bulgarian relations took a sharp turn for the worse. On February 28, the British Minister to Sofia warned the Bulgarian Government that Britain would be forced to sever diplomatic relations if the flow of German "technicians" and "tourists" was not checked. This statement was not supported by the presence of strong British military forces on the Bulgarian borders, and it is an old truth that military power is diplomacy's most persuasive argument. Moreover, coordination was lacking between Soviet and British policies toward Bulgaria, which might have offset this adversity. The British warning was virtually ignored. One week later, on March 5, London recalled its envoy from Sofia and broke off diplomatic relations with Bulgaria, but to no avail. Bulgaria was now one of Hitler's avowed satellites. Nine months later when the temporary successes of Germany seemed to assure the Axis total victory, Filoff spoke to the Sovranije with no effort to conceal the truth about the motives of Bulgaria's past foreign policy. He said:

Bulgaria is a small country, but her policies undoubtedly overturned the plan for a Balkan coalition, which was widely discussed at that time. In fact, only because of Bulgaria's steadfast policies, such a coalition never took shape and the plan for the concentration of one hundred divisions against the Germans failed. These events underline the fact that Bulgaria constantly followed these policies in order to be in harmony with the Axis Powers. (Pippinelis, p. 176.)

INTIMIDATION IN BELGRADE

Following the entrance of strong German forces into Bulgaria, detachments of British troops, already gathered in Egypt, were ordered to board ships. On March 3, 1941, the first British troops landed at Piraeus.

Campbell, British Minister to Belgrade, met Eden in Athens the day before their arrival. Campbell expressed the opinion that notwithstanding the apprehensions of the Yugoslav Government and the political difficulties by which it was confronted, there was a possibility of gaining its cooperation provided British intention to extend sufficient help to Greece was assured.

Eden and the Greek officials feared that such information, if given to the Yugoslav government whose policies in the recent past had been questionable, might leak out to the Germans, thus endangering the secrecy of the operations. In the confidential letter Eden wrote to the Regent, he avoided any mention of the British intention to assist Greece; he only assured him that Greece and Turkey were determined to fight if attacked. He instructed Campbell to inform the Regent verbally that the British had decided to help Greece with land and air forces. He also invited a Yugoslav staff officer to participate in the military discussions which were held in Athens.

This lack of trust was by no means unjustifiable. Recent policies of the Yugoslav Government were all but convincing of its intention to resist the German pressure. Already in November 1940, Marcovic, the Yugoslav Foreign Minister, had visited Berchtesgaden in secrecy. Although he avoided then committing his country to the Axis, a few weeks later, on December 12, 1940, a Pact of Eternal Amity was signed by Yugoslavia and Hungary, the minor Axis partner. On February 14, 1941, Zvetkovitch, the Yugoslav Premier, accompanied by Marcovic, visited Berchtesgaden on Hitler's invitation. By that time, Turkey was about to be neutralized by the Turko-Bulgarian Pact, and Hitler wanted to eliminate Yugoslavia as the "most dangerous factor" in the controversy with Greece. He was aware of the feelings of the Yugoslav people toward Germany. Therefore, he avoided pressing Yugoslav officials for concessions unacceptable to the majority of the Yugoslav nation, concessions which might stir the brewing opposition to governmental plans for alignment with the Axis. Hitler promised not to march through Yugoslavia in attacking Greece, but only to use the Yugoslav railways for the transportation of military supplies, provided that Yugoslavia would join the Tripartite. The frightened and depressed Yugoslav ministers returned to Belgrade to confer with the Regent and other members of the cabinet. They felt that the domestic and the external situation was almost hopeless. The Serbs would never accept any cooperation with Germany, while to fight Germany might cause conflict in Croatia; and it was no secret that the ties which connected the Croats with the Yugoslav crown were always weak. Greece was engaged in a difficult fight with more than two hundred thousand Italians and threatened by an oncoming German invasion. Turkey's attitudes were ambiguous as its pact with Bulgaria indicated. In addition, no signs of sufficient British military assistance were in sight.

The Yugoslav leaders realized now that the time had come to taste the bitter fruits of their policy of individual neutrality. Their anxiety was intensified as the first German motorized elements drove through Bulgaria and reached the Yugoslav borders on the evening of March 2; the ring had closed around Yugoslavia.

Campbell found an atmosphere of distress when he returned to Belgrade on March 4. Immediately he gave Eden's letter to the Regent and verbally assured him that British assistance would be extended to Greece.

These assurances were to no avail. Under the circumstances, the Yugoslavs saw no possibility for successful resistance to the German demands.

On March 18, Prince Paul, Regent of Yugoslavia, left Belgrade for a
secret visit to Berchtesgaden. During this meeting Hitler used a very
convincing argument; he spoke of his efforts to protect Yugoslavia from
Communist and Jewish infiltration. Communism had been always appal-
ling to Prince Paul, whose relationship to the Imperial family of Russia
was well-known; therefore, Hitler's argument provided an emotional outlet to the Regent's anxiety and bewilderment, and convinced him that, by
joining the Germans, he was actually serving his country and his people.
Relieved at last from the doubts and apprehensions which had tortured
him for months, Prince Paul yielded and verbally promised that the Yugoslavs would follow the example of Bulgaria and join the Tripartite.

Soon the oral pledge of Prince Paul was fulfilled. On the evening of
March 24, Zvetkovitch and Marcovic crept out of a suburban station in
Belgrade on the Vienna train. The next day, a pact was signed in secrecy
by the Yugoslav ministers and the German Government. In exchange for
an outlet to the Aegean Sea and the whole province of Salonika, Yugoslavia had joined the Tripartite.[5]

The commitments of Yugoslavia did not include military cooperation
with Germany. In two official notes signed by Joachim Von Ribbentrop,
it was specifically declared that:

the Governments of the Axis Powers will not ask the Yugoslav Government to allow the transit or transportation of troops through Yugoslav sovereign territory.

Also that:

in the event the Yugoslav Government should regard the participation in the military operations of the Powers of the Tripartite to their
own interest, the Yugoslav Government may conclude the necessary
military agreements with the Powers of the Tripartite. (*German Doc.*,
No. 70, No. 71.)

What Hitler wanted from Yugoslavia was not military assistance but her
benevolent neutrality. By the German-Yugoslav agreements of March
25, 1941, Hitler had finally accomplished the elimination of Yugoslavia as
"the most dangerous factor in the controversy with Greece." His insight
did not betray him. At the very moment of the Pact's signature, he whis-
pered to Ribbentrop that the ceremony was like a funeral; and it was.
Three members of the Yugoslav cabinet resigned as soon as the text of the
agreement was presented. The crisis threatened the very existence of the
Zvetkovitch Government. At this moment of commotion and despair, the
anti-Axis elements stepped on the stage.

A BELATED COUP D'ETAT

On March 26, Premier Churchill, who was aware of the Yugoslav negotiations with the Germans in Vienna, wired to Campbell:

Meanwhile . . . do not neglect any alternative to which we may have
to resort if we find present Government has already gone beyond recall. . . . (Churchill, II, p. 161.)

There was only one alternative since the Yugoslav Government had already gone beyond recall: General Simovic and his men had been working clandestinely for several months. When the news of Yugoslavia's
adherence to the Tripartite reached Belgrade they decided to move. A
clause of the Vienna agreement, which provided for the demobilization
of the Yugoslav Army, became the immediate cause for their coup d'etat.
During the night, they seized key points in Belgrade and by dawn of
March 27, the police, who had joined the mutineers, arrested Zvetkovitch
and brought him to Simovic's headquarters. There, he was forced to sign
a letter of resignation. Prince Paul, on a trip to Zagreb, was requested to
return to Belgrade where, together with the two other Regents, he signed
the act of abdication of the Regency. A few hours later he left for
Greece with his family.

On March 28, young Prince Peter, heir to the throne, took the oath
in Belgrade's Cathedral and, amid fervent acclamations became King of
Yugoslavia. But this spirit of independence and determination disappeared
astonishingly soon, and every one in Belgrade realized that the step to
overthrow the Zvetkovitch Government had been taken too late. No
strategic plans were made; neither were they under preparation. General
Simovic and his staff soon realized that to liquidate the Regent's regime
was by no means a measure sufficient to save the country. Confronted
with pressing problems, the jubilant mutineers of yesterday who tore into pieces the Vienna agreement, forsook their anti-Axis rage and, just like
their predecessors, attempted to appease Hitler. Simovic himself met the
German Minister to Belgrade and expressed the desire of the Yugoslav
Government to continue on friendly terms with Germany. He declared
that his government would carry out "all the open and public engage-
ments of the Pact," as a proof of his sincerity. He made clear to the British "that the Yugoslav Government, mainly for fear of the effect to the
internal situation, were determined to take no step which might be considered provocative to Germany." The internal situation was going out
of control. Communist demonstrators demanded a pact with USSR and
carried placards with slogans against both "Imperialist England" and
"Nazi Germany." Repeated British appeals to attack the demoralized
Italian forces in Albania from the rear were disregarded by the Yugoslavs,
although such a stroke would have provided the Yugoslav army with

masses of modern equipment and would have relieved considerable Greek forces which could then be deployed at the Macedonian front. General Simovic deceived himself by hoping that Yugoslavia would avert the German avalanche by decent behavior. Non-provocation became the keyword of his policy and one would have thought from their mood that they had months ahead in which to make their decision about peace or war with Germany. Very soon Simovic was to find out that Hitler was not at all impressed by his expressions of friendship and good will.

Document 1746-PS, (I. M. T., XXVIII, p. 23.) under the general title *Besprehung*, contains the minutes of a discussion in Hitler's headquarters immediately after Simovic's coup d'etat. During this discussion, the Führer declared that he was "determined without waiting for declarations of good faith from the new Government to make all preparations to destroy Yugoslavia militarily and as a national unit. No diplomatic inquiries will be made; no ultimatum presented. Politically it is especially important that the blow against Yugoslavia is carried out with unmerciful harshness and military destruction is done in a lightning-like undertaking. . . . The main task of the Air Force is to start as early as possible with the destruction of the Yugoslav Air Force ground installations and to destroy its capital, Belgrade, in waves of attacks. . . ." The date of this document is March 27, 1941; the decision of Yugoslavia's destruction was made as soon as the news of the revolt reached Berlin.

The confusion which prevailed in Belgrade was indicated by the spasmodic steps the Simovic's Government was taking. The British advice to attack the Italians in Albania and establish a solid front with the Greek and British forces was ignored.[6] Instead the Yugoslavs turned to Moscow and on April 3, Gavrilovich, the Yugoslav Minister to Moscow, opened negotiations for the conclusion of a Pact of Non-Aggression and Friendship. Two days later, the Pact was signed. Hitler accepted the challenge; he was sure that these agreements of the last moment were without any practical significance.

HITLER STRIKES

Early in the morning of April 6, German bombers blasted Belgrade mercilessly in execution of the Operation Punishment. At the same time German infantry and tanks crossed the Yugoslav and the Greek borders. There was no formal declaration of war, with the exception of the concluding sentence of a memorandum which was attached to the note handed to the Greek Minister in the dawn of April 6. ". . . the Reich Government can no longer close their eyes to the fact that Greece is making common cause with Britain and must therefore be regarded as Germany's enemy in the present war with all the consequences that this entails." (*German Doc.*, p. 28.)

As an additional precaution, heavy German artillery on the Turko-Bulgarian borders, was ready upon orders from Berlin to start shelling Constantinople. On April 9, Saracoglou summoned the British, Greek, and Yugoslav diplomatic representatives in Ankara and informed them of Turkey's final decision to remain outside the conflict. German diplomacy, supported by a ruthless military machine and exploiting to the full the mistakes of Germany's adversaries carried the day.

Greece and Yugoslavia fell under the blows of the German army, but it was not an easy victory. Hitler, on March 27, 1941, in view of the pending action against Greece and Yugoslavia, had decided that "in connection with this (Operation Marita), the beginning of the Operation Barbarossa must be postponed for four weeks." (I. M. T., XXVIII, p. 23.) He was compelled, however, to postpone the beginning of the Russian campaign from the middle of May—his original plan—to late June, as Crete, the last line of Greco-British resistance did not fall until May 29, 1941,[7] fifty-four days after the launching of the Operation Marita. This delay played no inconsiderable part in the final outcome of World War II.

As the gray curtain of Nazism dropped over the Aegean Sea, the world had witnessed a superb demonstration of conquest by disintegration and terror. The advocates of individual neutrality and isolationism, speechless before the inconceivable disaster, wept over the ruins of the new Babylon, but to no avail. History had pronounced its final decision.

FOOTNOTES

1. See letter of Ciano to Mussolini, dated November 18, 1940 in, *Ciano Diplomatic Papers, op. cit.,* p. 408.

2. Presumably Horia Sima's revolt was instigated by Mussolini who apparently disliked Rumania's penetration by Germany. Following the failure of his mutiny, Horia Sima fled the country and sought refuge in Italy.

3. ". . . wird das Bulgariache Heer . . . nicht offensiv . . . eingesetzt . . ." Doc. No. 1746-PS in *I. M. Tribunal, Proceedings, op. cit.,* Vol. XXVIII, p. 17.

4. Winston Churchill, in his speech of April 27, 1941, asserted that "there was a very real hope that the neighbors of Greece would by our intervention be drawn to stand in the line together with her while time remained."

5. See Hitler's speech of May 4, 1941 in *Der Volkischer Beobachter,* May 5, 1941. Also A. Papagos, *op. cit.,* p. 347.

6. The only meeting the Yugoslavs held with Greek and British officials took place at the railway station of Kenali the night of April 3 to April 4, 1941. The Greek Commander-in-Chief, Gen. Papagos, and the Deputy Chief of the Yugoslav General Staff, Gen. Yiankovitch, were present. See details in, Alex. Papagos, *op. cit.,* p. 349.

7. It is a striking coincidence that the fall of the Byzantine Empire occurred also on May 29 (1453).

PART TWO
Under Nazi Rule

UNDER NAZI RULE

GREECE, BY FIGHTING to the last ditch had delayed by more than six crucial weeks the launching of Hitler's operation against the USSR. Gratitude, however, is a virtue unknown among nations. As Alexander Hamilton once wrote in the Federalist Papers (July 10, 1793), "between individuals occasion is not unfrequently given for the exercise of gratitude . . . but among nations . . . such occasions . . . perhaps never occur. It may be said as a general principle that the predominant motive of good offices from one nation to another is the interest and the advantage of the nation which performs them. . . ."

If good offices among nations are motivated by interests and advantages, exactly the same can be said about the hostile policies occasionally employed by a nation against another. Soviet policies form no exception to the rule.

In order to comprehend clearly what interests and advantages caused the Soviet animosity against Greece in the postwar years, it is necessary to trace briefly the main developments in Greek political affairs during the Axis occupation. It is also imperative to examine the evolution of the international rivalry over the Balkans.

Background material for this second part comes from original sources of information. Among these are: the Memoirs of Winston Churchill and Cordell Hull, the Forrestal Diaries, the Diaries and Diplomatic Papers of Count Ciano, the informative works of James Byrnes, Edward Stettinius, Emmett Robert Sherwood, Admiral Leahy, the information and documents included in the books of E. I. Tsouderos and George Papandreou, the Greek Premiers during the war, underground publications of the Greek resistance organizations, reports of American and British newsmen, the Records of the House of Commons, and others.

As the reader follows the developments in the Second Part, he will see clearly that the so-called cold war had already started back in 1941, long before public opinion in the democratic countries became aware of this new type of warfare.

CHAPTER EIGHT

THE DISEASE CALLED DEFEAT

VIEWED FROM AN ORTHODOX Communist standpoint, Nazi Germany represented one of the last efforts of "dying Capitalism" to retard decay by
abandoning the "disintegrating methods of democracy." In the opinion of
the Soviet leaders, there was no essential difference between collaboration
with Hitlerite Germany and cooperation with the Western Democracies;[1]
for them, the Soviet-German agreements of August 1939, were merely a
matter of political expediency. Lenin, in his work, *Left-Wing Communism*, gave his followers a basic formula for use in their dealings with
the capitalistic world. He advocated the application of "zig-zag tactics,"
that is, cooperation, compromise or even withdrawal, but he emphasized
that the Communists should never lose sight of the ultimate goal, the
overthrow of "bourgeois society." Since that time, Lenin's formula has
become a keynote of Soviet foreign policy.

UNIFORMITY OF SOVIET FOREIGN POLICY

During the inter-war period, the prophesy of the fathers of Communism, that world Sovietization would come through social revolutions
of the working masses and the colonial peoples, failed to materialize. The
proletariat, far from becoming a majority suffering even greater impover-
ishment with the advancement of industrial society, tended to enjoy a
constantly rising standard of living. A vast middle class of technicians,
managers, professional people and a growing army of skilled workers
replaced the Marxist conception of proletariat. The Marxist-Leninist fore-
cast of proletarian world revolution was wholly wrong; thus, Stalin
decided to advance the Communist cause by using the old-fashioned, but
never out-dated, methods of power politics. He dusted off the Testament
of Czar Peter the Great, and the traditional imperialist policies of Czarist
Russia became a useful tool in the service of world Communism.

This new approach, noticeable already during the Montreux Conference of 1936, became manifest at the time of the German-Soviet collaboration of 1939-41; Communist ideology and Russian imperialism had
become the two constituent parts of Soviet Foreign Policy.

The Danubian-Balkan region and, particularly, the Balkans are a key point in intercontinental transportation. This location has made them one of the principal areas of Czarist imperialist aspirations. Under the new approach of Soviet foreign policy, the domination of these areas became one of the major objectives of the Communist master-plan for world Sovietization. In November 1940, during the German-Soviet negotiations for the drafting of a Four Power Agreement, the Soviet demands concerning the Balkan region and the Straits became one of the principal causes for the collapse of the negotiations.

This failure was by no means an indication that the Soviet objectives were unattainable; it was merely a temporary setback. After the Nazi assault against the USSR, the Soviet leaders readjusted their policies to the new world developments. They displayed such remarkable persistency and unique subtlety that, by the end of World War II, they had attained with the support of the Western Powers most of the objectives outlined in the Molotov memorandum of November 25, 1940, which had been rejected by Hitler.

THE MISTRUSTED ALLIES

Following the launching of Operation Barbarossa on that dawn of June 22, 1941, Premier Churchill promptly decided to establish a closer contact with the Soviet Union. Shortly after June 22, 1941, Eden went to Moscow to determine the Soviet needs for military assistance. Stalin immediately made it clear, even though the Soviet armies were in retreat, that the Soviet Union was less interested in military aid[2] than in a political alliance and in territorial settlements affecting the Soviet borders. He was particularly interested in the recognition of the frontiers of 1941. The Russians apparently suspected that the German assault was part of a gigantic plot of capitalism "to foster an armed conflict between Nazi Germany and Soviet Russia and then remain outside of the conflict as a happy bystander."[3] The correspondence between Premier Churchill and Stalin during the summer of 1941, clearly reflects the Soviet mistrust. Later in September 1941, the visit of Lord Beaverbrook to Moscow revealed that a dangerous misunderstanding overshadowed the relations of the two countries. Churchill was anxious to clarify the disturbing issues and wrote to Stalin accordingly. In his reply of November 8, 1941, Stalin stated that a clarification of the relations between the USSR and Britain cannot be achieved as long as "there is no definite understanding between the two countries on war aims and on plans for the postwar organization of peace. . . ." (Churchill, II, p. 529.)

In view of Britain's inability to win the war without the cooperation of other major Powers, Premier Churchill decided to make a further effort to smooth relations between the USSR and the United Kingdom. Once again he decided to send Eden to Moscow to discuss with the Soviet leaders all the points at issue. Stalin agreed to Eden's trip to Moscow, and plans were made immediately for the journey. But the night Eden sailed from Scapa Flow on his way to Russia, the news of the Japanese attack on Pearl Harbor was breaking upon the world.

Japan's entrance into the war and the unexpected disaster of the United States Navy tremendously improved Stalin's bargaining position. The United States Government was compelled to withdraw its naval forces from the Atlantic in order to meet the Japanese challenge in the Pacific. This would leave the British Navy alone to protect the transocean communications from the menace of the German U-boats. At the same time British positions in the Far East were threatened by the Japanese avalanche. Soviet resistance and the severe winter had halted the German divisions outside of Moscow and Leningrad, and had frustrated Hitler's expectation to annihilate the USSR in a swift campaign.

On December 16, 1941, during a conversation with Eden, Stalin presented in some detail his views on the postwar territorial arrangements in Europe. With regard to the Balkans, he suggested that Yugoslavia should be restored and even receive certain additional territories from Italy. Albania should be reconstituted as an independent state; and Turkey should receive the Dodecanese Islands with possible adjustments in favor of Greece as regards islands in the Aegean important to Greece. Turkey might also receive certain districts in Bulgaria and possibly also in Northern Syria.

The reasons for Turkey's very favorable treatment by Stalin were quite obvious. The Soviet leader suspected that the ten-year German-Turkish Pact of Friendship, Neutrality and Non-Aggression of June 18, 1941 might possibly develop into a closer cooperation between Germany and Turkey in the near future. Should this happen and the Turks allow a German attack on the Caucasus through Turkish territory, the Soviet military position would be seriously endangered. Since an openly pro-German policy by Turkey would also threaten the still precarious position of the British in the oil fields of the Middle East, Stalin proposed this favorable treatment of Turkey in the hope that he might induce Eden to accept the Soviet proposals as a whole.

As to the particular suggestion concerning the postwar fate of the Dodecanese, it can be fully explained if viewed in the light of the Soviet conviction that the Dodecanese Islands form a sort of outer gate to the Dardanelles. From a Soviet standpoint, it was advisable that the Dodecanese belong to the same country which controls the Straits. Stalin probably expected that such an arrangement, if eventually approved, would cause serious discord between Turkey and Greece, whose claims on the Dodecanese, based on the Greek nationality of the islanders, were well

known. Obviously Stalin had not forgotten that the Soviet Turkish amity
of the twenties had been seriously impaired during the thirties by the
impact of the Greek statesman, E. Venizelos, upon the Turkish leaders.
The further suggestion by Marshal Stalin, concerning possible adjustments in favor of Greece "as regards islands in the Aegean important to
Greece," was without practical significance since there are no islands in
the Aegean upon which Greece has any aspirations, unless Stalin meant
the British-controlled island of Cyprus, which is not in the Aegean.

Stalin did not limit his proposals to the rearrangement of the European
frontiers. He declared to Eden that he was prepared to support "any
special arrangements for security bases, etc., in Western European countries," in exchange for the recognition of the Soviet frontiers of 1941 and
"certain special facilities for bases, etc., in Rumania." (Churchill, II, p.
629.) Stalin's objective to bring about a division of Europe into zones of
influence was easily detected in these proposals. Eden resisted the temptation and did not commit his country. He explained to Stalin that "in
view of prior British undertakings to the United States it is impossible
for H. M.'s Government to commit themselves at this stage to any postwar frontiers in Europe without previously consulting with the United
States Government and the governments of the Dominions." Stalin's effort to exploit the difficult position of Britain after the Japanese assault
had failed to produce any results.

THE UNDERGROUND

Stalin's failure to extract any specific political commitments from Eden
made it clear that the Western Powers would never yield to the Soviet
claims unless forced to do so by pressing political realities. In preparing
the ground for these developments, the Soviet leadership displayed remarkable realism and shrewdness.

In the Balkans, particularly in Greece and Yugoslavia, the task of creating proper political conditions for the eventual showdown with Britain
was entrusted by the Soviet leadership to the underground movements of
national resistance. Stalin was apparently influenced by a sound appraisal
of the existing local conditions and the anticipated postwar developments
in choosing the underground movements to carry out this task. The German conquest had destroyed the pre-war political framework in these
countries and opened the way to the formation of new political forces.
Communist parties were able to achieve political predominance by leading the virtually headless nations in their struggle against the conqueror
and, thus emerge in the postwar period as the most powerful political
forces in these countries. There were two possible eventualities should
this be accomplished. The Communists might hope to impose their po-

litical system and help advance the Soviet sphere of influence to the Aegean Sea shores, with all the consequences that such a tremendous improvement of the Soviet positions entails. Should this fail the Soviet Union would be able to force the other Allied Powers to make concessions in other areas by using as a threat the strong Communist-led movements.

The Kremlin cautiously avoided open intervention and Soviet manipulation of the resistance movement never came to the surface. Such intervention was unnecessary; a fully-indoctrinated Communist leader hardly needs detailed advice in taking the necessary steps for the advancement of the Communist cause. Contrary to what is commonly believed, the Communist leader enjoys considerable freedom of action as long as he is acting strictly within the party line; any deviation or mistake, however, is easily remedied through ruthless purges.

Josip Broz or Tito, the Secretary General of the Yugoslav Communist Party, was one of the most competent leaders in the international Communist movement. Upon his shoulders fell the responsibility of not only leading the resistance movement in Yugoslavia but also supervising the movement in Greece, where there was a scarcity of Communist leaders of Tito's caliber. The author recalls that for the Communist-led Greek guerrillas, Tito was a sort of higher, most revered authority.

According to traditional practice, the Communist parties of both countries eagerly sought the cooperation of other leftist elements in forming the leadership of the resistance movement. On September 27, 1941, an organization was formed in Greece by Communist and left elements under the title, National Liberation Front (EAM). Among the most important political parties affiliated with the organization were: the Communist Party of Greece (KKE); the Union of Popular Democracy (ELD); the Socialist Party of Greece (SKE); and the Agrarian Party of Greece (AKE). Throughout the period under discussion, KKE was the dominant force, since ELD and SKE were newly founded parties without political power as the postwar elections in Greece have proven, and AKE was actually a branch of the Communist Party (KKE), which had never enjoyed an independent status. The composition of the EAM leadership was cautiously concealed from the Greek public, while EAM was presented as a non-partisan organization of national resistance with its ranks "open to all freedom-loving and patriotic Greeks."

EAM was not the only resistance organization formed in Greece during the Axis occupation. By the end of 1941, former officers of the Greek Army, who had distinguished themselves on the battlefield during the Italian aggression, together with their soldiers, had formed small groups of guerrillas in many parts of the country. These independent organizations had no political objectives and their primary purpose was the liberation of the country. But without a central authority which could provide a common plan of action their military undertakings were not coordinated. This lack of coordination cannot be ascribed exclusively to the personal ambitions of their leaders. These leaders repeatedly attempted to establish contact with the Greek Government-in-exile and the British military authorities in the Middle East in order to secure military assistance. But their appeals for procurement of equipment and supplies were conspicuously discarded by the British authorities who advised the Greek Government to avoid any action in favor of these independent organizations lest such policies "displease the extreme left elements in Greece."[4]

The British authorities apparently based their attitude on the reports of young British Intelligence officers who cooperated with the EAM movement in Greece. These officers represented the EAM movement as having by far the strongest appeal among the Greek people, particularly the youth of the nation. This was true; the EAM movement had spread throughout the country with remarkable speed. What these British agents had neglected to ascertain were the factors which had contributed to the EAM's rapid growth. This negligence finally resulted in a disastrous misinterpretation of EAM's progress; the eager response of the Greek people to EAM's call for resistance against the conqueror was falsely attributed to widespread left-wing leanings of the people and especially of the youth.

Subsequent events proved that this assumption was far from sound. The enthusiastic response of the Greek people to the appeals for national resistance sprang from their indignation because of the brutal behavior of their conquerors. The Greek Generals had signed the armistice agreement on April 23, 1941, only after Hitler's personal promise that Greece would not be dismembered nor would the Italians be allowed to cross the border and enter Greek territory. A few weeks later Greece was carved among the Axis partners. By "a common decision of Hitler and Mussolini," Italy annexed the Ionian Islands; Albania was given the territory lying within the line of Florina-Pindus-Arta-Preveza; and Bulgaria was granted the long-coveted outlet to the Aegean. This included western Thrace and eastern Macedonia up to the Struma River, together with the islands of Thasos and Samothrace (*Ciano's Dipl. Papers*, pp. 437-39.) This was only the beginning. Famine, terrorism, and persecutions soon rendered life in occupied Greece so unbearable that Mussolini himself once exclaimed according to Ciano's *Diaries* (p. 531) that "the only way to explain such a bestial attitude on the part of the Germans is that they are lost and, since they have to die, they want to create general confusion." The Com-

munists were experienced in clandestine operations and displayed remarkable ability in channeling the common sentiment of distress and indignation toward the resistance movement. Their efforts met with considerable
success, as the Communist frame of the EAM organization and the political objectives of its leadership were unknown to the public, being carefully concealed under the cloak of the national resistance. As a result, the
ranks of the organization were rapidly manned by thousands of patriots
who wanted to fight in the underground against the conqueror.

In December 1941, EAM proceeded to form its military arm, the
Greek People's Liberation Army (ELAS). It is characteristic that the
establishment of ELAS coincided with Stalin's failure to extract political
concessions from Eden, during his visit to Moscow in December 1941.

Strangely enough the fight against the occupation forces was not the
main task assigned to ELAS by the EAM leadership. Instead ELAS became engaged in strange practices, inexplicable at that time. These practices were: the monopolization of the resistance movement, and the
infiltration of the Greek military forces which were organized by the
Greek Government-in-exile with British assistance in the Middle East.

REALIZATION OF ELAS OBJECTIVES

The monopolization of the resistance movement was to be accomplished through the gradual liquidation of the aforementioned independent (non-Communist) resistance groups, on the grounds that the resistance movement should be unified in order to be effective. During the
year of 1942, the efforts of ELAS to disband the various independent
guerrilla groups met with success in many parts of the country. Numerous groups were disarmed by persuasion and, when persuasion was ineffective, by armed attacks or treachery. A noteworthy and at the same
time characteristic case is that of Colonel Stefanos Sarafis. A well-known
liberal officer, Colonel Sarafis, together with other officers and soldiers
had formed a resistance unit in the mountains of central Greece. Suddenly, early in 1942, his group was attacked by an ELAS detachment
acting under the command of Aris Velouchiotes or Klaras, a known Communist from Lamia. Sarafis' group was disbanded and he was captured.
Six weeks later, Colonel Sarafis yielded to the exerted pressure[5] and
accepted the ELAS terms. Under these terms, he was to become the military head of ELAS while Velouchiotes would remain the political commissar. Thus a dual system of command was established, apparently
inspired by the Soviet Army prototype. This system of combined political
and military leadership was gradually introduced into the whole structure
of ELAS, down to the company level and lasted until the final disband-
ment of ELAS in 1945. The real power rested in the hands of the politi-

cal commissars, while the military leaders were confined strictly to the direction of military undertakings.

The Sarafis incident was not the only one. In spite of ELAS persistent efforts to liquidate the other groups and monopolize the resistance movement in the country, some independent organizations survived. By the end of 1942, the Greek Democratic National Army (EDES) under Colonel Zervas was operating in Epirus, the National and Social Liberation (EKKA) under Colonel Psaros in Sterea Ellas, and several others of minor importance in Macedonia, Pelloponesus, Thessaly, and Crete. Yet ELAS was by far the strongest armed resistance organization.

The second objective of the Communist-led EAM was the infiltration of the Greek Armed Forces in the Middle East. The conditions in Greece under Axis rule had forced thousands of Greeks to seek refuge in the Middle East and there continue the fight against the common enemy together with the British. The flow of volunteers soon enabled the Greek Government-in-exile to form, the nucleous of a military force with British assistance. The Greek Premier, E. Tsourderos, had already requested British assistance in the organization of one Brigade on December 11, 1941. On March 9, 1942, an agreement was finally signed by the two Governments, defining the extent and the form of the British aid. It is noteworthy that, under the important clause of Article 2, "the complete liberation of Greece. . . ." became for the first time "one of the war aims. . . ."

The organization of an armed force in the Middle East by the Greek Government-in-exile caused grave concern to the Communist-led leadership of EAM. Should these forces grow into a strong army, loyal to the constitutional government of Greece and eventually return to the country as liberators, the EAM ultimate objective to seize absolute control over Greece through the liquidation of the independent resistance organizations would be seriously endangered. Therefore, in order to avert such an eventuality, the Greek armed forces of the Middle East should either be manned by EAM followers and sympathizers or infiltrated to such an extent that they would cease to be a menacing factor.

In carrying out this task ELAS detachments gradually gained absolute control over most of the shores which served as points of departure. Then they began to screen carefully every person who attempted to escape to the Middle East from points controlled by ELAS forces. The purpose of this screening was to hinder the departure of those whose allegiance to EAM was doubtful. Under such conditions, the time came when Greek patriots attempting to escape to the Middle East were less afraid of German or Italian persecution than of ELAS interception.

It was evident that even complete success of ELAS intrigues would not assure the final accomplishment of the Communist objectives. There was a possibility that the Greek Government in Cairo might influence the British in counteracting the ELAS maneuvers. It was therefore necessary, in the opinion of the EAM leadership, that the prestige of the Greek Government and especially of King George should be undermined so that any admonition concerning the Communist plans in Greece would be interpreted by the British as arising from political antagonism.

POLITICS IN THE MIDST OF WAR

On the evening of April 20, 1941, while the German divisions marched toward Athens and the Greek nation was torn in despair, E. Tsouderos became head of the Greek Government. Three days earlier, Premier Koryzis, I. Metaxas' successor, had committed suicide; the King immediately approached several prominent political figures, including Sofoulis, the veteran democrat leader, but no one was willing to shoulder the Premiership at this moment of national emergency. Finally E. Tsouderos, a distinguished Cretan economist, accepted the King's offer, although he was not on very good terms with the Metaxas regime and had never been a royalist. Tsouderos' Cretan descent became a helpful asset when, three days later, the King and his Government were compelled to seek refuge in Crete because of the German advance.

The Battle of Crete became one of the most renown incidents of World War II, and one of the first large-scale operations of air-borne troops in modern warfare. The heroism and the sacrifices of the Greek and Imperial troops could not avert Crete's fall into German hands. Once again the King and his Government had to seek refuge elsewhere, this time abroad. There they concentrated their efforts on the pursuit of the Greek national claims, the organization of an armed force in the Middle East, and the relief of the Greek people who suffered famine in occupied Greece. The appraisal of their accomplishments falls outside the scope of the present work; it is necessary to limit this study to the examination of the international rivalry over the Balkans as reflected by the political developments in Greece.

It has been mentioned previously that, in the opinion of the EAM leadership, the King and the Greek Government represented a threat to the complete realization of the communist designs and, therefore, the international position of the King and his Government should be undermined through well-calculated intrigues.

In undermining the prestige of the King, the Communists exploited with masterly subtlety the old political dispute between the royalists and the democrats. This issue had originated during World War I as a result of the serious rift between King Constantine and E. Venizelos, and had divided the Greek nation throughout the inter-war period with disastrous consequences. The establishment of the Republic in 1924 failed to reunite the people and to solve the pressing national problems. In 1935 a plebiscite restored the Constitutional Monarchy and King George II, son of King Constantine, was invited to the Greek throne. The return of the King and the subsequent establishment of the Metaxas dictatorship with the King's approval was little help in bridging the gap between the two antagonistic factions. Only the Italian attack of October 28, 1940, brought about the dramatic unification of the people, a unification that proved to be only temporary. The Greek political leaders were indignant because they had been deprived of any political activity and influence during the Metaxas regime and revived the old political feud during the occupation. They turned against the King whom they held responsible for the establishment of the dictatorship. They ignored the national interest at a time when national unity was paramount and, in their embitterment they contributed to the disunity of the people. Once Churchill wrote that the Greeks are one "of the most politically minded races" in the world. It is not clear what he meant by politically minded, but it is a fact that the Greek political leaders, twice within the last thirty years, displayed deplorable shortsightedness and lack of political responsibility. In 1920, while E. Venizelos, the creator of Greater Greece, was striving to materialize the national aims and consolidate the previous national achievements, the royalists of that time incited the people against the great statesman and finally led the nation to the Asia Minor catastrophe of 1922. Two decades later the blunder was repeated by the opposite faction, the democrats. Because of their hatred toward the King, they unleashed the old animosities and undermined his tremendous prestige abroad, to the detriment of the national interest.

Whatever faults the King had, their duty, as political leaders, was to wait until the liberation of the country and the achievement of the national aims. Only then should they guide the people to the solution of the political issues by democratic means. Instead, they aroused the latent passions and, with their shortsighted policies, served the Communist objectives better than the Communists themselves. They not only paved the way for the outbreak of civil war, but also impaired the international prestige of Greece to such an extent that even the Western Allies were reluctant to supporting the Greek national claims when the time came.

The first sign of the brewing disorder was a letter from the liberal Gonatas, forwarded to the Allied Governments in December 1941. Gonatas declared in that letter that King George had been deposed by a common decision of the political parties in Greece because of his cooperation in the establishment of the Metaxas dictatorship. "From now on," he declared, "Greece is a republic." (Tsouderos, *Anomalies*, p. 46.)

Tsouderos, the Greek Prime Minister, to whom a copy of the letter was handed, discussed the matter with the British Government in London. The British officially stated that they had no intention to intervene in the internal affairs of a friendly country. Tsouderos made an effort to forestall the looming discord in view of the international conditions. In his speech from London of February 8, 1942, he advised the Greek people "to guard against those who dream political anarchy or dictatorship, and because they find no other way to undermine our national life, they talk about individual rights and political liberties, at a time when the enemy occupies our country and does not allow us even to breath freely."

This wise advice was ignored by the political parties in Greece—or rather by their titular leaders, since the free expression of political opinions by the people was impossible under Axis rule. In a secret meeting on March 30, 1942, these politicos signed a manifesto, whereby the constitutional issue should be decided by a free plebiscite after the end of the war. They hastened to pledge, however, that, "all the signed political parties will take an unqualified position in favor of the Republic, in the belief that, thus, they contribute to the political concord within the country, and serve the true and permanent interests of the nation and the people." Copies of this resolution were forwarded promptly to the Allied Governments. Although this document annuled the previous letter of Gonatas, it still impaired the prestige of the King, whose position as a national leader was questioned by the overwhelming majority of the Greek politicians.

The Communists did not fail to exploit the revived political feud. On February 23, 1943, their agents in the Middle East, supported by the EAM followers whose journey had been facilitated by the ELAS control of the points of departure in Greece, instigated a mutiny in the Greek armed forces. Committees of soldiers took over the command of the military and naval units, while anti-royalist officers pressed the Tsouderos Government to replace certain members of the Cabinet by more democratic personalities. It is characteristic that they conspicuously avoided to request the appointment of even a single Communist or EAM leader to a government post. Apparently, they realized that such a demand, at this moment, would simply expose the driving force behind the mutiny and alarm the Greek political circles at home and the Middle East, all too soon. Tsouderos, who until that time had displayed notable political realism, failed to comprehend the real objectives of the mutineers and accepted their demands. Certain members of the Cabinet were relieved of their duties and new appointments made.

Tsouderos, wired the political leaders in Greece a few weeks later and proposed that three representatives of the parties should be sent to the Middle East, in order to discuss with the Government various issues of national interest. To this telegram, Sofoulis, the titular head of the Liberal Party after the death of E. Venizelos, replied that "the liberation of the country is the expectation of all the political parties and the people. But neither can the liberation be complete, nor the country saved, as long as the plague of the Royal issue remains open." He suggested that only an official declaration by the King, agreeing to the settlement of this issue by a free election, "would bring about the conciliation of the people." This communication was soon followed, in May 1943, by a similar message signed by Sofoulis, Kafanderis, Gonatas, Papandreou, and others.

In view of these declarations, the Cabinet discussed the situation on July 1, 1943, and unanimously resolved that:

    1. As soon as the return of the Government to national soil is possible, we will submit our resignations to the King in order to facilitate the formation of a new Government of National Unity, which will conduct, as soon as possible, elections for a Constituent Assembly.

    2. The Constituent Assembly will settle the royal issue and all shall abide with its decision.

    3. The King will soon declare his determination to guarantee the above resolution. . . .

The king promptly accepted the suggestion of his Government and agreed to submit the fate of the Royal House to the free verdict of the Greek people. On July 4, 1953, he addressed the nation from Cairo; in his speech, he affirmed his resolution to accept the decision of the Constituent Assembly, and he promised that the elections would take place within six months after the liberation of the country.

According to secret reports from Greece, the royal declaration had been received with appreciation by the political circles in Greece, but the next day (July 5, 1943) new disorder broke out in the Greek military units in Egypt. Sailors and soldiers defied the orders of their superiors and openly declared that "they do not heed orders, other than those of EAM." Apparently the instigation of these riots aimed at minimizing the favorable impression in Greece and abroad produced by the conciliatory gesture of the King. The mutiny was easily suppressed, but a few days later, Exindaris, a prominent Greek journalist, arrived from occupied Greece at the Turkish port of Smyrna, and stated that the political leaders in Greece were not satisfied with the royal declaration. He added that the King should remain outside of Greece until a plebiscite had determined the future form of the state, and that should the King return to Greece before this step had been taken, complete anarchy would follow.

Shortly after the arrival of Exindaris to the Middle East, the British Envoy to the Greek Government informed Tsouderos that four representatives of EAM and the Communist Party (KKE), together with two representatives of the other resistance organizations (EDES and EKKA), had arrived at Cairo by British plane from a secret allied airstrip in Thessaly. The Greek Premier was given the impression that the arrival of Exindaris was "somehow coordinated" with the arrival of the resistance representatives. In many instances, the British authorities of the Middle East played an inexplicable role; General Smuts, Premier of South Africa, who apparently was fully aware of these strange policies, wrote to Churchill on August 20, 1943, then at Quebec, that:

> . . . there is strong suspicion that British Intelligence agents, who brought Greek patriots and other representatives to Cairo, are antiroyalists, and that patriot representatives have even communist leanings . . . With politics let loose among those peoples we may have a wave of disorder and wholesale communism set going all over those parts of Europe . . . The Greek situation brings matters to a head. . . . (Churchill, III, p. 537.)[6]

Official British policy favored the solution of the royal issue in Greece by the free vote of the people when proper conditions of public tranquility would be established in the country. Yet there is a strong suspicion that there were certain British political groups who desired to prevent the settlement of the question of Cyprus or Northern Epirus, or even to thwart the rectification of the Greco-Bulgarian border. Presumably these groups anticipated that Greece, torn by the plague of civil strife, would very likely be unable to present these national claims with the necessary prestige. There is no documentary evidence leading directly to this assertion. However, the unfavorable reaction of responsible British officials toward the Greek claims,[7] the concern of members of the House of Commons for the independence and territorial integrity of Albania, and above all, the policies of certain British authorities undoubtedly constitute an indirect, but not negligible indication.

On August 17, 1943, Exindaris, acting as representative of the Greek political parties, together with the aforementioned resistance leaders and Mr. Kanelopoulos, head of the Unitarian Party, handed to Premier Tsouderos a resolution demanding an official declaration by the King that he should not return to Greece before a plebiscite had decided the form of the state. On August 19, the Cabinet examined the situation and concluded that, since this memorandum presumably represented the will of the majority of the Greek people, they should advise the King accordingly.

King George turned to Premier Churchill and President Roosevelt for consultation when faced with these new demands. His message reached the Allied leaders at Quebec during their conference. They both agreed that the King should return to Greece as soon as possible and submit the question of the royal house to the people. (Hull, II, p. 1240.) Churchill offered voluntarily to instruct the British agents, "working with Greek guerrilla groups, to refrain from encouraging those elements to put forward political claims at this time as to the future form of government." Churchill's statement is another indication of these strange practices which paved the way to the civil war.

President Roosevelt stressed his conviction that the royal declaration of July 4 provided the best solution to the constitutional issue on September 7, 1943, in a personal message to King George. The President expressed the hope that the Greeks would defer their political differences to a later period, "in view of the urgent need to win the war and liberate their country." (Tsouderos, *Anomalies*, p. 68.)

Encouraged by the warm support extended to him by the two allied leaders, King George refused to yield to the demands of the Greek politicians. The representatives of the resistance movements went back to Greece without definite results. Shortly after their return the balance of power and political conditions in Greece were deeply affected by the surrender of Italy on September 8, 1943.

GRECO-YUGOSLAV AGREEMENT OF JANUARY 1942

The distressing events of the recent past, when the Balkans were first politically disintegrated and then militarily subjugated by the Axis, had proven once again that the security of the Balkans depends entirely upon the solidarity of the Balkan countries. The leaders of Greece and Yugoslavia had clearly perceived that the security of their respective countries lies fully on their close and sincere cooperation. With this in mind, the two Governments negotiated, with the approval and support of the British Government, an agreement "concerning the Constitution of a Balkan Union," which was finally signed in London on January 15, 1942. In the preamble of this agreement, the parties declared that: "because of past experience, and more particularly recent experiences, which have demonstrated that lack of close understanding between the Balkan peoples has caused them to be exploited by the powers of aggression in their aim toward political and military penetration of the peninsula, and considering that . . . the fundamental principles of their policy must be the principle of 'the Balkans for the Balkan peoples' . . . ." they decided to form the nucleus of a Balkan Union. They established a Permanent Bureau composed of three sections: Political, Economic-Financial, and Military. Articles VI (1) A, and VIII (3) provided in detail for the functions of the said Permanent Bureau. On the eve of the signing, Tsouderos met with Bogomolov, the Soviet Ambassador to London, and emphasized the peaceful objectives of the agreement. Bogomolov showed no indication of disapproval. But when Molotov, who visited London in the spring of 1942, met with the Yugoslav leaders, he flatly expressed the Soviet displeasure for the agreement and counter-proposed the conclusion of a Soviet-Yugoslav agreement of friendship and non-aggression. This would be a blow to the newly born Balkan Union because an agreement of that nature, concluded between a small country and a big power, almost inadvertently results in the open or concealed domination of the foreign policy of the small country by the great power, on the pretext that the common interest will be better served by a concerted foreign policy. Therefore, the proposed arrangement would be inconsistent with the fundamental principle, "The Balkans for the Balkan peoples," upon which the new "Balkan Union" was founded.

The Soviet proposal failed to produce any definite results, chiefly due to British opposition. In order to avert the looming trend of separate agreements between the Great Powers and the small countries, which eventually would result in serious misunderstandings and friction among the allies, the British Government suggested the conclusion of an agreement whereby the Great Powers would pledge to avoid any separate agreements with the small countries during the war. Molotov agreed in principle to such an arrangement. He requested, however, that the ratification of the Soviet-Yugoslav agreement of April 5, 1941, which had been proposed by the Yugoslav Government as proof of its friendly policies toward the USSR, should be exempted from the proposed arrangement. Finally, the Soviet-Yugoslav agreement was not ratified and the British proposal was abandoned.

As a result of the Soviet reaction, the Greco-Yugoslav agreement for a Balkan Union gradually faded out. It is characteristic that when Tsouderos visited the Yugoslav Premier on January 15, 1944 to congratulate him on the anniversary of the Agreement, the Yugoslav expressed surprise, as he had "almost forgotten the occasion."

Soviet opposition to the formation of a Balkan Union was not due exclusively to the fact that the arrangement was sponsored by the British Government. In the postwar years, when the Balkans, with the sole exception of Greece, came under the domination of the Soviet Union, a Balkan Federation which was proposed by the Communist leaders of Yugoslavia and Bulgaria, (Marshal Tito and Georgi Dimitrof) met with the same opposition from the Kremlin. Finally this became one of the issues behind the dramatic breech between Tito and Stalin in 1948. Obviously, Soviet foreign policy strongly opposes any arrangement in the Balkans which may block the Soviet drive toward the warm waters of the Mediterranean. The incident of the unfortunate Greek-Yugoslav agreement provides indeed another indication of the uniformity of the Soviet foreign policy.

FOOTNOTES

1. Stalin in his address to the Congress of the Communist Party in 1939, stated that the only differences between Germany and Soviet Russia are ideological and these differences are exaggerated by others who wanted someone else to "pull their chestnuts out of the fire" for them. See also, James F. Byrnes, *Speaking Frankly*, New York: 1947, p. 283.

2. On the contrary, during the visit of Harry Hopkins to Moscow in July 1941, Stalin confined himself to requests for military assistance and avoided any political talks. The discussions were important because they convinced Hopkins that "no longer should Anglo-American calculations be based on the probability of early Russian collapse." After Hopkins' visit "the whole approach to the problem was changed." Robert E. Sherwood, *Roosevelt and Hopkins; An Intimate History*, New York: 1948, p. 343.

3. Excerpt from the introduction to the 3rd volume of *The History of Diplomacy*, Moscow: 1946, quoted by P. Pipinellis, *op. cit.*, p. 306.

4. Letter by Tsouderos to Premier Churchill, in E. I. Tsouderos, *Ellinikes Anomalies sti Messi Anatoli*, Athens: 1945, p. 176.

5. Later, during the Lebanon conference in May 1944, Papandreou, the Greek Premier, mentioned the incident in front of Colonel Sarafis who participated in the conference as the military head of ELAS. Colonel Sarafis remained silent. See, G. Papandreou, *The Liberation of Greece*, Athens: 1945, p. 49.

6. See Arthur S. Gould Lee, *The Royal House of Greece*, London: 1948, p. 159, "the growth of the republican intrigue was helped from an unexpected direction—none other than General Headquarters, Middle East . . . These men (officers of the Intelligence Staff, engaged in organizing guerilla resistance in Greece), some of whom were in their early twenties, were apparently so occupied by their efforts to damage King George that they forgot the purpose of the war (and) helped to influence responsible British leaders in abandoning the King in favor of a bunch of unknown toughs whose sole aim was to make Greece safe for Communism."

7. E. I. Tsouderos, *Diplomatica Paraskinia*, Athens: 1950, pp. 92, 150, 177, 183-187. Note Eden's statement to Tsouderos, "I regret very much the fact that you caused serious trouble in a part of the Empire. . . ." He had been displeased at the enthusiastic response of the Cypriots to Tsouderos' speech of November 15, 1941, in which he pictured Cyprus as "one of the daughters of Greece." (p. 184). Also note; on November 28, 1941, the Greek Under-Secretary of the Press, scheduled to speak on the first anniversary of the liberation of Korytza (N. Epirus), was pressed by the British not to mention the Greek nationality of the inhabitants. He preferred not to speak at all. (p. 177).

CHAPTER NINE

VICTORY FOR VICTORY'S SAKE

THE SURRENDER OF THE Italian occupation army in Greece on September 8, 1943, deeply affected the balance of forces in the country. The ELAS army had detachments in most parts of the country and was able to obtain, with the assistance of a well-organized underground in the cities, most of the Italian military and other equipment including the weapons of an entire division. The operation was carried out with remarkable coordination and rapidity. When the Germans stepped in to restore Axis control, the EAM-ELAS forces had already transported all the equipment to their outposts on the mountains.

Had the purpose of this operation been to reinforce the ELAS army in order to intensify the fight against the enemy, it would have been classed as one of the outstanding exploits of the Greek underground during the Axis occupation. But their objective was to use the Italian weapons for the liquidation of the remaining independent (non-communist) organizations and to eventually dominate the entire country.[1]

NO ALLIED OPERATION IN THE BALKANS

The fall of Fascism, the surrender of Italy, the victories of the Allies in Africa, the failure of the Germans to overcome the defenders of Stalingrad, and the success of the Soviet army on the Ukrainian plains, were signs of the approaching end of the war in Europe and of the liberation of the occupied countries. Before this occurred, the communist masterplan apparently provided for communist-led organizations to gain complete predominance. Thus immediately after the evacuation of the Axis troops from the occupied territories, they could move in and fill the newly produced vacuum of authority.

Early in October 1943, the reinforced ELAS army openly attacked the EDES forces in Epirus[2] in a last attempt to eliminate the only remaining significant armed opposition to the communist objectives. Tito had also succeeded in capturing sizable quantities of weapons from the surrendering Italian forces in Yugoslavia; his People's Army numbered about 200,000 armed men and women, while the forces of General Mikhailovitch, Tito's major opponent, had been gradually reduced to only 15,000. Reliable reports from Yugoslavia indicated that Tito was planning to establish his own government and denounce King Peter of Yugoslavia and his government.

During the Quebec Conference in August 1943, the combined Chiefs of Staff proposed that the British "should prepare forces to occupy the Athens area and pave the way for the establishment of law and order and the beginning of relief. . . ." The proposal was approved and initialed by both President Roosevelt and Premier Churchill. Churchill viewed with anxiety the signs of brewing disorder and shortly before the ELAS attack on EDES, ordered General Ismay on September 29, 1943, "to prepare five thousand British troops with armored cars and Bren-gun carriers to be sent to Athens as soon as the Germans evacuate Greece . . . The troops need not be organized to contend with more than rioting in the capital or incursion from the countryside . . . The Greek troops in Egypt would accompany them . . . Once a stable government is set up, we should take our departure." (Churchill, III, p. 538.)

Information concerning the explosive conditions which had developed in October in Greece and Yugoslavia led Churchill soon to realize that the military measures he had suggested a few weeks earlier in his communication to General Ismay were far from adequate to cope with the situation. Only a major British operation in the Balkans, subsidiary to the Allied operation in Italy would be an effective countermeasure.[3] The successful execution of such an undertaking would very likely induce Turkey to enter the war on the side of the Allies and march into Bulgaria. British forces, pursuing the retreating Germans, would probably advance as far north as the Rumanian and Hungarian borders, before the Soviet armies could reach the Danube-Balkan region.

Apparently with this in mind, Churchill on October 20, 1943, telegraphed Eden, who was then at Moscow participating in a conference with the Soviet and the American Foreign Secretaries:

. . . You should try to find out what the Russians really think about the Balkans. Would they be attracted by the idea of our acting through the Aegean, involving Turkey in the war, opening the Dardanelles and Bosporus . . . It may be that for political reasons the Russians would not want us to develop a large-scale Balkan strategy. . . . (Churchill, III, p. 286.)

Churchill had correctly anticipated the Russian reaction to any large-scale British undertaking in the Balkans. Political reasons had constantly played a major part in the formulation of the Soviet war plans. The Soviet leaders realized that there is no value in winning a war for victory's sake; what really counts is how and to what extent, military victory could serve the communist cause. Unfortunately, other statesmen did not apply an equally realistic approach.[4] Viewed from a strictly military standpoint, a British operation in the Balkans should have been welcomed by the Russians because it would engage considerable German forces, relieve the Russian armies in the Eastern Front, and speed up the general retreat of the Germans. But it would also result in the penetration of the Balkans by sizable British forces; Soviet designs for the Balkans would be overturned if this happened.

As Churchill had anticipated, the Russians rejected the idea of a British undertaking in the Balkans. Eden, in his reply to Premier Churchill, pointed out that "the Russians were completely and blindly set on our invasion in Northern France." (Churchill, III, p. 288.) They agreed to undertake a joint effort with the British to convince Turkey to enter the war. The Kremlin did not like the idea of Turkey's entering the war as an ally, because should this happen, Soviet plans to press for extensive concessions in the Straits would meet with almost insurmountable obstacles. But since it was evident that Turkey would not enter the war as long as the Germans were still in the Balkans and a major allied operation in that area was out of the question, the Russians agreed to the proposed joint action and on November 2, 1943, they signed a protocol with the British that was without any practical significance.

On his way home from Moscow, Eden met the Turkish Foreign Minister in Cairo and discussed the advantages the Allied cause would derive from Turkey's entrance into the war. The Turks were unmoved. The recent successes of the Germans in wresting the Aegean islands of Cos and Leros from the British forces, which had landed there after the surrender of Italy, had deeply impressed the Turks; under the circumstances one could hardly blame them for their caution. An allied operation in the Balkans, which would have been the only convincing argument, was unfortunately unavailable.

Eden's inquiry about the Soviet views with regard to a British operation in the Balkans revealed to the Soviet leaders that the British intended to press for the approval of such a subsidiary operation, during the coming Conference of the Big Three in Teheran. This necessitated the speedy consolidation of the communist gains in Yugoslavia and Greece. In November, Tito summoned a political Congress of his organization at Jajce, Bosnia. This Congress established a Provisional Government "with sole authority to represent the Yugoslav nation," and formally deprived the Royal Yugoslav Government in Cairo of all its authority. Efforts of British officers to stop the conflict in Greece, between ELAS and EDES failed to produce any results. These developments made more and more evident to the British Government that only an operation in the Balkans would prevent the Sovietization of those countries. The coming Conference in Teheran offered Churchill an opportunity to win the approval of his colleagues.

During the Teheran Conference, Churchill stressed repeatedly the strategic merits of an operation in the Aegean, but in vain he pressed President Roosevelt and Marshal Stalin for the approval of a British landing in the Balkans. This time the major opposition came not from the Soviet leader but from the Americans.[5] The President was seriously "oppressed by the prejudices of his military advisers, and drifted to and fro in the argument with the result that the whole of these subsidiary but gleaming opportunities were cast aside." The Americans "were comforted in their obstinacy by the reflection that "at any rate we have stopped Churchill entangling us in the Balkans." (Churchill, III, p. 386.) Of course, in view of the American reaction to Churchill's proposal, it was unnecessary for Stalin to intervene and by a too strong opposition arouse the suspicion of the President. He merely questioned the wisdom of dispersing the Allied forces.

Churchill's proposal was dropped and the British fell in line with the American position. The Big Three agreed to intensify their efforts in bringing Turkey in the war. This decision enabled Churchill to avoid a definite answer to Stalin's request for an allied commitment concerning the revision of the Montreux Convention, on the grounds that the time was awkward for such a decision since they were planning to bring Turkey into the war; Turkey would regret this because it would probably entail some infringement to her sovereignty over the Straits. Stalin necessarily agreed; he emphasized, however, that the time for the discussion of this issue would come later.

On their way home from Teheran, Roosevelt and Churchill met with the Turkish leaders at Cairo, and strongly insisted upon Turkey's participation in the war. Their arguments failed to convince the Turks, since an Allied operation in the Balkans had been rejected at Teheran. Once again Churchill attempted to persuade the President that an operation in the Balkans would not divert any forces from the major Allied operation Overlord; rather it would mean important advantages for the Allies. President Roosevelt and his military advisers were adamant in their opposition.

REPERCUSSIONS OF THE TEHERAN DECISIONS

An operation in the Balkans was now entirely out of the question and the possibility of Turkey entering the war had vanished. Churchill came to the conclusion that the only course left was to establish closer contact with the communist-led resistance movements in Yugoslavia and Greece, apparently with the prospect of retaining British influence in these two countries. He met Brigadier Maclean, the astute British liaison officer at Tito's headquarters while still at Cairo and informed him that "as a result

... of talks ... with Stalin and Roosevelt ... it had been decided to give all-out support to the Partisans." Maclean promptly observed that Tito's movement was "avowedly communist and that the regime which he might set up later would surely be strongly oriented towards the Soviet Union." He was told by Churchill that he should not worry about the future form of the Yugoslav government, being only concerned with "which local leader was doing the Germans the most direct harm." (Armstrong, p. 30.) It is significant that even Stevenson, the British Envoy to the Yugoslav Royal Government, in his reports suggested that the British policy toward Yugoslavia should be based on "three factors: The Partisans (Tito) will be the ruler of Yugoslavia. They are of such value to us militarily that we must back them to the full, subordinating political considerations to the military. It is extremely doubtful whether we can any longer regard the Monarchy as a unifying element in Yugoslavia." (Churchill, III, p. 468.)

The British Government withdrew its support from General Mikhailovitch, Tito's major opponent, and recalled the British mission operating in his territory. Eden asked the Soviet Government to send a military mission to Tito, obviously in order to establish a kind of cooperation with the Russians in Yugoslav affairs. Mikhailovitch's record during the period under discussion is still a controversial issue. There is some evidence that at times his troops cooperated with the Axis forces in the struggle against Tito. The policies of Mikhailovitch were narrow-minded and strictly oriented to the old Serbian tradition; he was rather incompetent to lead the Yugoslav nation as a whole.

Tito's support by the British did not prevent the communization of Yugoslavia after the end of the war; it did provide, however, a closer contact between Tito and the West, a fact which undoubtedly facilitated Tito's deviation from the Soviet orbit when the time came in 1948. There is no evidence that the British foresaw such a development when they abandoned Mikhailovitch and turned their support to Marshal Tito. In any case, once the decision had been made in Teheran to make Tito the chosen instrument of all the Allies, his supremacy over Mikhailovitch became certain.

The conflict in Greece between ELAS and EDES continued unceasingly throughout the autumn of 1943, causing the British grave concern. It was evident that only decisive political measures could prevent anarchy in Greece and avert the establishment of a communist-controlled regime. The British decided to halt the civil war by every possible means; in December, Headquarters in Cairo suspended all shipments of arms to ELAS. These supplies were no longer vital to ELAS because of sufficient Italian equipment. But the moral repercussions were not at all to the liking of the

EAM-ELAS leaders, as they did not think that the time was ripe for an outright break with the British. Thus, in February 1944, an uneasy truce was signed by ELAS and EDES at Placa, Epirus. Under this agreement ELAS succeeded in retaining control of almost the entire countryside, as the EDES region of operations was limited to a small area in Epirus, actually held by EDES forces at the time of the truce.

POLITICS AGAIN

The Greek royal issue was once again brought under consideration on October 15, 1943, when Eden stopped in Cairo on his way home from Moscow. He met the Greek Premier and suggested that the King should not return to Greece before the royal issue had been settled by a plebiscite. Only a few weeks earlier, on August 19, 1943, Premier Churchill had written to Eden that "in any case, he (the Greek King) would make a great mistake to agree in any way to remain outside Greece while the fighting for the liberation is going on and while conditions preclude the holding of a peaceful plebiscite." (Churchill, III, p. 536.) This complete reversal cannot be explained unless viewed in the light of the Soviet reaction to the British plan for an operation in the Balkans. The British, apparently, in order to win the cooperation of the Greek political leaders and prevent anarchy in Greece, adopted their proposals as presented by Exindaris in August, and decided to urge the King to make further political concessions.

On October 28, 1943, a statement by the British Ambassador to the Greek Government further revealed the anxiety of the British. In a conversation with Tsouderos, he suggested that the Archbishop of Athens, assisted by a committee of reliable persons, should be authorized by the King to assume the administration of Greece with the cooperation of the Allied military authorities as soon as the German forces evacuated Greece.

In view of the obvious reversal in the British policies, and in order "to facilitate the discussions," the King addressed a letter to his Prime Minister, on November 8, 1943. In this, he declared his determination "to reexamine, in consultation with the Government, the question of (his) return to Greece, taking into consideration the political and military conditions which will exist at the time of the liberation of the country." (Tsouderos, *Anomalies*, p. 74.)

Political circles in Greece interpreted the King's letter as an indirect promise that he would not return to Greece before a plebiscite had decided the issue. However this did not put an end to the importunity displayed thus far by the Greek politicians. They demanded that the King put this promise in the form of an official declaration. This new demand was discussed by the Allied leaders and the Greek King during the short stay of the former in Cairo after the Teheran Conference. This time,

Churchill's policies were oriented to the decisions of Teheran, and he pressed the King for the issuance of an official declaration such as the one demanded by the Greek leaders. The President maintained that the King should not be deprived of his right to return to his country after its liberation. He agreed with the King that the royal issue should be decided by the Greek people as soon as conditions of public tranquillity would permit the conduct of free elections. Finally an agreement was signed by the British and the Greek Government whereby the King agreed to re-examine the question of his return under the conditions outlined in the letter of November 8, 1943. The agreement also provided that the King and his government should authorize the Archbishop of Athens and other reliable personalities to represent them in Greece; and that the question of the future form of state in Greece should be decided by the people in free elections conducted according to the royal declaration of July 4, 1943.

The Greek Government ordered Colonel Fradelos, a Greek officer, to parachute into Greece and secretly contact, as a government representative, the Archbishop and other personalities in Athens. Two months later, on March 6, 1944, Colonel Fradelos returned to Cairo carrying with him some extremely interesting documents.[6] These documents offered a revealing picture of the situation in Greece. Their authors, prominent political leaders, displayed genuine anxiety for the future, and a fairly clear understanding of the real causes of the situation. Yet they clung to their anti-royalist preoccupation and furthered their previous demands by asking for the issuance of a Constitutional Decree whereby the King should appoint the Archbishop of Athens as the Regent of Greece.

Meanwhile, signs of brewing disorder in the Greek armed forces of the Middle East caused grave anxiety to the Greek Premier. On March 1, 1944, he telegraphed to the King who was in London:

I consider it necessary that the First (Greek) Brigade be transported to Italy as soon as possible. Political elements are expected to come from Greece and stir up several political issues, a fact which will very possibly impair the discipline in the army. This will be disastrous from a national standpoint because the only prestige our country still enjoys among the Allies comes from the National Forces of the Middle East. I understand that the promised transportation of our army to Italy has been postponed. . . . (Tsouderos, *Anomalies*, p. 85)

Churchill had suggested two months earlier that "the Greek Brigade, if necessary without vehicular equipment, should be sent from Egypt to Italy to take part in the Allied offensive," because "by remaining idle in the Middle East they (the Greek troops) are liable to be contaminated by revolutionary and communist elements there." (Churchill, III, p. 540.)

The British authorities disregarded this sound advice along with similar admonitions from Greek officials, and, continuing their unexplicable policies, they kept the Greek forces in Egypt until it was too late to prevent the uprising.

Serious political developments foreshadowed the impending clash in occupied Greece. On the very same day the truce between ELAS and EDES was announced (March 14, 1944), a broadcast from a secret radio station in Greece spread the news of the establishment by EAM-ELAS of a Political Committee of National Liberation (PEEA) which evidently was a counterpart of Tito's provisional government. This was a direct challenge to the future authority of the Greek Government-in-exile, as an alternative communist-controlled administration was thus formed as a rallying point for all Greeks. Soviet troops were already on the Rumanian border and the Greek Communists reasonably expected the Germans to evacuate the Balkans within the next few weeks. The possibility of the King's return to Greece with the Army of the Middle East supported by British troops was already in sight. Should this happen, all past efforts and accomplishments of the Communists would have been in vain. Therefore, they decided to press for the quick development of the situation while time remained.

THE MUTINY OF MARCH 31, 1944

The establishment of PEEA was only the first step. On March 15, 1943, the Greek Premier received through General Headquarters of the Middle East a telegram from the Political Committee (PEEA). It declared that "the primary purpose of the Committee is to form a Government of General National Unity." (Tsouderos, *Anomalies*, p. 117.) This was obviously an outright demand for the formation of a new government. Tsouderos immediately communicated with the titular leaders of the political parties in Greece and requested their cooperation in the formation of the proposed new government. Before the leaders could reach any decision, the communist-dominated leadership of PEEA and EAM-ELAS proceeded to the second and far more important step, namely, the disintegration of the Greek armed forces.

On March 31, 1944, a group of Greek officers presented Tsouderos with a manifesto asking the Greek Premier to take the necessary steps for the formation "of a government, representing the fighting people and based on the Political Committee of National Liberation (PEEA) otherwise, he would bear the responsibility for the outbreak of civil war. . . ." Mutineers of several Greek military units simultaneously declared allegiance to PEEA and refused to obey the orders of their superiors. Soon the revolt spread to the First Brigade and to the Greek naval units in Alexandria. The replacement of Tsouderos by Sophocles Venizelos (son of the late Greek statesman) failed to satisfy the mutineers, although they had previously pressed for the appointment of Venizelos to the Premiership.

It is questionable whether the primary purpose of the Communists in instigating such a revolt had been to establish a new government, even one based on the Political Committee (PEEA). Such a development would have little effect upon their position in Greece. This being the case, one may wonder why they should attempt to disintegrate the Greek forces in the Middle East which had been so successfully infiltrated by their agents. It seems that under the circumstances, the revolt was a tactical mistake. This is partially correct. Their decision to give the signal for the uprising had been prompted by the expectation that the Germans would evacuate Greece during April 1944 at the latest. They apparently thought that if at the time of the evacuation the Greek Government in Egypt would be fighting an uprising of the Greek armed forces, EAM-ELAS would be the only significant political and military force in the evacuated areas of Greece. To their discomfiture the evacuation did not occur until the next October, a condition which allowed the British Government to react effectively.

The revolt continued for twenty-three days. During that time, the prestige of Greece among the Allied nations fell to such an extent that President Roosevelt remarked in a telegram to Premier Churchill (April 18, 1944) that "I join you in a hope that your line of action toward the problem (of the revolt) may succeed in bringing Greeks back into the Allied camp. . . ." (Churchill, III, p. 548.)

The line of action to which the President referred in his telegram is superbly summarized in a cable dated April 9, 1944, from Premier Churchill to Leeper, the British Ambassador to the Greek Government. In this telegram Churchill said:

Our relations are definitely established with the lawfully constituted Greek Government headed by the King who is the ally of Britain and cannot be discarded to suit a momentary surge of appetite among ambitious *emigrè* nonentities . . . Our only desire and interest is to see Greece a glorious, free nation in the Eastern Mediterranean, the honoured friend and ally of the victorious powers . . . All the time I have been planning to place Greece back high in the councils of the victorious nations . . . The King is the servant of his people and he submits himself freely to the judgment of the people as soon as normal conditions are restored. He places himself and his Royal house entirely at the disposition of the Greek nation . . . Why then cannot the Greeks keep their hatreds for the common enemy?

The revolt was finally suppressed by force, and S. Venizelos was replaced in the premiership by George Papandreou, an astute political leader who came to Egypt from occupied Greece on April 15, 1944.

The British Government had kept the Russians constantly informed of its actions during the revolt. The Soviet Government, however, "confined itself to criticism" and on May 5, it turned down a formal British request for cooperation in Greek affairs, on the grounds that "it would be improper to join in any public pronouncements on political matters in Greece."

TOO HIGH A PRICE TO BE A BARGAIN

With the disintegration of Greek military forces in Egypt, one of the immediate objectives of the EAM had been secured. ELAS was finally the decisive military factor. Churchill realized that nothing could prevent the Communists from taking over in Greece should the Germans withdraw, and decided upon drastic measures. On May 30, 1944, Lord Halifax, the British Ambassador to Washington, handed a written communication from his Government to Secretary of State Hull, asking whether the United States Government had any objection to an agreement between Britain and Russia whereby the main Rumanian affairs would be the concern of the Soviet Union while the Greek affairs would be the responsibility of the British Government. A few days earlier the British had made such a proposal to the Soviet Government which agreed in principle, pending the consent of the United States Government.

This British proposal was obviously the result of overall strategic and political considerations. The Russians were already on the Rumanian borders and naturally the responsibility for the occupation of Rumania would fall in their hands. The conditions in Greece that had developed after the events of March-April 1944 foreshadowed the need of British intervention to forestall the domination of the country by the Communists. If the Russians choose to interfere and openly oppose the British actions in Greece, the position of the British would be very difficult. Therefore, an understanding between the Soviet Union and the United Kingdom was necessary. The moment was right for such an arrangement. The launching of the Second Front was approaching and Stalin would not display too avaricious an attitude under the circumstances, and jeopardize Allied cooperation.

Hull was "flatly opposed to any division of Europe or sections of Europe into spheres of influence," (Hull, p. 1452.). He immediately rejected the British proposal. The next day, Churchill wired directly to the President and argued strongly for the approval of the proposed arrangement. On June 8, another message to Lord Halifax from the British Foreign Office brought into the picture also Bulgaria to be dealt with by Russia and Yugoslavia to be dealt with by Britain. Following the launching of the Second Front on June 6, the Russians presumably felt that it was an

opportune time to broaden the arrangement and gain control not only in
Rumanian but also in Bulgarian affairs. At long last, they had accomplished most of their objectives in the Balkans, as outlined in the Molotov
memorandum to Hitler on November 25, 1940, and in Stalin's proposals
to Eden on December 16, 1941. At that time (1941), Eden had refused to
commit his country to what actually entailed the advancement of the Soviet positions toward the Mediterranean. In May 1944, Stalin's shrewd
maneuvering and cunning utilization of the resistance movements in the
Balkans—strangely enough aided by the inexplicable practices of certain
British authorities—forced Churchill to propose arrangements that he had
rejected in 1941.

Churchill's strong desire to keep at least Greece and Yugoslavia outside
the Soviet orbit was quite evident in the proposed arrangement. Stalin,
of course, would prefer to advance to the Aegean Sea as well, but the war
in Europe was still going full swing and he needed the cooperation of the
Western Allies, at least until the German Reich was totally defeated. He
was aware that in Yugoslavia Tito's forces were strong enough to dominate the political scene even while ostensibly cooperating with the British. The communist movement in Greece was considered strong enough
to play a decisive role even under parliamentary political methods.

On June 10, 1944, the President replied to Churchill's message of June
8; he pointed out that the proposed arrangement would lead to the persistence of differences between Britain and Russia, and concluded that
the United States Government would prefer to see consultative machinery set up for the Balkans to resolve misunderstandings and to prevent
the development of exclusive zones of influence. The next day the British
Premier answered with a long, forceful telegram. He explained with concrete examples why consultative machinery would simply paralyze any
effective action, and concluded his message by suggesting that the proposed arrangement should be given, at least, a three-month trial, following
which it would be re-examined by the Three Powers. President Roosevelt
then acted without consulting the Department of State. In a reply to
Premier Churchill, he personally approved the proposed arrangement under the condition of a three-month trial; he added, however, that care
should be exercised to make it clear that no postwar spheres of influence
were being established. This message virtually freed Churchill's hands
and he proceeded to the conclusion of an agreement which finally kept
Greece outside the Soviet sphere—a situation that made possible the deviation of Marshal Tito in 1948.

FOOTNOTES

1. See letter of Gonatas to the Greek Government in Cairo (Feb. 1944). "Last October, EAM, in the belief that it had grown sufficiently, waged a kind of revolution, unveiled its purposes and attacked Zervas. They thought that they would be able to liquidate him too, as they had eliminated Sarafis and Psaros previously, in order to turn against Athens and seize complete control of the city as well." In E. Tsouderos, *Ellinikes Anomalies, op. cit.,* p. 111.

2. "The responsibility of KKE, as the leading force within EAM-ELAS . . . for the recent general attack against EDES, remains unquestionable . . . proven by the most competent authority—the General Headquarters of the Middle East . . ." as Papandreou replied to the Communist Party (KKE) in December 1943. G. Papandreou, *The Liberation of Greece op. cit.,* p. 14.

A few months earlier, ELAS forces had disbanded the other major independent organization EKKA, taken its leader (Colonel Psaros) prisoner and slaughtered him brutally.

3. General Mark Clark, Commander of the Fifth U. S. Army in Italy and later American High Commissioner in Austria, in his book *Calculated Risk* wrote on pp. 348-51: "Not alone in my opinion, but in the opinion of a number of experts who were close to the problem, the weakening of the campaign in Italy in order to invade Southern France, instead of pushing on into the Balkans, was one of the outstanding political mistakes of the War . . . Stalin knew exactly what he wanted in a political as well as a military way; and the thing he wanted most was to keep us out of the Balkans . . . I later came to understand in Austria the tremendous advantages that we had lost by our failure to press into the Balkans . . . Had we been there before the Red Army not only would the collapse of Germany have come sooner but the influence of Soviet Russia would have been drastically reduced."

4. Compare the Soviet attitude to the following passage: "It was a part (Churchill's opposition to the Southern France operation) of the long story of the differing attitudes of the British and American toward the war. We (the Americans) were concentrating in the early defeat of Nazi Germany. The British wished to defeat the Nazis but at the same time to acquire for the Empire postwar advantages in the Balkan States." W. D. Leahy, *I Was There,* New York: 1950, p. 242.

5. Admiral W. D. Leahy, in his book *I Was There,* although the book was published in 1950, still clings to the idea that an operation in the Aegean was a mistaken plan to which the British "insisted stubbornly" and with "bulldog tenacity."

6. See excerpts in Appendix III, Note A.

CHAPTER TEN

THE SHORT INTERMISSION

THE REPERCUSSIONS OF THE British-Soviet understanding were immediately felt in Yugoslav and Greek political affairs. In May 1944, King Peter of Yugoslavia dismissed Mikhailovitch from his post as Minister of War, and by August a new government was formed abroad under the premiership of Subasitch. With British mediation, the new Yugoslav Government concluded an agreement with Tito whereby they jointly guaranteed "the fullest collaboration to free Yugoslavia from the common enemy" and let the question of monarchy rest until liberation was accomplished. A few days later, King Peter signed a decree severing all official ties with Mikhailovitch. The British obviously favored a conciliatory policy in order to bring about an understanding between the Royal Yugoslav Government abroad and Tito's regime within Yugoslavia; since Mikhailovitch appeared to be a serious obstacle to this, he was removed.

INTERLUDE IN CIVIL WAR

George Papandreou was now the leading figure in Greek politics. As soon as he became Premier on April 26, 1944, he concentrated his efforts on forming a Government of National Unity; he regarded himself "a crusader for the National Unity." The day of liberation was apparently approaching; but the recent developments in Greek affairs, the formation of PEEA, the disintegration of the Greek armed forces, and the expansion and strengthening of ELAS domination over the Greek countryside, made it evident that an agreement with the communist-dominated organization was necessary if the sovietization of Greece after the evacuation of the occupation forces was to be averted. Papandreou was afraid that PEEA might proclaim itself a government with sole authority to represent the Greek nation and deny the King and his government the right to enter the country after the liberation. Should this happen, open British intervention to support the Royal Government, as the "lawfully constituted Greek Government" might be condemned by uninformed or misinformed world opinion as an imperialistic action against the independence of an allied nation. The Greek army, whose landing in Greece could hardly be presented as an "imperialist intervention," no longer existed as an or-

ganized force after the mutiny of April 1944. In view of the existing conditions in Greece, a Government of National Unity, with the participation of the EAM, was the best alternative. If such a government were
formed in Cairo before the liberation, it would be accepted by all as the
National Government of Greece; should the Communists decide later to
overthrow the constitutional authorities and seize absolute control of the
country, the Government of National Unity already established in Greece
would represent the nation instead of being an *èmigrè* setup abroad. On
the other hand, the Communists instead of claiming to be the Government would represent the Revolution against the State. The British would
then be able to rush to the support of the lawfully constituted government without fear of being condemned as "imperialists" by the other allied governments and the world opinion.

On May 17, 1944, a conference of the representatives of all Greek political parties and organizations, including EAM-ELAS, opened in Lebanon under the presidency of Premier Papandreou. The conferences
lasted only three days and, in spite of many difficult moments, an agreement was finally reached, which became known as the National Contract
of Lebanon. By this agreement, it was generally accepted that the question of King's return to Greece should be reexamined by the Government
at the time of liberation. It was stressed however that the "expressed
opinion" of the political leaders was that the King should not return to
Greece before the plebiscite.[1]

EAM agreed to (a) the formation of a Government of National Unity,
(b) the re-organization of the Greek armed forces in the Middle East,
(c) the unification of the resistance organizations under the command of
the Government of National Unity and, (d) to the official condemnation
of all terroristic activities of underground organizations in Greece.

The acceptance of such important terms by the EAM leadership cannot be explained except in close connection with the British-Soviet understanding of May 1944. Presumably the Soviet Government was willing to
prove its sincerity on the eve of Operation Overlord, and advised the
EAM leaders accordingly. Thus the British were able to bring about an
understanding between EAM and the other Greek political parties. The
launching of Operation Overlord on June 6, 1944, effected a slight modification in the Soviet policies, which was immediately reflected in the
actions of EAM. Notwithstanding the approval of the Lebanon Contract
the leaders of EAM delayed under several pretexts the participation of
their representatives in the new Government of National Unity.

On July 6, 1944, Premier Papandreou informed the Cabinet that two
telegrams had arrived from Greece. One was signed by General Sarafis,
the military chief, and C. Porphyrogennis, the political commissar of

ELAS; the other, by the Political Committee of National Liberation (PEEA). In both telegrams the Communists presented new pretexts for their obstructionism and asked for further concessions. The PEEA leaders, in particular, were very specific in their new demands. They demanded that "the present organization of ELAS (political commissars etc.) be continued until the liberation," that "the Supreme Commander of all the guerrillas be an ELAS senior officer," that "out of fifteen ministerial posts . . . the Ministries of Interior, Justice, Education, Agriculture, Labor, Public Welfare and the Under-Secretariat of the Army be given to PEEA." They also demanded that "a branch of the government should be sent immediately to Free Greece." Obviously the posts claimed by PEEA should be among those to go to Greece, because of their very nature. Papandreou, without demur rejected the communist terms and declared that these conditions, if accepted, would bring about the "subjugation of Greece to EAM." It is obvious that should these terms be accepted EAM would possess in Greece the armed forces (ELAS) and also the administration, this time vested in the cloak of legitimacy.

The British reaction to the new communist demands was immediate and forceful. On July 27 and August 2, 1944, Eden and Premier Churchill, respectively, blasted EAM as bearing "the responsibility for the failure to bring about unity in Greek politics at this ultimate moment of the common struggle." They wholeheartedly endorsed the policies followed by Papandreou, whom the British Premier compared to the "Great Venizelos."[2] This denounciation would have been ineffectual, had it not been for instructions by the Kremlin; by the end of July, the First Counselor of the Soviet embassy forwarded official instructions to the EAM representatives in Cairo, advising them to show less obstructionism and enter the Papandreou Government. As a result, on August 2, 1944, the EAM leaders retracted their previous terms and, instead, based their participation in the government upon the removal of Papandreou from the premiership. Apparently, they had been alarmed by the successful handling of Greek affairs by Papandreou, and, particularly, by his methods in exposing the communist game to the public; naturally, they preferred more tractable personalities in the Cabinet posts.

Papandreou immediately offered to resign in order to facilitate national unity, but his offer was not accepted by the other members of the Cabinet. In a telegram, Papandreou informed the EAM leaders on August 4, of this decision and invited them to advise their representatives to take over the Ministerial posts originally allotted to their organization. In the same telegram, he expressed "the nation's indignation for the tragedy of Amphilohia, where ELAS troops slaughtered the families of EDES guerrillas," and demanded that "the culprits of this horrible fratricide be severely punished. . . ."[3] The incident of Amphilohia was neither unusual nor unprecedented; but this was the first time the Greek Premier himself had presented to world opinion a communist crime in concrete terms; not even EAM-ELAS could afford such publicity.

On September 2, 1944, six representatives of the EAM movement were sworn in as members of the Greek Government of National Unity. Two days later, Secretary Hull officially declared the satisfaction "of the United States Government and the American people that representatives of the resistance groups inside Greece have now joined the Government-in-exile."[4]

This development as well as the agreement concluded in August between Tito's movement and the Yugoslav government abroad, was to some extent the reflection of a fresh turn in the Balkan policies of the Soviet Union. After the slight wavering which followed the launching of the Second Front, the Soviet leaders decided to abide with the British-Soviet understanding of the previous May and to speed up conciliation between the opposing camps in Greece and in Yugoslavia. This new approach apparently had been prompted by the realization that Germany, contrary to expectations, was not yet on the verge of collapse. A plot against Hitler's life in July had failed and he still controlled firmly the situation in Germany. More disturbing to the Russians were indications that even top Nazi officials favored cooperation with the Western Powers in a crusade against Communism. Even the plot against Hitler had been interpreted by some political quarters as an effort to eliminate him and then proceed with the Western Powers in a joint action against the USSR. One must never forget the Soviet thesis that the rest of the world represents an opposing camp, and that by historical necessity, an ultimate conflict between the Communist world and the "decadent capitalistic countries" is inevitable.

The fact that the western armies were once again on the Continent, revived the Soviet apprehensions that they might join the Germans in a holy crusade against Communism. The Soviet Union ought not foster such a development by too pertinacious a policy.

The decision of the Allies to open a Third Front in Southern France instead of the Balkans made it almost impossible for the British to employ any significant forces in the Balkan region. The small Greek army, which had been reorganized during the summer and was now participating in the allied offensive in Italy, was obviously inadequate to stand up against the ELAS forces in Greece. Consequently, the Greek Communist Party (KKE) and its military arm (ELAS) would be able to dominate the political scene even while ostensibly cooperating with the other parties in the Government of National Unity. Because of these considerations, Soviet approval was granted and EAM joined the Government of National Unity on September 2, 1944.

Papandreou was not deceived by the pompous patriotic declarations of EAM. Like the Soviet leaders, he also was aware of the fact that EAM possessed the armed forces in Greece while his government was practically unarmed. He clearly realized that the vacuum of authority which would be necessarily produced in Greece by the gradual evacuation of the German forces, would be saturated by the most powerful military force within the country. Already reports received from Greece disclosed "the gradual spread of a terroristic occupation of the country by EAM, following the retreat of the Germans."[5]

The anxiety of the Greek Premier was aggravated by reports stressing the unwillingness of the Bulgarians to evacuate the Greek territories they had occupied in 1941 with German assistance. He communicated repeatedly with General Wilson, Commander-in-Chief in the Mediterranean, and emphasized the anxiety of the Greek Government because of the Bulgarian attitudes; he also stressed the point that the Bulgarians hoped to gain the cooperation of EAM and keep the Greek territories.[6] He requested the exertion of British pressure on the Bulgarians, and also the sending of sizable British forces to Greece. His admonitions produced no results; no British forces were available.

On September 22, 1944, Papandreou received reports from Greece stressing that "the EAM terrorism in the Capital (Athens) continues to increase . . . After the tragedies in Pyrgos and Kalamai (where the Communists slaughtered hundreds of people) the people are afraid of ruthless massacres." The following day another report disclosed that "the leaders of EAM made it clear that they are determined to occupy Athens immediately after the departure of the Germans . . . ELAS has received orders to avoid fighting with the Germans and be ready for action by September 23." (Papandreou, p. 121.)

In a final effort to forestall the gradual occupation of the country by EAM-ELAS, Papandreou summoned General Zervas, Chief of EDES, and General Sarafis, military head of ELAS to Cazerta (Italy) on September 26. After stormy negotiations, during which the Communist political counselor to General Sarafis fiercely opposed the dispatching of British troops to Greece, an agreement was signed whereby "the guerrilla forces (were) placed under the command of the Greek Government which will delegate this authority to British General Scobie." (Papandreou, p. 123.)

It was evident, however, that even this agreement would not suffice to defeat the communist designs. The Greek political leaders who had paved the way for these developments with their irresponsible policies in the past, lamented now in agony and in distress for the gradual subjugation

of the country to EAM, and urged the sending of sufficient British forces
which only could prevent sovietization of Greece.[7]

On October 8, 1944, Premier Churchill and Eden paused for a while in
Italy on their way to Moscow. During their stay, Papandreou met with
the British leaders and analyzed the situation in Greece; he stressed that
only the immediate dispatching of British forces to Greece and the early
formation of a National Army in the country based on general conscrip-
tion would enable the Government successfully to withstand communist
pressure. In view of the pending British-Soviet agreement on the Danube-
Balkan region, the British leaders assured Mr. Papandreou that the whole
matter would be settled in the near future; they also promised that the
Bulgarians would be compelled to evacuate Greek territories of eastern
Macedonia and western Thrace.

In Moscow, the original British-Soviet understanding of the previous
May was broadened and put in an unusually precise form. The two governments even defined by percentages the extent of their respective responsibility in settling the internal affairs of the various Danube-Balkan
countries. According to cables from Moscow and Ankara, the Soviet
Union should have 75 percent predominance in Bulgaria, Hungary, and
Rumania; Britain should have 100 percent in Greece; and the two powers
would share equally the responsibilities in Yugoslavia.

This agreement has been criticized in many instances and it still remains
one of the controversial issues of the war. Subsequent events fully justified Churchill's farsightedness and political realism. Without this agreement, British intervention in Greece during the communist revolt of
December 1944, would have faced tremendous opposition by the other allied governments; it is doubtful indeed whether such intervention would
have been possible.

The assertion that this agreement facilitated the subjugation of Bulgaria,
Hungary, or Rumania by the Communists, cannot be taken seriously. The
Soviet troops were already in these countries when the agreement was
signed in October. On August 20, 1944, the Soviet Generals Malinovski
and Tolbukhin had launched a converging attack against the German positions in Bessarabia. Three days later, a new government in Rumania
made peace and simultaneously changed sides as a sequel to negotiations
that had been proceeding for some time. With their passage thus cleared,
the Russians pushed through the mountain barrier into Transylvania and
up the Danube valley to the Yugoslav frontier. At the same time another
spearhead reached Bulgaria where no resistance was met. Thus, when
Mr. Churchill concluded the Moscow agreement he merely sanctioned
a situation which already existed. In fact, the Moscow agreement was a
desperate measure on the part of the British to offset the repercussions of

the Teheran decisions for no operations in the Balkans. The fact that Czechoslovakia or Poland were not included in this or any other similar agreement did not prevent their subjugation by the Kremlin.

THE LIBERATION OF GREECE

With two Allied armies north of Florence, and the Russians holding Rumania and Bulgaria, Hitler gave Field Marshall Maximilian von Weichs, Commander-in-Chief in the Balkans, the order to abandon Greece. The evacuation started early in October and by October 12, the last German troops had left Athens. On the morning of October 18, 1944, the Greek cruiser Averoff sailed slowly into the Saronikos Bay. Under the clear sky of Attica, the marble columns of the Parthenon were shining in the morning sun. Hundreds of thousands of people from all walks of life had gathered on the seashores, the roofs of houses, along the sideways, wherever they could see and cheer the Greek Government of National Unity. The nightmare of slavery was over; and more important, the even worse calamity of civil war seemed to have been finally averted.

The Greek Communists, however, were not willing to give up their wartime gains. There is no evidence as yet proving that in preparing the December Revolution, the Greek Communists followed Soviet instructions. On the contrary, several Communist leaders loyal to the Kremlin had criticized the December Revolution as a tactical mistake. In any event, the fact remains that during the Communist Revolution in Greece, the Soviet Union cautiously avoided any interference in or criticism of the British actions there.

A direct cause for the Communist Revolution was the decision of the Greek Government to demobilize all the guerrilla forces and proceed to the organization of a national army based on general recruitment. This decision, incidentally, was in full accord with the terms of the Lebanon Contract (Ch. II), which had been endorsed by the Communists as well. According to Chapter II of the Contract, all the parties and the organizations had agreed that "the guerrilla form of the armed forces cannot become a permanent situation," and that "the Government of National Unity shall proceed as soon as possible to the organization of a national army. . . ." Following the liberation of the country and the establishment of the Government of National Unity in Athens, the participating parties discussed in detail the question of the guerrilla demobilization and the organization of a national army. On November 27, 1944, these negotiations produced an agreement approved by all the parties concerned, including the Communists. The next morning Papandreou announced to the nation the agreement and expressed the hope that it would be signed by all members of the Cabinet.

THE RED REVOLUTION OF DECEMBER 1944

On the afternoon of November 28, Zevgos, one of the Communist Ministers, visited Papandreou at his home and presented the Greek Premier with new demands. These new demands concerned "EAM's refusal to disarm and disband its militia, the ELAS" as the *New York Times* reported on December 5. Papandreou refused to yield and stated that the Government would abide with the previous agreement. The conversation was stormy and Zevgos left the Premier's house in excitement without even bidding good-bye. The following day, Svolos, Professor of the University of Athens and one of the original leaders of EAM,[8] called upon Papandreou. He was very depressed and confessed to the Greek Premier that the change of the Communists "had been sudden and inexplicable." He added that under the circumstances he was unable to exert any influence upon them. At last, it had become clear to Svolos that no cooperation with the Communists is possible, only subordination to their policies. As long as Svolos was in agreement with them, he was a welcome friend, or, more precisely, a welcome "label" good enough to attract the Greek people with his prestige as a professor and deceive the foreigners with his liberalism. Now he was an unnecessary burden, with no voice within the organization which he had helped so much to gain political power.

No one can tell as yet what really caused this "sudden and inexplicable" decision of the Communists. The only logical explanation may be that, after they discovered the British forces in Greece were actually insignificant, they thought a sudden coup d'etat by ELAS would drive them out of the country, shatter the small regular Greek forces, and subjugate Athens[9] before any effective reaction would be possible. The author recalls that the keyword among the EAM followers during that period was, "now or never." Until the truth behind this inexplicable decision of the Greek Communists is revealed, one can only study the facts and by impartial reasoning reach certain conclusions.

According to the available information, the Greek Communists acted on their own initiative. However, no one can dismiss the supposition that the Soviet Union might have secretly permitted the revolt under the condition that the Greek Communists would assume all responsibility and expect no Soviet intervention in their favor. Should their coup meet with success, the Soviet position would improve immensely; in case of failure, the Soviet Union would claim complete innocence, in faithful conformity with the British-Soviet agreement of October 1944. The Soviet leaders had important reasons to abide with the October agreement. The Yalta Conference was approaching, and Stalin was unwilling to offend his British allies by an open violation of their agreement and thus jeopardize important Soviet interests. In addition, he was on his way to communize

Poland and Rumania, and, apparently, he expected that conformity with the October agreement would silence possible British opposition. It is interesting to note that Churchill himself in a message to President Roosevelt, dated March 8, 1945, wrote:

> We have been hampered in our protests against these developments (in Rumania) by the fact that, in order to have the freedom to save Greece, Eden and I at Moscow in October recognized that Russia should have a largely preponderant voice in Rumania and Bulgaria while we took the lead in Greece. Stalin adhered very strictly to this understanding during the thirty days' fighting against the Communists and Elas in the city of Athens, in spite of the fact that all this was most disagreeable to him and to those around him."[10]

It is doubtful, however, that in the absence of this agreement, Stalin would have any difficulty in imposing the Communist rule over those countries.

The Communist revolt broke out on December 3, 1944. There has been considerable discussion in the past on the question of who started shooting.[11] The answer to this question is immaterial. No revolution has ever started because of an isolated and minor incident; and no revolution has ever been postponed because of the lack of incidents. Revolutions always spring from much deeper causes and aim to achieve far broader goals than the obvious ones.

The United States Government adopted from the beginning of the conflict a hands-off policy which was outlined by Secretary Stettinius in his statement of December 7, 1944. He declared that he was in agreement with Churchill's statement of December 6, 1944, to the House of Commons when the British Premier said that "whether the Greek people form themselves into a monarchy or a republic, whether they form a government of right or left, is for their decision."[12] But Stettinius refused to comment on Churchill's further statement that the British Government was determined to use the British army in order "to see that peace and order are maintained in Greece." American public opinion was uninformed or misinformed and even government officials had misinterpreted the British actions in Greece. It is characteristic that Admiral King ordered Admiral Hewitt, the United States Commander of the Mediterranean Fleet, not to allow any American LSTs to be used for the transportation of supplies to the fighting British forces in Greece. This order was withdrawn only after forceful British protests which led Harry Hopkins and Admiral Leahy to suggest to Admiral King the withdrawal of this ban. The American official position is really superbly defined by Admiral Leahy in his book in the following statement: ". . . there still remained a hope that we might succeed in avoiding entangling ourselves (USA) in European political affairs." (W. D. Leahy, p. 285.)

The Soviet Government followed a policy of non-intervention, as the attitude of Lieutenant-Colonel Gregory Popov, Soviet representative in Athens, indicated during the dramatic meeting of December 27. The day before, Premier Churchill and Eden had flown to Athens; their objective was to find some way to stop the bloodshed. On the 27th, a conference was convoked with the participation of the Greek Cabinet, the representatives of the Allied governments in Athens, and the representatives of EAM-ELAS, under the chairmanship of the Archbishop of Athens. During the meeting, when Premier Churchill declared that the British had come to Greece "with the knowledge and approval of President Roosevelt and Marshal Stalin," Iieutenant-Colonel Popov remained silent. Obviously, he could not object to Churchill's statement in view of the British-Soviet agreement of the previous October. Three days later, on December 30, Vyshinsky summoned Politis, the Greek Ambassador to Moscow, and announced the appointment of Sergeyev as the Soviet Ambassador to Athens. The Soviet gesture was interpreted as a formal disapproval of the Communist revolt, and caused grave distress and confusion in the ELAS ranks, as the author had the opportunity to witness personally.

When ELAS efforts to seize Athens crushed upon the staunch resistance of the British and Greek troops, the Communists kidnapped thousands of citizens of all political leanings—with the exception of Communist, —and dragged them to the mountains, in the middle of the severe winter, with the purpose of blackmailing later the Greek Government in achieving lenient armistice terms. The revolution was finally suppressed by force, and the ELAS army was crushed in the streets of Athens. Deprived of their military arm, the Communists promptly asked for a truce, which was signed by General Scobie and the EAM-ELAS leadership on January 15, 1945.

During the Big Three Conference at Yalta, Stalin underlined the Soviet policy of nonintervention in Greek affairs. At the meeting of February 8, 1945 he stated to the allied leaders that he "would like to ask . . . what was going on in Greece." He immediately explained, however, that he "was not criticizing the British in Greece, but merely seeking information." (E. R. Stettinius Jr. p. 217.) Premier Churchill replied that he was hopeful that peace would come soon, and added that the British Government was very much obliged to Marshal Stalin for "not having taken too great an interest in Greek affairs." Stalin repeated that he had no intention of criticizing the British actions in Greece nor interfering in that country. The next day, when Premier Churchill officially invited a Soviet observer in Greece, Stalin sarcastically remarked that he thought it would be exceedingly dangerous, had Churchill allowed any but British forces to go into Greece. Then hastened to add in a serious manner that he had "complete confidence in British policy in Greece."

On February 12, 1945, the civil war in Greece was officially ended by the signing of the Varkiza Agreement. The wartime communist plot to seize absolute control over Greece, by exploiting the national desire for resistance against the conqueror, and for freedom and social progress, had finally failed, and the British had succeeded in keeping Greece outside the Soviet sphere.[13]

THE INTERMISSION IS OVER

The Soviet policy of non-intervention in Greek affairs did not last long. The signal was given on July 8, 1945, by Marshal Tito of Yugoslavia, who spoke openly against the "Monarchofascist" regime of Greece and its oppressive measures against the "Democratic citizens" and the "Slavic minorities" in Macedonia. The USSR no longer needed a policy of non-intervention in Greece. Stalin capitalized at Yalta upon the dream of President Roosevelt to create a new world of peace and international cooperation for generations to come,[14] and succeeded in achieving most of the immediate Soviet objectives, although many prominent political writers have denied that there were any real "concessions." Immediately after Yalta, the Russians in violation of the Yalta agreements for the political organization of the liberated European countries, started a "pattern of unilateral action" aiming at imposing absolute Communist control of the eastern European countries. By the spring of 1945, their efforts had already met with significant success in Poland and Rumania; consequently, keeping away from Greek affairs no longer served any practical purpose. But above all, the collapse of Germany had freed the hands of the Soviet leaders. For them, the war was over, while the Western Allies were still entangled in a difficult struggle against Japan.

Indications of the oncoming rift between the Allies appeared during the preparation for the San Francisco Conference. The obstructionism of the Soviet leaders once caused President Truman to exclaim that "our agreement with the Soviet Union so far had been a one-way street, and that (he) could not continue; it was now or never. (He) intended to go on with the plans for San Francisco and if the Russians did not wish to join us, they could go to hell . . ." (The Forrestal *Diaries*, p. 50.)

Tito's speech on Greek affairs virtually coincided with another Soviet diplomatic move in the Balkans. In late June, the USSR renewed pressure on Turkey for the revision of the Montreux Convention and the readjustment of the Soviet-Turkish borders in the frontier districts of Kars and Ardahan. The Turks flatly rejected the Soviet suggestion that there could be a unilateral adjustment between Russia and Turkey. Thus, when the Big Three met in Potsdam, on July 17, 1945, the wartime spirit of Allied cooperation was slowly dying.

The time when Stalin was "merely seeking information about Greece," was gone and Greece had been chosen by the Kremlin as the first point at which to reopen the strife. During the Potsdam Conference, Stalin asked for a military base in Salonika or Alexandroupolis (northern Greece), as Churchill disclosed in August 1947. And when the United States delegation submitted to the Conference a paper in which it was flatly stated that the obligations assumed in the Yalta Declaration of Liberated Europe had not been carried out by the Soviet Union, particularly in Poland, Rumania, and Bulgaria,[15] Molotov counteracted with a severe attack against Greece. Eden angrily termed the attack a "travesty of fact" and pointed out that in contrast to what had happened in Rumania and Bulgaria, international observers, including representatives of the Soviet Union, had been invited to observe the Greek elections.

The Soviet move at Potsdam was merely the prelude. The dispute was brought into the open on January 21, 1946, when the Soviet Union officially attacked in the Security Council of the United Nations the British policies in Greece.

The short intermission was over. The traditional Russian-British rivalry over the Balkans merged in the over-all strife between Communism and Democracy, and was resumed under a new form. Another chapter of bitterness, suffering, and bloodshed had begun in Greece.

The sorry tale of communist conspiracy which has been related in the previous pages will serve no useful purpose unless it becomes a guide to future policies of the democratic nations in their struggle to preserve free society from communist subversion. Wartime experiences indicate that strength is the only quality the Communists understand and respect, while disintegration and weakness serve as an invitation to disaster. Above all, one must never forget that the Communists may "cooperate, compromise or even withdraw" in their dealings with the free world, but they will never lose sight of their ultimate objective, the overthrow of "bourgeois society."

FOOTNOTES

1. Minutes of the first meeting of the Government of National Unity (June 12, 1944) in G. Papandreou, *The Liberation of Greece*, p. 76
2. See full text in *British Speeches of the Day*, New York: British Information Services, September 1944, Vol. 11, No. 9, p. 14.
3. G. Papandreou, *op. cit.*, p. 108. It is a deplorable fact that during the occupation the Greek people suffered not only from the atrocities of the Germans, Italians, and Bulgarians but also from the rage of killings and reprisals among the guerrillas.

4. *Documents on American Foreign Relations*, ed. Leland M. Goodrich, World Peace Foundation, Boston, 1942, Vol. VII, p. 889.

5. Telegrams from the Secret Information Service *Kodros* in G. Papandreou, *op. cit.*, p. 121.

6. See also reports on the intentions of the Greek Communists to detach Macedonia from Greece and "fall in with a Bulgarian plan for a free independent state to form part of a Balkan Union," in *New York Times*, December 10, 1944, p. 21. See also the Yoannides-Daskalov agreement of July 1943 concerning the formation of a Macedonian State to be incorporated directly into the Soviet Union.

7. See for example, the telegram of Sofoulis and Kafandaris to the Greek Premier in Papandreou, *op. cit.*, p. 121.

8. Svolos was not a Communist; he was a socialist, head of the Union for Popular Democracy.

9. The rest of Greece, with the exception of few districts in Epirus and Crete, was under the actual administration of EAM-ELAS. The representatives of the Government (Nomarchs) were virtually captives, with no power at all.

10. From a statement by James F. Byrnes in *The New York Times*, October 18, 1947.

11. According to a telegram by the United Press "at least ten persons were killed and sixty wounded, including six policemen, when members of the left-wing EAM, defying a Government ban, staged a mass demonstration." The British Exchange Telegraph Agency reported that "the shooting began when one youth, seeking to break police lines, threw a hand grenade." John Nixon, BBC correspondent in Athens reported that "the Greek police opened fire on the procession . . . and that as far as Mr. Nixon could see the demonstrators were not armed." Quotations from *The New York Times*, December 4, 1944, pp. 1 and 5.

12. *The New York Times*, January 5, 1945, p. 7. Note also reported statement of Mr. Lincoln MacVeagh, the United States Ambassador in Athens, "the American policy is to stay clear and take no part in Greek politics." *The New York Times*, December 6, 1944, p. 13.

13. On December 10, 1944, Raymond Daniell, an American journalist who obviously believed that this was the war to end all wars and render power politics obsolete, wrote while analyzing Churchill's decision to uphold the Papandreou Government: "To him (Churchill), armagedon is still ahead. He is a product of nineteenth-century thought, fighting a twentieth century war for eighteenth century aims." *The New York Times*, December 10, 1944, Sec. 4, p. E3.

14. The views of the President appear to have been summed up in a memorandum prepared by the United States War Department before the Quebec Conference of August 1943. This paper said: "Since Russia is the decisive factor in the war, she must be given every assistance and every effort must be made to obtain her friendship. Likewise, since without question she will dominate Europe on the defeat of the Axis, it is even more essential to develop and maintain the most friendly relations with Russia." Quoted by R. E. Sherwood, *op. cit.*, p. 748.

15. Even before the death of President Roosevelt, Soviet practices in Poland and Rumania had caused the exchange of bitter messages between Stalin and Roosevelt. The Yalta Declaration of liberated Europe had been forgotten too soon. See, J. Byrnes, *op. cit.*, pp. 53-58.

PART THREE
Bitterness is the Reward

BITTERNESS IS THE REWARD

THE END OF WORLD WAR II and the collapse of the totalitarian regimes in Germany, Italy, and Japan, did not mark the end of the story; it only brought the major question of our time to a head. During the pre-war period, the riddle which puzzled Western political leaders was whether Communism or Nazism represented the most serious threat against democratic freedom and human dignity. When the war broke out and the moment came for a decision, the responsible Western leaders decided that Nazism was the paramount menace which should be eliminated from the face of the earth; to that end they devoted all the resources and the power of the Western world.

Having decided that Nazism was the major threat against mankind, they cooperated with the Soviet Union and helped save Communism from certain defeat. At the end of the war, Hitler's swastika had been torn down and, in its place, the red banner with the hammer and sickle was flying over the Gate of Brandenburg in the heart of Europe. The time had come when their decision, which was bound to affect the fate of mankind, was to be tested under the ruthless criterion of reality.

The question whether or not they were right in that decision was answered with alarming clarity in the postwar years. Greece, located on the crossroads, soon became a testing ground.

CHAPTER ELEVEN

THE ALLIES AND
THE GREEK NATIONAL CLAIMS

ON SEPTEMBER 5, 1945, one month after the end of the Conference at Potsdam, the United States delegation to the Council of Foreign Ministers, headed by Secretary Byrnes, boarded the *Queen Elizabeth* for London. There, the Foreign Ministers of the five major Powers were expected to lay down the cornerstone of the new world order.

MODERN PEACE-MAKING METHODS

The establishment of the Council of Foreign Ministers by the Potsdam agreements was somewhat of an innovation in peace-making procedures. In the opinion of the American policy-makers, "the logrolling, the interplay of conflicting interests plus the sheer number of issues and people" should be avoided this time and, in their stead, a system should be devised which would "facilitate agreement among the major powers and at the same time provide the smaller states with ample opportunity to express their views." (J. Byrnes, p. 70.)

With this general notion in mind, the United States Delegation had proposed at Potsdam the establishment of a Council, composed of Foreign Ministers from the major powers, entrusted with the task of examining the several issues, agreeing on certain general principles and appointing deputies to draft treaties based on these principles. The peace treaties, based on these general agreements then would be presented to all the United Nations for consideration and amendment in the same way the Dumbarton Oaks proposals were reviewed at the San Francisco Conference. Conflicting interests and objectives of the major powers had been, as a rule, the principal factor which dominated peace-making efforts in the past. The American plan appeared to be not only practical and promising but also an honest recognition of the fact that the small nations, whether participating actively in these efforts, were generally compelled at the end to conform to the decisions of the great powers.

The British and the Soviet leaders had no difficulty at all in agreeing in principle on the American proposal. There was disagreement, however, as to which countries should be considered eligible for membership in the proposed Council. Premier Churchill and Generalissimo Stalin questioned the eligibility of China for participation in the Council while the Soviet leader refused to admit France to the ranks of the great powers. A remark by Generalissimo Stalin is characteristic of his attitude on the whole matter; when Churchill suggested consideration of whether the Council should be composed of four or five members, Stalin quickly added, "or three members." In his opinion the participation of more countries was unnecessary since "the three powers would represent the interests of all." (J. Byrnes, p. 72.)

A compromise agreement was reached to the effect that China would participate only in the discussion of Far Eastern problems and those of world-wide importance. It was also agreed that each treaty should be drafted by the states which had signed armistice agreements with each enemy country. France would be regarded as a signatory of the armistice only in the case of the treaty with Italy. This arrangement practically limited participation in the drafting of the peace treaties with the eastern European enemy states to the Big Three, with the exception of Finland where only Britain and USSR would draft the treaty. Undoubtedly Stalin favored such a scheme which would obviously improve the bargaining position of the Soviet Union.

The full meaning of Stalin's remark that "the three powers would represent the interests of all," became evident with alarming clarity soon after the opening of the meeting of the Council of Foreign Ministers in London. Not many days had passed before it was apparent to all that the main task before the Council was not to make peace with the former enemies, but to reach a lasting settlement between the Soviet Union on the one hand and the Western Powers on the other. The separation line between allied countries and defeated enemies gradually vanished and a new classification, based on the relationship of a country to each of the two camps, produced strange developments. For example, the USSR supported Bulgaria—a defeated enemy—against Greece—one of the original allied countries, only because Bulgaria, had in the meantime become a satellite of the Soviet Union while Greece was on the other side of the Iron Curtain. On a similar basis, the Western countries opposed the Yugoslav claims on the Italian port of Trieste, not only because the city was populated mostly by Italians but also because Yugoslavia was at that time a pro-Soviet country, while Italy was expected to become one of the keystones in the Mediterranean defense system.

When Secretary Byrnes arrived at London, he was already aware that the war-time Great Alliance had travelled a long way from the Teheran and Yalta spirit of cooperation. The Soviet leaders had already given unmistakable evidence of their expansionist aspirations. Secretary Byrnes knew about the Yalta agreements on the Kuriles, Sakhalin, Dairen, and

Port Arthur; in Potsdam he, himself, had encountered the Soviet demands that Poland be given a large portion of eastern Germany as compensation for the cession of Polish territory to the Soviet Union, according to a preliminary agreement reached by the Big Three at Teheran. He had also encountered the Soviet demands for Königsberg, for a share in the administration of the Ruhr, and for control over the Straits of the Dardanelles. Even before the end of the war in Europe, the determination of the Soviet Government to acquire absolute control over eastern European and the Balkan states had become quite obvious, while at Potsdam Stalin had even made a bid for control over one of Italy's North African colonies through the device of trusteeship.

Signs of oncoming departure from the war-time cooperation with the West were also noticeable within the USSR shortly after the collapse of Germany. In the week of May 13-19, 1945, the Soviet press gave strong indications that, with the European war over, it would view both foreign and domestic affairs with renewed emphasis upon the uniqueness and superiority of the Soviet political and social system. A series of articles published in *Red Star*, official organ of the Soviet Army, demanded that the indoctrination of the army personnel on "the superiority of the Soviet system over capitalism" should be intensified. A few months later, in August 1945, Mikhail Kalinin, President of the Soviet Union, speaking at a conference of rural party commissars, said:

". . . But even now, after the greatest victory known to history we cannot for one minute forget the basic fact that our country remains the one socialist state in the world . . . The victory achieved does not mean that all dangers to our state structure and social order have disappeared. Only the most concrete, most immediate danger, which threatened us from Hitlerite Germany, has disappeared. In order that the danger of war may really disappear for a long time, it is necessary to consolidate our victory. . . .[1]

This passage superbly reveals the Soviet attitude toward the whole issue of the Second World War. For them, Hitlerite Germany was merely the "immediate danger" which threatened the "one socialist state in the world." "Capitalism," the paramount danger still remained and since, according to Marxism, war is the product of "capitalism" and "imperialism," only world sovietization would eliminate the danger of war. Fear, fanaticism, and ambition, the three elements of the Soviet complex, are looming through Kalinin's words.

The Soviet attitude made drafting of the Peace treaties a difficult task. With this depressing setting as a background, the Council of the Foreign Ministers held its opening meeting at the Lancaster House, London, on September 11, 1945.

THE GREEK NATIONAL CLAIMS

When General Metaxas rejected the Italian ultimatum in the early hours of October 28, 1940, there was no understanding between Greece and Great Britain concerning any postwar territorial arrangements in favor of Greece as compensation for her participation in the war. The only consideration which prompted the decision of the Greek Government to resist Italian aggression was the belief that Greece's independence was at stake.

Following the occupation of Greece by the Axis, the Government sought refuge abroad and, there it brought officially to the attention of the British Government the Greek national claims. In view of the uncertainties of the war, the British were very reluctant to commit themselves to support Greek claims on Northern Epirus or the rectification of the Greek-Bulgarian frontiers. Presumably, certain quarters cherished the hope that Bulgaria might still become a rampart of the British defense system in the eastern Mediterranean, and that British influence might replace the Italian in Albania after the defeat of Italy.

Greek national claims as officially defined[2] by the Greek Government were: (a) Dodecanese, (b) Northern Epirus, (c) rectification of the Greek Bulgarian frontiers, and (c) Cyprus. It is probable that the American reader of these lines may shake his head, wondering whether a strip of land in a tongue-twisting province is worth quarreling over. The Greek claims, with the exception of the rectification of the Greek-Bulgarian frontiers, were based on the principle of self-determination, which is approved by the American people. In order to help the reader form his own conclusions as to the merits, or demerits, of the Greek national claims, a brief analysis is necessary before we study their treatment by the Council of Foreign Ministers and the Peace Conference.

Dodecanese. On May 4, 1912, during the Italo-Turkish war in Tripolitania, Italian armed forces landed in Rhodes, the major of the Dodecanese isles, and with the assistance of the Greek inhabitants occupied the island. Thus, they took possession of all the Dodecanese islands. General Ameglio, commander of the Italian forces, in his Proclamation to the Rhodian Demogerontia (Assembly of the Elders) declared that: "Turkish supremacy has ended on Rhodes and on the other islands, by the temporary occupation of them by Italy, and the future of the islands cannot be other than their autonomy." These and other similar promises were later discarded and by the Secret Treaty of London, signed on April 26, 1915, Italy was assured full possession of all the islands of Dodecanese "at present occupied by her." As the Twentieth Article of the League covenant abolished all secret treaties, the question of the Dodecanese came again under the consideration of the great powers. A committee of American experts appointed for examination of the Italian boundary settlements, recommended in Article Four of Document 31, that "Rhodes and Do-decanese be assigned to Greece. Over 80 percent of the population of Rhodes and the Dodecanese are Greek Orthodox. They are bitterly op-posed to the present Italian occupation, and should be assigned to the mother country." Finally, under the pressure of the other powers, Italy consented to award the Dodecanese Isles to Greece. On August 10, 1920, the Treaty of Sevres was signed by the representatives of Italy and Greece. The first Article of this treaty awarded to Greece complete sovereignty over the Dodecanese with the exception of Rhodes which, under Article Two, was to remain for fifteen years under Italian admini-stration, governed by an autonomous system of local authority. After this period, the Rhodians were to decide their political future in a plebiscite, to be held under the auspices of the League of Nations. On the same day, Turkey affixed her signature to the Peace Treaty with the Allies, re-nouncing in Article 122 all her titles, rights, and interests in the Dodecan-ese in favor of Italy. This was a necessary step before Italy would be in a position to grant any rights to Greece.

The Italian army of occupation prepared to leave the islands. But Italy was very slow in transferring the islands to Greece. In fact, she was try-ing to find some pretext to repudiate the agreements and retain the islands. The opportunity was given by the collapse of the Asia Minor campaign. On August 9, 1922, the Greek Ambassador to Rome was orally notified that Italy had unilaterally renounced the Treaty of Sevres.

On July 24, 1923, the Treaty of Lausanne was signed. Article 16 pro-vided that "the fate of the islands is settled or to be settled by the parties interested." During the inter-war period, however, Italy did not settle the Dodecanesian question with the "parties interested."

Northern Epirus. The predominance of the Greek element among the population of Northern Epirus has been questioned in certain political quarters. But the Greek character of the area has been repeatedly recog-nized in the past by the following international acts: (a) Early in 1913, while the Italian and Austro-Hungarian governments were striving to es-tablish an Albanian state, the Greek population of Northern Epirus re-volted and, on March 2, 1913, the independence of Northern Epirus was proclaimed in Argyrocastro. The revolt of the Epirotes was brought to an end by the mediation of an international commission established by the powers. On May 17, 1914, an agreement was signed at Corfu between the Commission and the representatives of the Epirotes, whereby the latter obtained the autonomy for which they had struggled. This agreement was approved by the great powers on June 18, and by the Albanians on June 23, 1914. (b) In September 1914, Sir Edward Grey feared that the misery and famine which existed in Epirus, might precipitate disorder;

he proposed, therefore, that the Greek Government send one regiment to Argyrocastro to avert massacres, with the condition that, should the powers so desire, the Greek troops should be withdrawn immediately. He added that the Greek Government should further consent to the occupation of Valona by the Italians. Premier Venizelos agreed to the British proposal as a whole under the condition that the Greek action should be unequivocally approved by the Italian Government whose influence in Albanian affairs was well known. The Italian Premier Salandra approved the proposed arrangement, and Greek troops were dispatched to Northern Epirus. (c) Under Article 7 of the secret treaty of London (April 26, 1915), Italy had undertaken "not to oppose the possible desire of France, Great Britain, and Russia to repartition the northern and southern district of Albania between Montenegro, Serbia and Greece . . ." in the event of a small, autonomous, and neutralized state being formed in Albania. (d) The Paris Peace Conference (1919) referred all questions affecting Greek territorial claims to a special committee. This committee after a series of meetings from February 18 to March 6, 1919, presented its report. With regard to Northern Epirus, the delegations of the United States, Britain, and France, accepted the Greek claims with various modifications, while the Italian delegation insisted upon the demarcation line indicated in the Protocol of Florence of 1913. (e) The resignation of Orlando and the formation of a new Italian Cabinet on June 22, 1919, opened a new phase in the Italo-Greek relations. With the change in the Italian foreign policy, an agreement, known as the Venizelos-Tittoni accord, was reached on July 29, 1919. Under the terms of this secret accord, the Italian Government pledged its support to the Greek claim on Northern Epirus, at the Peace Conference. (f) On December 9, 1919, the Greek claim on Northern Epirus was recognized in a memorandum signed by Grey (Britain), Clemenceau (France), and Polk (USA). Italy approved this memorandum on January 10, 1920. (g) On May 17, 1920, the United States Senate passed the following resolution:

Resolved: that it is the sense of the Senate that Northern Epirus (including Corytsa), Twelve islands of the Aegean (Dodecanese), where a strong Greek population predominates should be awarded to Greece and become incorporated in the Kingdom of Greece. (Congressional Record, Vol. 59, No. 137, p. 7160.)

Finally, in spite of all the aforementioned international actions, Northern Epirus was allocated to Albania, due to the same political reasons which prevented the annexation of the Dodecanese. On November 9, 1921, the Conference of Ambassadors which dealt with the problem of the Albanian frontiers gave its long-awaited decision; the Conference accepted the Albanian frontiers as defined by the Florence Protocol of 1913, with the exception of four very small alterations in the North, three to the advantage of Yugoslavia and one in favor of Albania. Furthermore, the signatories—United Kingdom, France, Italy and Japan—recognized Albania as a sovereign and independent state.[3] Simultaneously, they formally accepted the pre-eminence of Italian influence in Albania.[4]

During the inter-war period, the Albanian Government attempted to change the ethnologic composition of the area by persecuting the Greek element. It is characteristic that while in 1913 more than two hundred Greek schools were functioning in Northern Epirus providing the only source of education,[5] by 1925 their number had decreased to only seventy eight, and in 1933-34 not a single Greek school was allowed to operate in that area.

At the present time, certain political circles question the preponderance of the Greek element in Northern Epirus, although the national sentiment of the inhabitants is unknown. If it were true that Greeks no longer exist in Northern Epirus, one may wonder what happened to those people who were able to achieve autonomy in 1913 without external aid, and to maintain two hundred schools which provided "the only source of education."

The rectification of the Greek-Bulgarian frontiers. This claim was based strictly upon military and strategic considerations, and it involved a narrow strip of mountainous land along the Greek-Bulgarian boundary, thinly populated by Bulgarians and Turks (Pomaks). Past experience had shown that the existing borderline permitted the Bulgarians to invade the Greek territories of eastern Macedonia and western Thrace, and it had also facilitated the German campaign against Greece during World War II. The Greek claim was in substance similar to the French claim on the rectification of the French-Italian frontier, although the area involved in the latter was significant from an economic as well as a strategic point of view.

The question of Cyprus. This island under the jurisdiction of Great Britain represented an entirely different problem. It was quite obvious that the political future of this British dependency could not possibly become the subject of consideration by the Council of Foreign Ministers or the Peace Conference. Any decision concerning Cyprus should be reached through bilateral negotiations between Greece and Britain. As yet Great Britain has shown no intention to cooperate in the settlement of the Cypriot question.

Great Britain took over the administration of Cyprus from Turkey under the terms of the Convention of Defensive Alliance between Great Britain and Turkey, signed on June 4, 1878. Article I of this Convention provided that:

> If Batum, Ardahan, Kars, or any of them shall be retained by Russia, and if any attempt shall be made at any future time by Russia to take possession of any further territories . . . England will join His Imperial Majesty, the Sultan, in defending them by force of arms . . . (and) in order to enable England to make necessary provision for executing her engagement, (the Sultan) further consents to assign the Island of Cyprus to be occupied and administered by England.

Under the terms of an Annex to this Convention, the Sublime Porte remained the nominal sovereign of the island and was to receive a tribute of a fixed amount of 92,000 pounds. This sum, however, was never paid by the British Government to the Sultan but it was used to offset previous debts of the Ottoman Empire to Britain.

The day Sir Garnet Wolseley, the first British administrator, landed at Larnaca in 1878, a Greek deputation headed by the Archbishop was waiting to welcome him. In the course of an address of welcome, the Archbishop of Cyprus declared:

> . . . We accept the change of Government inasmuch as we trust that Great Britain will help Cyprus, as it did the Ionian Islands, to be united with Mother Greece, with which it is nationally connected. (C. W. J. Orr, p. 160.)

The sentiments of the Greek inhabitants have remained unchanged ever since.

On the outbreak of the war with Turkey in 1914, Cyprus was annexed to the British crown. This was an important development because it left Britain free to decide the future of the island. The following year notwithstanding arguments presented by certain British quarters that "neither on historical nor on geographical grounds would there seem to be any real connection between Cyprus and modern Greece," on October 20, the British Government offered Cyprus to Greece on the condition that the latter aid Serbia, then being invaded by Bulgaria. Zaimes, the Greek Premier refused to enter the war and the British offer lapsed. "But the incident showed that England was prepared to recognize that on national grounds the claims put forward by the Greek-speaking Cypriots that the island should be united with Greece were not considered unjustifiable." (C. W. J. Orr, p. 163.) Finally, in 1925 the island became a British colony.

The predominance of the Greek element among the population of Cyprus is not questioned—not even by the British Colonial Office. According to the 1946 census,[6] the ethnologic composition of the inhabitants of the island was: Greeks 361,199 or 80.2 percent; Ottoman 80,548 or 17.9 percent; Others 8,367 or 1.9 percent. According to more recent estimates

(1951), there are 399,972 Greeks out of a total population of 492,297. Under these conditions, there is no question what the decision of the overwhelming majority of the population will be in case the principle of self-determination is applied. Unfortunately, the British Government still opposes the settlement of the Cypriot question in accordance with the expressed desire of the inhabitants.

It is characteristic that Winston Churchill wrote in 1907:

> . . . I think it only natural that the Cypriot people, who are of Greek descent, should regard their incorporation with what may be called their mother country, as an ideal to be earnestly, devoutly, and fervently cherished. Such a feeling is an example of the patriotic devotion which so nobly characterizes the Greek nation . . . (C. W. J. Orr, p. 163.)

His government, however, rejects to-day any proposal for a friendly settlement of the dispute, and bases its opposition upon presumably sound political and strategic considerations. The British oppose the transfer of the island to Greece on the ground that this might displease Turkey. The presence of some 90,000 Moslems in a population of almost 500,000 allows certain Turkish quarters from time to time to display too great an interest in Cypriot affairs. This by no means implies that four fifths of the population may be barred from pursuing and achieving their national emancipation. Besides, Greece and Turkey in the past have solved a far more extensive and complex problem of minorities. The 90,000 Moslems of Cyprus will never present an insurmountable obstacle to the continuation of friendly relations between the two nations. It is characteristic of Greek policies toward minorities that in the general election of November 16, 1952, three Mohammedans were chosen to represent the Moslem minority of western Thrace in the Greek parliament. The recently signed Greek-Turkish-Yugoslav Pact (February 26, 1953) is a further indication that the two nations realistically evaluate their common interests and overcome the minor differences which inevitably exist among neighbors. In brief, the British argument that Turkey is an obstacle to the cession of Cyprus to Greece does not hold much water.

The second British argument is based on strategic considerations. There is no question that Cyprus is of great importance as a base for the protection of the eastern Mediterranean region and the Middle East. Particularly after the recent developments in Egyptian-British relations, the strategic importance of Cyprus as a defense outpost for the Suez waterway has tremendously increased. The question arises whether a transfer of the administration of the island to Greece would endanger the strategic position of Britain in that area.

Although the strategic value attached to Cyprus is basically correct, the whole approach of those who oppose the solution of the Cypriot question according to the principle of self-determination is fundamentally wrong. Britain, Greece, and Turkey, all being members of the North Atlantic Treaty Organization and facing the same threat, are bound to cooperate in the defense of the eastern Mediterranean region. In the event of another world-wide conflagration, Cyprus will necessarily become an important defense base for the allied forces of these nations within the framework of NATO. Consequently, the political *status quo* of the island will matter little since its use by all the allied forces will be necessary for a successful defense of the area.

Should Britain agree to the transfer of Cyprus to Greece, her strategic position would be unimpaired. Britain might be permitted to retain her own bases on the island on a lend-lease basis by a special agreement. On a similar basis, she might be granted military facilities at strategic points in Greece proper.

Such a solution, while not affecting Britain's strategic position whatso-ever, would have a tremendous effect upon the morale of the Cypriot people. It may be commonplace to argue that in every enterprise, and even more so, in every military undertaking morale is a factor of decisive importance. Should the question be settled on the aforementioned basis, the British forces in the island would become welcome guests, instead of being looked upon by the population as foreign oppressors.

The continuous obstructionism so far displayed by the British Gov-ernment on this issue, seriously damages Greek-British friendship and enables communist propaganda to exploit the question of Cyprus and un-dermine the unity and solidarity of the countries concerned.

To the unquestionable advantages of such an arrangement, those who oppose a solution of the issue argue that in the event of a change in the political *status quo* of Greece the agreements concerning the lease of bases to Britain may be repudiated. In such a case, they argue, Britain may find herself in a situation similar to the one involving the British troops in Suez. This argument is unfounded. It is beyond any doubt that only a communist regime in Greece would renounce such agreements. But it is equally certain that subordination of Greece through internal commun-ist subversion is virtually impossible under the existing conditions. Only an external aggression from the north, supported by the Soviet Union, can overthrow the present democratic regime and draw Greece behind the Iron Curtain. Such an aggression, however, would necessarily lead to a general conflagration, since Greece is a member of NATO and she is also connected with Turkey and Yugoslavia under the Pact of February 26, 1953.

In the event of a general conflict, the status of Cyprus as a Greek or British territory would be immaterial. Whether Greek or British, Cyprus would be considered by the enemy as a hostile base and would be treated accordingly. It would be childish indeed to argue again in the manner the British authorities did in 1941. At that time, immediately upon the collapse of the resistance in Greece, the Greek Government requested the permission of the British authorities to transfer temporarily the seat of the government to Cyprus. The British refused on the grounds that a transfer of the Greek Government to the island might provoke a German attack; as though the presence of the Greek Government in the island would render Cyprus more hostile to Germany. Obviously, the reason behind their refusal was that they desired to avoid an action which might be exploited later by the people of Cyprus and the Greek Government in the solution of the Cypriot question. As to another British argument that Cyprus is too far away from Greece, one can only reply that, however far, Greece is much nearer than Britain.

It is beyond doubt that a transfer of the administration of Cyprus to Greece with possible lease of bases to Britain would not impair the security system in the eastern Mediterranean. On the contrary, the continuation of the present British policy is only to the advantage of the communist propaganda which continually presses the issue upon the Greek and the Cypriot people. No one can blame the Greek and Cypriot people for their indignation, in view of the fact that the natives of Sudan are accorded the privilege of self-determination, and the people of Cyprus whose contributions to civilization date thousands of years back—long before the appearance of the British nation in the foreground of history—are denied the right to determine freely their own political future.

THE LONDON MEETING OF THE COUNCIL

Soon after the opening of the meeting of the Council of Foreign Ministers on September 11, 1945, the settlement of the question of the Dodecanese became—beyond any proportion— a crucial issue of the treaty with Italy. The reason was that Molotov refused to discuss the Dodecanesian question until the fate of the Italian colonies in Northern Africa had been decided by the Council. In view of the Soviet claim for a trusteeship on Tripolitania, the colonial issue was far from being an easy one. In supporting his claim on Tripolitania, Molotov argued that United States Secretary of State Stettinius, while outlining the American position on the assumption of a trusteeship by the Soviet Union, had expressed the opinion that USSR was eligible to receive a territory for administration under a trusteeship. On the basis of this statement, Molotov demanded that one of the Italian colonies, preferably Tripolitania, should be placed under the trusteeship of the Soviet Union. Molotov was very outspoken in his remarks. He pointed out that the Soviet Union had a sea outlet in the north, but in view of its vast territory it should also have one in the south, "especially so since we (USSR) now have the right to use Dairen and Port Arthur in the Far East. The Soviet Union," he added, "should take the place that is due to it, and therefore it should have bases in the Mediterranean for its merchant fleet. We do not propose to introduce the Soviet system into this territory," he hastened to explain; but he added: "apart from the democratic order that is desired by the people." And he concluded sarcastically "this will not be done along the lines that have been used in Greece." (J. Byrnes, p. 97.) This remark obviously referred to the steps taken by the British during the Communist revolt of December 1944, and revealed that Stalin no longer had "complete confidence in British policies in Greece."

The Soviet demand for a trusteeship in Tripolitania was very well calculated indeed. Should it be accepted by the other powers, it would enable the USSR to establish a foothold on an important point of the North African coast. If Tripolitania, located as it is in the middle of the North African Arabic countries, was placed under Soviet administration, it would undoubtedly become the center of political influence upon the Arabic peoples, which would attempt to channel the endogenous nationalistic anti-Western currents into a communist movement. Strategically, a Soviet trusteeship of Tripolitania would upset the balance of power in the Mediterranean by the addition of the USSR to the constellation of powers directly concerned with that area. Furthermore, the Soviet Union, under the familiar pretext of preserving her communications with the trusteeship, would press even more vigorously for a basic modification of the regime of the Straits in order to obtain adequate facilities for the passing of her fleet through them.

British Foreign Secretary Bevin bluntly refused to support the Soviet claim. As the Soviet claim over Tripolitania was officially based upon the damage caused the Soviet Union by the Italian troops during the war, Bevin openly pointed out that Britain and the dominions were fighting Italy long before the Soviet Union was at war with her. He went on emphasizing that Great Britain had recognized Soviet interests in eastern Europe and had supported their claims there, but he expressed his surprise that the Soviet leaders were not willing to recognize a similar British interest in the Mediterranean. Such arguments coming from the socialist Foreign Minister of Britain were a remarkable display of the continuity of the British foreign policy regardless of changes in the administration.

The exchange of such arguments between the Soviet delegates and other members of the Council, with variations and embellishments, were to become a familiar feature throughout the following sixteen months until it became clear to all concerned that no agreement on the issue of the Italian colonies could be reached.

Greece again became the subject of Soviet criticism when Secretary Byrnes remarked that the Groza Government in Rumania was "installed as a result of a two-and-a-half hour ultimatum to King Michael by Vyshinsky," and refused to agree to the recognition of the puppet governments of eastern Europe. This infuriated Molotov. In retaliation, he attacked Greece and asked the American representative why he was maintaining a different attitude toward Greece whose Government, in his opinion, was no more representative than that of Rumania. Secretary Byrnes replied that the difference in attitude was rather a question of facts. "In Greece," he added, "correspondents had been allowed to go in, move about freely, and report without censorship what they had seen. As a result, the American people were informed about Greece and felt that the situation was not the same as that described by you. In Rumania correspondents have not been allowed any such facilities and the actions of the Groza government have led us to believe it is not representative of the people." (J. Byrnes, p. 98.)

"Apparently," Molotov remarked, "in Greece the correspondents are happy but the people are not; whereas in Rumania the people are happy but the correspondents are not. The Soviet Government attaches more importance to the feelings of the people." This was correct from the communistic standpoint, since the word *people* in the communist political dictionary has a very narrow connotation, meaning only the followers of the Communist ideology in each country.

When the Foreign Ministers parted they had reached no agreement on any of the major issues. Their first effort to put the cornerstones in the edifice of the new world order had ended in an impasse. The people who had been encouraged by the Yalta mirage of world unity began wondering whether the war that had just ended had any historical justification at all. Here and there voices could be heard, boldly pointing to the fallacy of the arguments presented by top leaders of the Western world, to the effect that "we must and can get along with the Soviet Government,"[7] and that "we know or believe that Russia's interests, so far as we can anticipate them, do not afford an opportunity for a major difference with us in foreign affairs . . . The Russians undoubtedly like the American people, (and) . . . they want to maintain friendly relations with us . . ."[8]

THE SECOND EFFORT: MOSCOW

Molotov's failure to impose the Soviet views upon the other Allies was a rather painful surprise to the Kremlin. So far the Russians had returned to Moscow from Teheran, Yalta, and even Potsdam with substantial gains; this time Molotov left London without any prize package. The repercussions of the Soviet dissatisfaction with the new shift in Western policy were soon felt in eastern Europe. The governments which had been established in these countries with the more or less open intervention and support of the Red Army hardly represented the peoples of these countries. The Western governments had withheld recognition of these governments on the grounds that they were not representative of the people. Since the Soviet Government had decided to consolidate victory and its gains in eastern Europe, those governments should be vested with a cloak of legitimacy so the argument of nonrepresentation of the people would no longer be applicable.

Following the London meeting of the Council of Foreign Ministers, Bulgaria, Albania, and Yugoslavia, the three countries bordering the southern flank of the European-Soviet sphere, conducted single-list elections which naturally resulted in the triumph of the participating parties which were led by the Communists. Any opposition to the Communist-dominated regimes was wiped out in terror. Secretary Byrnes witnessed with sincere anxiety the steadily widening gap between the Soviet Union and the Western Powers. It was plain that victory in war did not necessarily mean a successful peace. But now with the inconceivable development of science and technology, the world could not afford to jeopardize its own existence in another war adventure. Every effort should be made to forestall the looming rift between the Soviet Union and the other powers. According to the Protocol of Proceedings of the Crimea Conference, the Foreign Ministers of the three major Powers were expected to meet from time to time and consider the international situation. As they had met in Berlin and London, but not in Moscow, Secretary Byrnes asked the Soviet Government to prepare a meeting in the Soviet capital. The Soviet Government agreed to the American proposal and on December 16, 1945, the three Foreign Ministers met in Moscow.

The same problems and the same opposing views which harassed them in London were present again. With one difference; the Soviet policies and objectives had become so manifest in the meantime that no responsible leader of the Western Powers cherished any illusions as to the possibility of sincere cooperation with the Soviet Union. It was plain to all that the hard core of the problem which faced the Foreign Ministers was not the drafting of peace treaties with the enemy states, but to establish a way of living together in a united world. The particular issues were, in a last analysis, manifestations of the terrifying truth that the war-time Great Alliance was gradually shaping into two hostile international camps.

Among the questions discussed in Moscow was the procedure to be followed by the Peace Conference, and the number of countries eligible to participate in the final drafting of the peace treaties. In both issues, the desire of the Soviet Government to limit the participation to the least possible number, was stressed again in Moscow. Under the Soviet formula which was finally accepted by the other Powers as the only way to get the Soviets to agree to call a peace conference, Britain, the USSR, the United States, and France would participate in the final drafting of the peace treaty with Italy, with France dropping out for the Rumanian, Hungarian, and Bulgarian treaties, and both France and the United States dropping out for the treaty with Finland.

The Soviet leaders not only pressed for a limited participation in the Peace Conference, but they further proposed rules of procedure that would virtually strip it of any real power. All these Soviet policies were a striking return to the practices of secret diplomacy which the fathers of Communism had so fiercely denounced as one of the worse evils of Imperialism.

The Americans refused to agree to the Soviet proposals and insisted upon the participation of all "the members of the United Nations which actively waged war with substantial military forces against the European members of the Axis." (J. Byrnes, p. 112.) Finally, after a phone call from Marshal Stalin to Molotov, the American list of twenty-one states eligible for participation was accepted by the Russians. But little real power was left to the conference; under the approved rules of procedure, the smaller participants could do little in modifying the draft treaties as prepared by the big powers.

When the Foreign Ministers of Britain and the United States left Moscow, they felt that this time some progress had been made toward the solution of many important problems. They had no doubt that many trying days were ahead. Nevertheless, they faced "the new year of 1946 with greater hope as a result of the Moscow Conference." (J. Byrnes, p. 122.)

THE FOREIGN MINISTERS DELEGATE THEIR WORRIES

Notwithstanding the optimistic expectations of the Western Foreign Secretaries who only three weeks earlier had left Moscow more or less lighthearted, the atmosphere was less calm than ever when the deputies of the Foreign Ministers gathered in London on January 18, 1946,—entrusted with the solution of problems which their superiors had been unable to solve. A few days earlier, the first session of the General Assembly of the United Nations had opened in London, only a few blocks away from the Lancaster House where the deputies were holding their meetings.

The issues which divided the two camps quickly became sources of disunity among the members of the United Nations. Averill Harriman had come to London to report that the committee, which had been established by the Foreign Ministers in their last meeting in Moscow, had failed to make any progress in Bucharest toward the reorganization of the Rumanian Government of Groza. On January 13, Vyshinsky had announced from Moscow that efforts to broaden the Bulgarian Government had been equally unsuccessful. Thus, the efforts of the Western governments to reorganize the regimes of the eastern European countries according to the principles laid down by the Yalta Declaration had failed to produce any results; the Soviet Union was building steadily its eastern European empire.

The problem of the presence of Soviet troops in Iran was becoming more acute in the meantime. Finally, the filing of a complaint by the Iranian representative with the Security Council brought the issue to a head.

Soviet charges against the presence of British troops in Greece and Indonesia, and the acrimonious debates which ensued in the Security Council, hindered the smooth preparation of the draft treaties by the deputies. It is no wonder that when March came the deputies were still as far apart as ever on the major issues of the reparations, the colonies and the Italo-Yugoslav border and Trieste.

Greek national claims slowly sank in a turmoil of conflicting interests. Again and again the Soviet representative refused to discuss the question of the Dodecanese before the colonial question was settled, that is, before the establishment of a Soviet trusteeship over Tripolitania. The other two Greek claims concerning Northern Epirus and the rectification of the Greek-Bulgarian border for security reasons were supported only by the British. The Russians flatly rejected any such arrangement, determined to prevent any decision detrimental to the interests of Albania and Bulgaria, the two Communist-controlled Balkan countries. The Americans were undecided. Although a Congressional resolution passed on July 29, 1945 had suggested that "Northern Epirus (including Corytsa) . . . where a Greek population predominates should be awarded by the peace conference to Greece and become incorporated in the territory of Greece," Secretary Byrnes, who apparently did not foresee the important role Greece was to play in the coming years, maintained a middle-of-the-road attitude toward the question of Northern Epirus. As to the Greek claim for rectification of the frontier with Bulgaria, he argued that such an arrangement was unnecessary and that Greece should primarily rely on the United Nations for security.

The Foreign Ministers had agreed in Moscow that there should be a peace conference "after the completion of the drafts . . . (and) before May 1, 1946." The insignificant progress made by the deputies in drafting the treaties, rendered the convocation of a peace conference before May 1, practically impossible.

The delegation of responsibility for solving such intricate problems to deputies who lacked the necessary authority was unrealistic and impractical. The responsibility of the deputies should be limited to the solution of minor problems of detail, after the major issues were settled by the Council of Foreign Ministers. As a result of the inability of the deputies to prepare the drafts within the deadline, a meeting of the Foreign Ministers became necessary.

THE UNEXPECTED SETTLEMENT OF THE DODECANESE QUESTION

Again on the initiative of Secretary Byrnes, the members of the Council agreed to reunite and speed up the drafting of the treaties. Secretary Byrnes suggested Paris as the site of the meeting. He hoped that Molotov, in view of the active participation of the Communists in French politics, would not insist on opposing the participation of France in the preparation of all five treaties. Strangely enough, Molotov quickly agreed to rules of procedure which actually entailed France's participation in all five treaties.

This conciliatory gesture marked about the limit of the Soviet contribution to the lessening of the tension. After twenty one days of acrimonious debates and the exchange of charges and counter charges for imperialism and aggressiveness, they all wearily agreed on May 16, to take a recess and meet again in Paris on June 15, 1946.

They met on June 16, but for another eleven days progress was agonizingly slow. Suddenly, on June 27, the impasse showed signs of breaking up. After a long meeting that had followed the familiar pattern of constant disagreement, Molotov agreed to some of the economic clauses of the Rumanian treaty. This prompted Secretary Byrnes to say in humor as much as in hope, "We should make it a good afternoon and settle the question of the Dodecanese." To his amazement, Molotov immediately replied that "the Soviet delegation has no objection to that proposal." Bevin, who had tried repeatedly in the past to settle this question, asked in disbelief whether Molotov meant that the islands should go to Greece. The Soviet delegate promptly affirmed that this was the meaning of his statement and immediately asked his colleagues to proceed to the examination of the next question.

"Let me have a minute or two to recover," Secretary Byrnes exclaimed.

The promptness with which Molotov agreed to the transfer of the Dodecanese to Greece is really surprising. During the first meeting in Paris, only a few weeks before, "the discussions on the transfer of the Dodecanese . . . continued to produce no results, as Mr. Molotov insisted that the settlement of this question had to await the disposition of the colonies." His unexpected reversal indicates that the decision was already made in Moscow before he returned to Paris. What caused this sudden

change? Apparently the Soviet leaders were by now convinced that no
concessions were obtainable on the colonial issue and therefore they had
decided to defer the solution of this problem to a later period. During the
second meeting in Paris, Molotov agreed to postpone the decision for one
year, after which, if agreement had not been reached, the General Assembly of the United Nations would be asked to decide the issue.

The Dodecanese question no longer served as a bargaining instrument
in the discussion of the colonial issue, and therefore it would be unwise
to foster anti-communist sentiments in Greece and render the political
task of the Greek Communists even more difficult. The Soviet leaders
must have been aware that the extensive influence of the Communists in
Greek affairs during the war had faded out since the liberation of the
country, partly because of the Soviet opposition to the Greek national
claims. The results of the general election of March 31, 1946, which had
been conducted under the supervision of international observers, had
proved that the Greek people had followed closely the Soviet policies
toward Greece and had reacted accordingly.

On May 13, 1946, two days before the recess of the first Paris meeting,
the Regent of Greece had announced that a plebiscite would be held on
September 1, 1946, to decide the question of the Monarchy. The issue of
the national claims and the Soviet opposition to their settlement had been
one of the major issues of the political fight in Greece and, undoubtedly,
the outcome of the March 31 election was partly due to the Soviet policies.

The defeat of the Communists in the election would be easily offset by
the abdication of the Monarchy in the coming plebiscite, which was of
far greater importance for the political future of Greece. There was no
doubt that the defeat of the Monarchy would be acclaimed by the Communists as their own victory. Since the Red Revolution of December
1944 and the horrible experiences of the civil war, the Greek people had
come to realize that the old-fashioned anti-royalists would be unable to
contain the Communists in the event of a defeat of the Monarchy. As a
result, the Republic, supported too eagerly by the Communists, was identified in the minds of the majority of the Greek people with Communism.
The question of the Monarchy, from an issue concerning the form of the
state, had become basically a duel between Communism and the rest of
of the people. Consequently, the majority of the people, who previously
were more or less indifferent toward the King and the Monarchy, turned
to King George as to the only national element able to avert domination
of the country by the Communists. One may venture that the Soviet
leaders apparently well informed about the political developments in
Greece, decided to use the Dodecanese question, which no longer served

as a bargaining instrument, to influence the Greek people in the coming plebiscite.

The settlement of the Dodecanese question was the limit of Soviet willingness to facilitate the task of the Greek Communists. Soviet opposition to the settlement of the other two Greek claims remained stiff. Albania and Bulgaria had become by that time People's Republics and any cession of Albanian or Bulgarian territory to Greece would come out of the Soviet sphere.

The Soviet opposition to these two claims was matched by the indifference of the American and the French delegates who desired to avoid issues which might make worse the already precarious relations with the Soviet Union. Only the British delegation supported the Greek claims on Northern Epirus and the Greek-Bulgarian borderline but without any result.

THE PEACE CONFERENCE

Twenty-one nations were represented at the Conference which opened in Paris at the Luxemburg Palace, on July 29, 1946. Again the Greek national claims became part of the hardly concealed strife between the distinctly opposite camps. Particularly the dispute over the Greek-Bulgarian boundary was magnified beyond proportion, not because of the size or the importance of the territory involved, but because it concerned a segment of the frontier between the Soviet and the Western spheres.

This time, the Soviet delegation, in an effort to counterbalance the Greek claims, not only expressed its opposition but went even further; it encouraged Bulgaria to present a counter claim on the Greek province of western Thrace, "the return of which to Bulgaria . . . would remove a grave injustice committed against the Bulgarian people."[9] This Bulgarian counter claim involved exactly the same Greek territory which had been granted to Bulgaria by Hitler in 1941, as a reward for Bulgaria's collaboration in the Nazi campaign against Greece.

The opinion in certain quarters was that the Greek claim on the Bulgarian boundary had little to recommend it; but Bulgaria's presumption in putting in such a counter claim impressed the nations outside of the Soviet sphere as monstrous. This Bulgarian claim, followed by continuous Soviet diplomatic attacks against Greece, had the effect of rallying the small countries to the support of Greece. This support, however, had little practical significance since under the rules of procedure the decision rested with the Council of the Foreign Ministers.

The Soviet move to support the Bulgarian claim was a severe blow against the political position of the Greek Communists. In fact, were the Soviet leaders concerned with the position of KKE as a political force in Greece, this move would have been a serious political mistake. The Soviet leaders had to choose between influence in Greece bought at the price of Bulgarian territory, and consolidation of the Soviet position in Bulgaria at the expense of the Greek Communists. They chose the latter because it was no longer necessary for the Soviet Union to bother with the advancement of the communist cause in Greece through political means. The preparations for Greece's subjugation through armed subversion were already well under way; so, there was no reason at all to agree to the settlement of the other two Greek claims. Dodecanese was the limit of Soviet willingness to support politically the Greek Communists; and any way, Dodecanese was outside the Soviet sphere.

It is doubtful that the Soviet leaders expected the Bulgarian claim would ever be accepted by the other powers; more likely, their purpose in advancing the Bulgarian claim was to counter the Greek claims on Northern Epirus and the Bulgarian boundary, and force the other powers to a compromise. The Soviet maneuver finally met with remarkable success. When the Soviet delegation quietly dropped the Bulgarian claim, Secretary Byrnes found in this the opportunity for a compromise that exactly met the Soviet aims; he pushed the idea of prohibiting the fortification of Bulgaria's southern border. The same border had been demilitarized under the terms of the Treaty of Neilly (1919) but this had not stopped Bulgarian aggression against Greece in 1941.

To those advocating rectification of the Greek-Bulgarian boundary, the American representatives replied that Greece should rely for security on the United Nations, not on the acquisition of a few miles of territory inhabited by an alien population. But these American officials forgot the United Nations when they declared that "far from opposing . . . (they had) sympathized with . . . the efforts of the Soviet Union to draw into closer and more friendly association with her central and eastern European neighbors," and wholeheartedly subscribed to the Soviet "special security interests in those countries."[10]

The Conference accepted the demilitarization proposal over Soviet opposition, but in a surprise revolt the British dominions and the small western European nations refused to accept the view supported by the Soviet and the American delegates that no rectification of the borderline should be made. Twelve nations out of twenty-one participants abstained when it came up for vote, and the question went back to the Council of Foreign Ministers without a recommendation. The incident was without practical significance, but was characteristic of the widespread dissatisfaction among the smaller countries with the tactics of the major powers.

FINALE IN NEW YORK

The Council opened its final meeting in New York on November 4, 1946. But if it were not for the New York skyline as background, one might have thought he was back in London one year ago. The same arguments, the same disagreements, as though there had not been so many months of exhaustive negotiations. For three weeks, Molotov refused to accept any of the recommendations of the Peace Conference, not even those approved by a two-thirds majority. During the fourth week of fruitless negotiations, Secretary Byrnes decided to change his tactics. Taking advantage of a call by Molotov, he expressed his utter dissatisfaction because of the Soviet attitude.

"I must tell you," he said to Molotov, "that since you have rejected practically all of the recommendations of the peace conference adopted by at least a two-thirds vote, I see no hope for agreement . . . It is with the greatest reluctance, therefore, that I have come to the conclusion we will not be able to agree upon the treaties. Having become reconciled to this, I think we should agree to disagree without having any of the bitter exchanges that marked some of the debates at Paris." (J. Byrnes, p. 152.) Molotov's reaction, as soon as he became convinced that Secretary Byrnes really meant what he said and there was no possibility for further political gains, was genuinely Soviet in character. In order to secure what had been already conceded to the Soviet camp, Molotov changed his attitude radically, and, since he realized that the time had come for him to agree, he did it "in a big way." He proposed amendments which were merely changes in words rather than substance. His colleagues were quite willing to cooperate in this face-saving and within a few days the Council had reached agreement on all the controversial issues.

The Greek claims on Northern Epirus and the Bulgarian boundary were not among those controversial issues. Without the support of the American delegation, their fate already had been decided in the Peace Conference. Thus, when the peace treaties were finally signed on February 10, 1947, only the Dodecanese islands were allocated to Greece. The Soviet Union had succeeded in eliminating the Greek claims and had affectively protected the interests of Albania and Bulgaria, two former Axis satellites but now avowed members of the communist family.

The treaties "were not the best human wit could devise. But they were the best human wit could get the four principal allies to agree upon." (J. Byrnes, p. 137.) The Greek Government, although deeply disappointed by the treatment of the national claims by the allies, signed the peace treaties. It formally expressed, however, its determination to pursue the settlement of the Northern Epirus question by peaceful means. The Greek claim on Northern Epirus still remains open.

FOOTNOTES

1. Quoted from *Propaganda i Agitatsia*, Leningrad, 1945, No. 18, p. 3, in Frederick C. Barghoorn, "*The Soviet Union Between War and Cold War,*" *The Annals of the American Academy of Political and Social Science*, Philadelphia, 1949, Vol. 263, p. 4.

2. See Appendix IV, Note A.

3. *Official Journal*, League of Nations, December 1921, 2nd Year, No. 12, p. 1195.

4. *Treaty Series*, League of Nations, Vol. XII, p. 383.

5. During the Paris Peace Conference (1919), the Albanians did not deny the predominance of Greek schools in N. Epirus. They argued, however, that this was due to the fact that "the Greek language attracted them by its culture while the Albanian was less developed, and that Greek is the commercial language of the Near East." E. Pierpont Stickney, *Southern Albania or Northern Epirus in European International Affairs, 1912-13*, p. 61.

6. British Colonial Office: *Report on Cyprus for the year 1949*, London: H. M. Stationery Office, 1950, p. 8.

7. Opinion expressed by C. Hull quoted by Chester Wilmot, *op. cit.*, p. 639.

8. Memorandum by H. Hopkins, written on August 1, 1945, quoted by R. E. Sherwood, *op. cit.*, pp. 922-923.

9. *Paris Peace Conference, Selected Documents*, U. S. Department of State Publication 2868, 1947, p. 887. See also similar statement by Kulishef, Bulgarian Foreign Minister, to the Conference, on August 14, 1946, *ibid.*, p. 898.

10. Statement by Secretary Byrnes, on October 31, 1945, quoted by F. L. Schuman, *op. cit.*, p. 812.

CHAPTER TWELVE

GREECE, A TESTING GROUND

SOVIET OPPOSITION TO THE Greek national claims arose from far deeper causes than the mere protection of the new People's Republics of Bulgaria and Albania. The Soviet leaders, undoubtedly regretted that the wartime efforts of the Communists to subjugate Greece had failed. Therefore, they reversed their hands-off policy soon after the collapse of Germany.

PREPARING THE THIRD ROUND

As it has been previously mentioned, signs of this change were already evident during the Potsdam Conference. This time, the communist plan for the sovietization of Greece was modified to meet the existing international and domestic conditions. Taking advantage of the breathing space after the crushing of the December revolution, the Greek Government took steps which made it a very difficult enterprise to take control of Greece by seizing the government in Athens. Besides, the disorganization of the Communist Party (KKE) after the failure of the December revolution, excluded for a while any effective subversive activity.

However there was an alternative. Following the defeat of the Communists in December 1944, several thousand people fled from Greece across the border to the northern neighboring countries. According to Soviet sources more than 20,000 found refuge in Yugoslavia, more than 5,000 in Bulgaria and more than 23,000 in Albania.[1] Some of these people were members of ELAS who had fled in order to escape persecution for crimes committed during the occupation and the December revolution. Others were Slavo-Macedonians who crossed the border together with the Communist guerrilla groups. Most of them were persuaded by the Communists that a ferocious persecution of the minorities would follow the defeat of ELAS. Some others, particularly among those 23,000 who fled into Albania, were Czamuriots who had actively assisted the Axis occupation authorities during the war in the persecution of the Greek population of Epirus, and especially of that part which had been annexed by Albania. Finally, some had fled abroad to escape personal revenge for crimes committed during the war period.

Whatever the reason for their escape, the presence of these people in the Balkan People's Republics perfectly suited the Soviet plans. Since under the circumstances it was practically impossible to overthrow the government in Athens, the new Communist aggression should start from the north; those thousands of "refugees" provided the nucleus for the formation of a new guerrilla army. At the beginning, small guerrilla units trained in the neighboring countries should cross the border and enter Greece to form the basis of a new revolutionary army. Simultaneously, a well-prepared propaganda campaign should present the assault against Greece as the effort of persecuted "democratically-minded citizens and national minorities" to defend themselves against suppression and terrorism carried on "by the Greek gendarmerie, regular troops and rightist bands." This very realistic plan found support from many directions, some of which were really unexpected.

The inability of the Greek Government to assert its authority over some remote parts of the country had allowed anti-Communist bands to become self-appointed protectors of the civil order. The Communists did not fail to exploit this situation to the full. The civil war, which had ravaged Greece in the past years, had provided ample causes for hatred and revenge. It was very easy for the Communists to intensify the disorder by provoking more incidents in order to be able to claim that the rightist bands were persecuting innocent democratic citizens. Of course, these rightist bands, composed of extremists and persons of doubtful integrity, helped the improvement of the internal conditions in Greece very little. To assert, however, that the actions of these groups were the only cause for the new communist rebellion would be an oversimplification. But it did help the Soviet Union to support the allegation that the tense situation in Greece was the result of domestic causes only. The Soviet contentions frequently found valuable support by non-Communist observers. But these observers were often unfamiliar with the deeper causes of unrest and in some cases promoted relatively small matters to the level of international concern. Due to this lack of knowledge, fair-minded non-Communist journalists and political observers, supplied world opinion with information stressing beyond proportion the "ordeal of the Greek democratic citizens" who fled to the mountains to save themselves from the savage terrorism of the Athens regime.[2] So the Soviet myth was unexpectedly sustained by American and British observers who, even though they traveled freely all over the country, failed to comprehend the drama of the Greek people.

According to the general plan, the Communist Party of Greece (KKE) first launched the so-called "self-defense of the democratic citizens" which soon became "mass self-defense" and finally "armed mass self-defense." Slogans and labels used by the Communists always serve a practical purpose and reveal to a *connoisseur* the hidden communist objectives. This time the aforementioned slogans were primarily prepared for international consumption.

The preparation of the "third round" as the Communists called their third attempt to subjugate Greece started in the spring of 1945. But it was intensified only after Nicholas Zachariades, the Moscow-trained secretary-general of KKE, returned from Germany where he had been interned by the Germans during the war. Soon after his arrival in September 1945, the publication of inflammatory articles and provocative manifestoes in the two chief communist newspapers, *Rizospastis* and *Elefteri Ellada*, was increased. Frenzied propaganda, published freely under the "suppressive regime of Athens," called the people "in self-defense against the Greek Government and the Angloslaves of Athens." (*Rizospastis*, Oct. 11, 1945.) Slogans written on the walls of the houses in Athens and elsewhere at night demanded the immediate withdrawal of the British military forces from Greece and the establishment of a "democratic government." It is interesting to note that the main themes of these communist articles and slogans were later incorporated in the official charges brought by the Soviet Government to the United Nations and faithfully reiterated by the representatives of the Soviet-controlled countries.

THE GREEK QUESTION IN THE UNITED NATIONS

The first indications of the oncoming "third round" were given by Tito's speech of July 8, 1945, and by the allegations against the presence of British troops in Greece and the policies of the Greek Government, presented by the Soviet Government during the Potsdam conference in July 1945. These allegations were repeated during the London meeting of the Council of Foreign Ministers. Coupled with Soviet pressure on Turkey and the continued presence of Soviet troops in Iran, they indicated the intention of the Soviet Union to resume its expansionist policy in the Middle East, on the general lines contained in the Molotov memorandum to Hitler on November 25, 1940. The new Soviet scheme for the subjugation of Greece was, in fact, only part of a master-plan centered around the Straits of the Dardanelles and aimed at control of the Middle East and the eastern Mediterranean region by the Soviet Union.

As early as March 19, 1945, while the hopeful declarations of the Big Three for the establishment of a better world were still fresh in the memories of the peoples, the Soviet Government notified Turkey that she did not intend to renew the 1925 treaty of friendship, which was to expire the following November 7, 1945. A few months later, on June 22, 1945, the Soviet Government went much further and stated that it would not sign a new treaty with Turkey unless the latter would cede to the Soviet Republics of Armenia and Georgia the frontier provinces of Kars and

Ardahan, agree to the establishment of Soviet bases in the Straits, and be willing to revise the Montreux Convention. On July 10, the Turkish Government replied that although it was willing to cooperate in the establishment of some form of international arrangement for the Straits, it would not agree to the cession of Turkish territory. The purpose of the Turkish Government in proposing the establishment of some form of international arrangement for the Straits is quite obvious. It desired to bring the discussion from its bilateral frame, to an international level so that Turkey would not be alone in the negotiations with the Soviet Union.

It was only natural that the Soviet proposals to Turkey were considered during the Potsdam Conference. Winston Churchill desired to disprove the allegation that Britain was trying to hem the Soviet Union in the Black Sea. Thus, he expressed his willingness to join in a revised agreement that would insure free passage through the Straits for both the naval and the merchant ships of the Soviet Union in peace or war. He felt it important, however, that Turkey should not be alarmed unduly, and pointed to the concern aroused by Russia's request for the provinces of Kars and Ardahan, and for a naval base in the Straits. (J. Byrnes, p. 77.) Stalin and Molotov defended their proposals to Turkey by stressing that the two provinces had been part of Russia under the Czar and, in any event, the Soviet Union was justified when entering a new treaty of alliance to fix the boundaries it would be obliged to defend. As for the Soviet request for a base in the Straits, they maintained it resulted from the consideration that Turkey was too weak to give an effective guarantee of free passage, and it was, therefore, right that the USSR should be able to defend the Straits in case of emergency.

The American position was presented by President Truman who declared that the United States Government favored a revision of the Montreux Convention provided that "the Straits should be a free waterway open to the whole world and guaranteed by all of us."

In the discussion which followed, it became clear that the form of guarantee for the freedom of navigation through the Straits formed the heart of the problem. The Soviet leaders wanted free navigation guaranteed by the Soviet Union, or by the Soviet Union and Turkey, whereas the Western Powers preferred a United Nations guarantee. This was not a question of form, but a matter of substance. Should the Soviet proposal be accepted, Russian troops would be stationed on Turkish soil; and from this point to political infiltration and eventual subordination was too short a distance, as past experience had shown.

Although one may argue that under the present development of war weapons and global strategy the importance of the Straits as a water gate has to a certain extent diminished, their domination still remains one of the objectives of the Soviet foreign policy. This time, however, the Soviet interest to gain a foothold on Turkish soil arose rather from political considerations embracing the whole Middle East and exceeding (by far) the issue of the Straits proper.

The Western Powers refused to agree with the Soviet position and in the protocol of Proceedings of the Berlin Conference, issued on August 2, 1945, the three Governments recognized that "the Convention concluded at Montreux should be revised as failing to meet present-day conditions. It was agreed that as the next step the matter should be the subject of direct conversations between each of the three Governments and the Turkish Government." (Paragraph XVI) Apparently, the "present-day conditions" were primarily Russia's ability to press for terms more favorable to her than those of 1936. On the whole, this paragraph of the Protocol hardly concealed the failure of the conference to reach a constructive solution of the problem.

In accordance with the stipulation of separate communication with the Turkish Government, the Government of the United States dispatched a note to the Turkish Government on October 31, 1945, whereby it advocated the establishment of a new regime in the Straits. Under the terms of the proposed arrangement, the Straits would be open in time of peace to the warships of the Black Sea Powers only, and closed to those of other nations. In November 23, Britain handed a similar note to Turkey and on December 6, the Turkish Government announced its willingness to accept the American proposal as a basis for discussion.

The American proposal was fair; indeed, had the Soviet objective been merely the security of the Soviet Union and the free passage of its ships through the Straits, it should have been accepted by that Government without demur. But the goal of the Soviet Union was actually the penetration of the Middle East. The repercussions such a serious dislocation of the balance of power in that region entails are obvious.

The Soviet reaction to the conciliatory diplomatic efforts of the west, is characteristic of their objectives. Within a few days, the Soviet press opened a forceful campaign in support of the "rights " of the Soviet Republics of Georgia and Armenia on Turkey's northeastern provinces of Kars and Ardahan, and flatly raised the question of Soviet bases in the Straits.

On December 19, 1945, the day before the Soviet press launched its campaign on Turkey, Secretary Byrnes, then at Moscow for the meeting of the three Foreign Ministers, had met Stalin and Molotov and had expressed his concern about the situation in Iran, where 30,000 well-trained and fully-equipped Soviet troops were stationed. The Iranian Government had protested against Soviet intervention, when 1,500 Iranian troops marching toward the province of Azerbaijan to quell what the Iranians claimed to be an uprising instigated by foreign forces, had been stopped and ordered by the Soviet military authorities to turn back. Following this incident, the Iranian Government had asked for the withdrawal of all foreign troops. As a matter of fact, since the war had ended and Iran no longer served as a corridor for the transportation of supplies to the Soviet Union, there was no justification for the presence of foreign troops on Iranian soil. The United States Government promptly issued an order to the remaining American troops to evacuate Iran and urged the Soviet Union and the United Kingdom to take similar steps, thus fulfilling the pledge that President Roosevelt had entered into with Marshall Stalin and Premier Churchill at Teheran in 1943.

Stalin was unwilling to relinquish a position of such strategic importance as long as there was the slightest indication that such a step could be avoided. He argued that his desire to maintain troops in Iran was based solely on the fact that he could not place confidence in the Iranian Government, and that the Baku oil fields should be protected from possible activities of foreign saboteurs. He also claimed that the Soviet Union had a right, by treaty, to maintain troops in Iran until March 15, 1946.

On January 19, 1946, the head of the Iranian delegation to the United Nations addressed a letter to the Acting Secretary General. It stated that (1) owing to interferences of the USSR, through the medium of its official and armed forces, in the internal affairs of Iran, a situation had arisen which might lead to international friction, and (2) that in accord with Article 33 of the Charter, the Iranian Government had repeatedly tried to negotiate with the Government of USSR but it had met with no success. The Iranian delegate, therefore, requested the Acting Secretary General to bring the matter to the attention of the Security Council, in accordance with Article 35(1) of the Charter, so that the Council might investigate the situation and recommend appropriate terms of settlement. Secretary Byrnes discussing this subject in his book *Speaking Frankly*, asserts that both he and Bevin had advised the Iranian delegate to avoid this step which was likely to bring friction within the "young" Security Council. (J. Byrnes, p. 123.)

Two days later, the acting chief of the Soviet delegation requested the Security Council to discuss the situation in Greece, under Article 35 of the Charter. In his letter he declared:

. . . the presence of British troops in Greece after the termination of the war is not called for now in the interests of the protection of the communications of the British troops staying in the defeated countries. On the other hand, the presence of the British troops in Greece has turned into an instrument of pressure . . . not seldom utilized by reactionary elements against the democratic forces of the country. Such a situation . . . causes extraordinary tension fraught with grave consequences both for the Greek people and for the maintenance of peace and security . . . (U. N. Journal of S. C. No. 2, p. 14.)[3]

THE BACKGROUND OF THE SOVIET MOVE

The Soviet diplomatic move, only two days after the filing of the Iranian complaint, has been interpreted by some prominent political observers as an act of retaliation; this interpretation, however, is unworthy of the Soviet diplomacy. True, it was connected with the Iranian question; but not as a counter measure for the Iranian charges. As it has been previously pointed out, Greece, Iran, and Turkey were at the beginning of 1946 the three focal points of a concerted Soviet plan of infiltration and expansion toward the eastern Mediterranean and the Middle East. In this sense, the Soviet policies in Iran were fully related to those in Greece. But the preparation of the Soviet move in bringing charges against the British forces in Greece had begun long before the Iranian representative had even considered the possibility of an appeal to the Security Council. This preparation had taken the form of protests presented by the Soviet leaders in several occasions as in Potsdam, London, and Moscow. It had been also assisted by the Greek Communists who, during the summer and the fall of 1945, conducted a systematic propaganda campaign designed to supply the Soviet Government with the necessary "evidence" for their anticipated attack in the Security Council.

By December 1945, the efforts of the Greek Communists were intensified. Under the personal direction of N. Zachariades, the secretary-general of KKE, they instigated riots in Salonika, Volos, Kavalla, Kalamata, and other Greek cities. Zachariades himself, in his address to the Plennum (olomelia) of KKE of Macedonia and Thrace, openly declared that northern Greece had become the preparation camp for "Monarcho-Fascist" bands armed by the Athens regime and directed against the People's Republics of Albania, Yugoslavia, and Bulgaria. In conclusion, he said, "Comrades, we (Greece) are threatening international peace." (*Rizospastis*, Jan. 1, 1946.) Seven days later, a strike instigated by the Communists was launched in Athens and other major cities, with the too obvious objective of providing additional "evidence" in support of the impending Soviet move in the Security Council. On January 13, 1946, *Rizospastis*, the official organ of KKE published a leading article under the title "The ferocious persecution of the Slavo-Macedonian people." It maintained that the "tyranic Greek-English regime of Athens exerts an unimaginable terroristic oppression on the Slavo-Macedonian minority." Finally, on January 21, 1946, on the very same day the Soviet representative filed his letter with the Security Council in London, the Politbureau of the Central Committee of KKE released a manifesto in which it at-

tributed "the principal and major responsibility for the situation in Greece
. . . to the English occupation forces." It listed a series of allegations
against the British troops and particularly against the British instructors
of the Greek army. The manifesto further included a demand for the
"immediate withdrawal of British troops from Greece" and an appeal for
the organization "of a voluntary corps consisting of faithful democrats,
tested in the national resistance, who will clean up the Monarcho-Fascist
dirt from the country . . ." The perfect timing and the almost identical
wording of this manifesto with the Soviet letter to the Security Council,
is a truly remarkable display of communist coordination.

In bringing charges against the presence of British troops in Greece,
the Soviet Government had, as usual, two objectives in mind; one maximum and one minimum. In the first place, should their move bring about
the withdrawal of the British troops from Greece, the penetration of that
country by communist bands would be tremendously facilitated. The
small and poorly-equipped Greek army was not a serious threat to the
Soviet plans. But as long as there were British troops in Greece, there was
a possibility that they might be involved in the conflict, a fact which
might have serious international complications. Therefore, the withdrawal
of the British troops from Greece was highly desirable to the Soviet leaders. Should this fail, the Soviet Union would have at least a priceless opportunity to disseminate its propaganda through the medium of the
United Nations, and to present the launching of communist bands and the
fomenting of disorder in Greece as the uprising of "persecuted democratic
citizens and oppressed minorities." At the beginning these plans met with
a certain amount of success; finally they were foiled by the successful
counter-measures, taken by the United States.

DISCUSSION OF THE SOVIET CHARGES IN THE SECURITY COUNCIL

The Greek question came before the Security Council for discussion
on February 1, 1946, when Vyshinsky presented the Soviet charges. Vyshinsky reminded his audience that the Soviet Government had repeatedly
expressed its concern about the situation in Greece. The Soviet admonitions had not received, he asserted, proper attention in Potsdam, London,
or Moscow. The Soviet Government, however, could no longer remain
impassive. The presence of the British troops in Greece, "although it is
not necessitated by circumstances, because there is no need to protect
these communications as in the case of troops in defeated countries . . . it
has become a means of pressure, and it has resulted very often in support
of reactionary elements in the country against democratic elements."
Vyshinsky concluded his speech with a very important statement. He
denied that the presence of British troops in Greece "still is in accordance

with the views of the Allied Governments." He admitted that the Soviet
Government had agreed "once upon a time" to the presence of British
troops on Greek soil, but the objective of that agreement was only to
facilitate the war against the Germans. Now with Germany defeated and
the war ended, there was no serious justification, in the opinion of the
Soviet Government, for the presence of British troops in Greece. Therefore it insisted upon "the quick and unconditional withdrawal of the British troops from Greece."[4]

The answer of Bevin shed a new light upon the whole issue. He pointed
out that "it is significant that whenever the problems of Greece has arisen
in any negotiations with the Soviet Union, it has always come about when
we have been discussing Rumania or Bulgaria or Poland." He stressed the
case of N. Zachariades, the leader of KKE, who went back to Greece
without any obstacle "to agitate his cause." Soon after his arrival, Zachariades had spoken in Salonika on August 24, 1945, and in a violent attack against the British had said:

> If Mr. Bevin is not in a position to impose order in Greece with his
> occupation forces, let him withdraw them from our country. Then,
> the Greek people, in spite of the one-sided application of our Peace
> Agreement (the Varkiza Agreement), will be in a position to restore
> order and quiet in the country with their own unaided efforts.

Bevin further recalled that during the incident of Kalamata, when rightist
bands started a putsch against the legal authorities, the Communist leader
Xianthos called on the British ambassador to complain of the failure of the
British troops there to interfere in the incident. "He complained that our
troops were not there to protect them (the Communists). I suggest this
is a glorious inconsistency," Bevin exclaimed, "in view of the fact that
the Communist Party demands the withdrawal of the British troops."
Bevin also reminded his audience that the Soviet Government had been
invited to participate in the supervision of the elections which were to be
held in Greece soon, "but they have refused." He answered, further, the
charges that the situation in Greece endangered the peace, by pointing
out that in the countries bordering on Greece "there is not far short of
seven to eight hundred thousand Russian, Yugoslav, and Bulgarian troops
within a reasonable range of communication, from Hungary right down
to the frontier of Greece." And he concluded: "Can you imagine Greece,
even with the aid of the British army there, which is a very small one,
declaring war or attacking these countries? Where, then, are we endangering peace?"

On the second day of the discussion, Vyshinsky continued the attacks
against the British. He disclosed that on July 21, 1945, the Soviet Foreign

Minister had stated at Potsdam that the formation of a democratic government in Greece together with the withdrawal of the British troops would certainly help improve the situation in that country. After reciting the statements of several British left-wing politicians, he quoted a statement by Sophianopoulos, the Greek Foreign Minister and head of the Greek delegation to the United Nations. Sophianopoulos had been ousted a few days earlier from his post when he refused to follow the instructions of his government and defend the position of the British. In that statement Sophianopoulos, whose connections with the Soviet circles were well known, explained why he left the United Nations and returned to Athens. "And now," Sophianopoulos concluded, "I avail myself of the opportunity to observe that as I have said to British officials in London, we cannot speak about the possibility of free and genuine elections until a wide amnesty is granted . . . Secondly, terrorism by responsible organizations and by state organs must cease . . . Thirdly, the state machinery must be purged of all Fascist and reactionary elements which remain at their posts although they are remnants both of the dictatorship and of the enemy occupation." (*The News Chronicle*, Feb. 4, 1946.)

The emphasis put by Vyshinsky on the internal political conditions in Greece, together with his suggestion that recognition of the governments in Bulgaria, Hungary, and Finland would undoubtedly relax the existing tension, revealed the wide scope of the Soviet move. Far from being merely a retaliation against the Iranian appeal, the Soviet attack was not only part of the scheme for expansion in the Middle Eastern region, but also a means of extortion, an attempt to force the Western Powers to recognize the Communist-controlled regimes of the eastern European countries. It is truly amazing how rich in objectives every Soviet move is.

The exchange of heated arguments—which was to become a familiar feature of the Security Council sessions in the following years—finally ended in a compromise. As soon as Vyshinsky realized that there was no disposition on the part of the majority of the Security Council members to agree with the Soviet thesis, he reversed his tactics. In fact, it was not very advantageous to press the issue any more. The comments of the press in the non-Communist countries showed that the Soviet move, instead of convincing world opinion of the vice of the Greek government and of the imperialist policies of Britain, had brought exactly the opposite result. Bevin's dramatic appeal for either open condemnation or unconditional acquittal had impressed the public more than the furious attacks launched by the Soviet representative. At the tenth meeting of the Security Council on February 6, Vyshinsky proposed that "a formal resolution of the Security Council on the question of the situation in Greece in connection with the presence there of British troops should be dispensed with." The other representatives realized that Vyshinsky was actually withdrawing his charges, and promptly helped him with this face-saving effort. With unanimous approval, the following statement was made by the president of the Council, in lieu of a resolution:

I feel we should take note of the declarations made before the Security Council by the representatives of the Soviet Union, the United Kingdom and Greece, and also the views expressed by the representatives of the following members of the Security Council; U.S.A., France, China, Australia, Poland, the Netherlands, Egypt and Brazil in regard to the question of the presence of British troops in Greece, as recorded in the proceedings of the Council and consider the matter as closed." (U.N. Journal of S. C. No. 10, pp. 176-177.)

This decision, if this statement can be called a decision, was received with warm applause by the delegations and the galleries who unaccustomed as yet to the exchange of bitter arguments between the Soviet representatives and the other delegates had been alarmed during the debate on the Greek question.

The warm applause notwithstanding, the impression was left in diplomatic quarters and in public opinion that "the Greek question had not been brought to the Security Council only because of the conditions in Greece. It appears that there is a deeper cause, known only to the Soviet Government." (U. N. Journal of S. C. No. 7, p. 95.) In the following years that deeper cause became known to the world.

A TELEGRAM FROM UKRAINE

On August 21, 1946, while the fate of the Greek national claims was decided by the peace conference, the Greek question came before the Security Council for the second time, as a result of a telegram from the Minister of Foreign Affairs of the Ukrainian SSR to the Secretary General of the Security Council. In his telegram, the Ukrainian Minister charged that "the situation in the Balkans which has resulted from the policy of the Greek Government . . . endangers the maintenance of peace and security." He further requested the examination of the situation by the Security Council under Article 34 of the Chapter. The essential difference between the first Soviet attack in January 1946 and the Ukranian charges, was that this time the charges were brought by a Soviet Republic and not by the Soviet Union itself, and were directed primarily against the Greek Government and only by implication against Britain. Apparently the Soviet policy-makers realized that it had been a tactical mistake to attack Britain directly the previous January.

This time the charges against Greece served an additional purpose. They were an effort to discredit the Greek Government and prevent favorable treatment of the Greek national claims by the peace conference. It is characteristic that on September 6, 1946, two days after the opening of the discussion of the Ukranian charges by the Security Council, Novikov, the Soviet representative, argued at the peace conference that Greece, having been satisfied with the acquisition of the Dodecanese, should cede western Thrace to Bulgaria. Pijade, the Yugoslav representative, openly presented the Yugoslav claims on Greek Macedonia or "Aegean Macedonia"—the territory that Hitler had promised to Yugoslavia in 1941.

A further incidental objective of Ukrania's move undoubtedly was, to disavow the Greek plebiscite on the Monarchy, scheduled for September 1, 1946. Indeed, the statements of Gromyko, the Soviet representative and the other Soviet-led delegations leave little doubt that these two additional objectives were also on the list.

It is worth mentioning that although the Soviet representative charged Greece with pursuing an imperialist, expansionist, and chauvinistic policy with respect to her northern neighbors, EAM, the communist-led Greek organization, not only had supported the Greek claims on northern Epirus and the rectification of the Greek-Bulgarian frontiers but it had laid claims to the Turkish territory of eastern Thrace, in cables addressed to the Paris peace conference on July 31, 1946. Thus, EAM appeared to be even more "chauvinistic" than the "imperialist" Greek Government. Obviously, the attitude of EAM toward the Greek claims was prompted primarily by domestic considerations; the denunciation of the Greek claims by EAM would amount to political suicide. As to the EAM claim on eastern Thrace, obviously, it was designed to cause difficulties in the relations with Turkey.

At the beginning, the discussion of the Greek question by the Council, followed the same familiar pattern as the previous January. The same allegations and the same arguments harassed the members of the Council for days. With remarkable realism, Dendramis, the Greek representative to the United Nations who had been invited to participate in the discussion, rebuffed the Ukranian charges, and openly stated that "if the representative of the Ukraine was as sincerely attached to the cause of peace as his words seem to indicate, all he had to do is to give some words of advice to the proper quarters. In that case I can assure him that incursions into Greek territory would stop immediately (and) order would be restored as if by magic and the concern of the Ukranian representative for peace would be given complete satisfaction." (U.N., S. C. Off. Rec., No. 9, p. 239.)[5] The validity of this statement was to be proved later, when after the crushing of the communist conspiracy, order was restored in Greece "as if by magic."

On September 18, 1946, as no solution of the problem was in sight, the Western Powers decided to adopt a positive approach and pass to the offensive. Hershel Johnson, the United States representative, in a counter move, suggested "the establishment of a sub-committee of enquiry" to conduct an on-the-spot investigation in order to ascertain the facts as to the disturbed situation along the northern frontiers of Greece. The committee should be able to move freely on both sides of the frontier, and investigate wherever they deem it necessary.

Gromyko, the Soviet representative, quickly grasped the full repercussions of the American proposal. The communist preparations for the penetration of Greece were not yet completed; should such a committee be allowed to visit the three Communist neighbors of Greece, the whole scheme might be exposed and, probably, checked in time. Because of these considerations, the Soviet representative abandoned all efforts to bring about the condemnation of Greece, and instead he concentrated his attention on preventing the adoption of the American proposal. He finally succeeded, by using the veto.

The United States draft resolution for the establishment of "a commission of three individuals to be nominated by the Secretary-General," to investigate the facts relating to the border incidents along the frontier between Greece on the one hand and Albania, Bulgaria, and Yugoslavia on the other, and to submit a report on the facts as disclosed by its investigation, was voted for by eight members of the Security Council. Australia abstained and the USSR together with Poland voted against. Since one of the permanent members (USSR) had voted against, the draft resolution was rejected.

On September 20, only two days after the presentation of the American proposal for a committee of inquiry, the discussion of the Greek question ended, and the Ukranian item was removed from the agenda of the Council. Once again the Security Council had reached no decision. The general impression was, however, that the Soviet attempt to present Greece as a threat to the peace and security of the Balkans had turned out to be a pitiable fiasco. Instead, it had been ascertained during the discussions that quite different sources were responsible for the disturbed situation along the northern frontier of Greece.

THE GREEKS APPEAL TO THE UNITED NATIONS

Since the Security Council had refused for the second time to accept the thesis that Greece was threatening international peace and security, the Soviet Government abandoned the idea of presenting the Greek question again to the United Nations. In fact, a new diplomatic attack against Greece was no longer necessary. The Greek national claims on northern Epirus and the boundary with Bulgaria had not been sustained by the peace treaties. On the other hand, the military preparation for the "third round" had been almost completed in the meantime, and already bands consisting of political refugees armed and trained in the three northern neighboring countries (Yugoslavia, Bulgaria, and Albania), had begun to cross the frontiers and enter Greek territory.[6] The period of diplomatic maneuvers was over.

The first task assigned to these bands was to liquidate one by one the small guards of the frontier villages. When this first assignment had been accomplished, reinforced groups of guerrillas started passing through the opened gaps into the interior of Greece. There, together with ELAS veterans and forcibly recruited villagers they formed more and more bands.

Finally the incessant frontier incidents and the explosive situation in the northern Greek provinces, forced the Greek Government to appeal to the United Nations. It requested that under Article 35(1) of the Charter, the Security Council give early consideration "to a situation which is leading to friction between Greece and her neighbors, by reason of the fact that the latter are lending their support to the violent guerrilla warfare now being waged in northern Greece against public order and the territorial integrity of (that) country. This situation if not promptly remedied, is . . . likely to endanger the maintenance of international peace and security." The Greek Government also drew the attention of the Council to "the urgent necessity for an investigation to be undertaken on the spot in order that the causes of this situation may be brought to light." The letter was accompanied by a memorandum containing detailed evidence of communist aggression. (U. N., S. C. Off. Rec., No. 10, pp. 170-172.)

This time, with the preparation for the "third round" completed, the Soviet Union adopted a much milder attitude toward the Greek problem and especially toward the request for an on-the-spot investigation. In fact, a different policy would be a tactical mistake, as it would simply prove to world opinion that the Soviet Union and the Balkan People's Republics had really something to hide. Therefore, the Soviet representative agreed to an investigation. He insisted, however, that the investigation should be conducted "only in Greece; and also in the frontier districts of Albania, Bulgaria, and Yugoslavia . . ." He argued that such an investigation if carried into the interior of the People's Republics would be a violation of Article 2, para. 7 of the Charter. This was a rather peculiar logic to maintain that an investigation conducted in Albania or Yugoslavia would constitute an intervention "in matters which are essentially within the domestic jurisdiction," and a similar investigation conducted in Greece would not.

Finally as it became evident that the other members were inclined to adopt the proposal for an investigation of all four countries, the Soviet representative withdrew his objections. On December 19, 1946, the Security Council unanimously adopted a resolution establishing, under Art. 34 of the Charter, a Commission of Investigation "to ascertain the facts relating to the alleged border violations along the frontier between Greece on the one hand and Albania, Bulgaria, and Yugoslavia on the other." The Commission was empowered "to conduct its investigation in northern Greece and in such places in other parts of Greece, in Albania, Bulgaria, and Yugoslavia as the Commission considers should be included in its investigation . . ." (U. N., S. C. Off. Rec., No. 28, p. 646.)

The Commission, composed of representatives from the eleven member-countries of the Security Council, together with liaison representatives from Albania, Bulgaria, and Yugoslavia, arrived in Greece on January 29, 1947. On the next day it held its first meeting in the Acropol Palace Hotel in Athens. A new chapter in the long story of Communist attempts to subjugate Greece had begun. This time, the whole question was to be investigated by an international body which was expected to establish the real causes for the disturbed conditions in Greece. This was not, however, the major problem facing the Commission. Even more important and incomparably more difficult was to prove that the world organization as a super-national body could conduct through its organs an impartial investigation of an international dispute: in other words, the policies of the eleven delegations gathered in Athens would show to the world whether or not the United Nations was able to operate effectively and perform the duties for which it had been established.

FOOTNOTES

1. See the conclusions prepared by the Soviet Delegation in the U. N. Commission of Investigation, Chapter II, Sec. G, of the Report. U. N. Doc. S/360 in *The United Nations and the Problem of Greece*, Dept. of State, Publication 2909, 1947, p. 70.

2. See among others, Smothers and McNeil, *Report on the Greeks*, New York: The Twentieth Century Fund, 1948, pp. 29-32.

3. *U. N. Journal of the Security Council*, U. N. Publication 1946-1949.

4. Quotations from the *U. N. Journal of the Security Council, op. cit.*, No. 7, pp. 88-97.

5. *U. N. Security Council Official Records*, U. N. Publications, 1946-1947.

6. See the Report by the Commission of Investigation Concerning Greek Frontier Incidents. U. N. Doc. S/360 Vol. I, Para. 2, in *The United Nations and the Problem of Greece, op. cit.*, pp. 52-54.

CHAPTER THIRTEEN

THE TIDE BEGINS TO TURN

THE PRESENCE OF THE Commission of Investigation in Greece, however useful, did not serve as a protective shield against the Communist assault. Its purpose was merely to investigate the causes of disorder and notify the Security Council accordingly. Its task was an examination, not a cure of the disease.

A PRESIDENTIAL MESSAGE

While the Commission was struggling against serious difficulties to establish the actual facts, the military situation in Greece deteriorated rapidly. Numerous isolated guards of strategically located villages were liquidated in surprise attacks by Communist bands, while troops stationed in nearby villages were barred from rushing to the rescue of those attacked without orders from General Headquarters in Athens—orders which arrived always too late. This mistaken tactic, introduced by the British military mission, caused heavy losses to the Greek army and the Gendarmerie, while it enabled the guerrillas to invade many villages, plunder the meager supplies of the inhabitants, and recruit forcibly or voluntarily young men and women for the reinforcement of the bands. Thus, by the beginning of 1947 the guerrilla forces had increased up to 13,000 men and women with the initiative absolutely in their hands. They were able to choose their targets and the time of attack, while 130,000 regular troops dispersed all over the country guarding every single town or important village, were waiting for the Communists to strike.

The Greek Government was busily occupied with the conduct of the warfare, and in no position to heed admonitions for economic and social reforms, occasionally proposed by foreign quarters. Almost the whole of the country was a battleground, with a vicious enemy attacking at night against towns or villages, only to disappear at dawn, leaving behind smoking ruins and corpses. Strict security measures were unavoidable if the government was to cope effectively with the nefarious tactics of the guerrillas. This situation permitted Vyshinsky to blast the Greek Government as oppressive, and also to question the sincerity of Western leaders in attacking the eastern European governments as undemocratic. He overlooked the fact that the Greek Government was fighting against an armed assault, while the governments of the People's Republics, safely seated in these countries with the support of the Red Army, were engaged in the emasculation of their peoples through persecution and terrorism.

In that confused situation, it is no wonder that innocent people were occasionally hurt by the government measures. It is also true that some people were forced to join the bands voluntarily because of these measures; but it would be an oversimplification to imply that the policies of the Greek authorities were the only or even the major cause for the intensification of the guerrilla warfare. The number of those who joined the bands because of persecution remained insignificant throughout the revolt. The bulk of the Communist forces consisted of ELAS veterans who, obeying Party orders, had joined the bands as soon as they had been released from the prisons, thanks to the amnesty granted by the Greek Government. There were also Slavo-Macedonians under the leadership of NOF fighting for a Macedonian People's Republic within the Yugoslav federation; and there were forcibly recruited young villagers; and the hard-core Communists trained in neighboring countries.

Early in 1947, the distress caused by the deterioration of the military situation was aggravated by rumors that Britain was unable to support Greece any longer and would soon withdraw. Indeed, on February 24, 1947, the British Government officially gave notice to the Governments of the United States and Greece of the impending withdrawal of British troops and the discontinuation of financial support to Greece, due to economic difficulties at home. "The English must leave," the first goal of the Communist attack, which had been the standard theme of the Soviet statements in the United Nations, of the broadcasts of the secret guerrilla radio, and of the slogans written at night on the walls of the Athenian houses, was near to accomplishment.

It was plain to all that should the British abandon Greece there would be little hope for a non-Communist Greece to survive—unless, some other power would come to Greece's assistance. The discussion of the Greek question since January 1946 had shown that United Nations action was practically impossible. According to Article 39 of the Charter, "the Security Council shall determine the existence of any threat to the peace . . . and shall make recommendations or decide what measures shall be taken in accordance with Articles 41 and 42, to maintain or restore international peace and security." A decision on such a subject being a matter of substance should be made according to Article 27, that is, "by the affirmative vote of seven members including the concurring votes of the permanent members"; in that case, a Soviet veto would block the way to any United Nations action to restore peace in Greece.

Consequently, should the British withdraw, Greece would be left help-less, with the Commission of Investigation present only to witness the gradual subjugation of the country. Greece, however, was too important a strategic key-point to be handed over gratis to the Soviet Union. There-fore, on March 12, 1947, President Truman went before the United States Congress to ask for $400,000,000 in aid for Greece and Turkey. The former was to receive, as it was disclosed later, $150,000,000 for relief and an equal amount for military supplies, while the latter would receive the remaining $100,000,000 in arms and military advice. In his message to Congress, President Truman said:

. . . The very existence of the Greek State is today threatened by the terrorist activities of several thousand armed men, led by Com-munists, who defy the Government's authority . . . Greece must have assistance if it is to become a self-supporting and self-respecting demo-cracy . . . The United States must supply that assistance . . . There is no other country to which Greece can turn . . .

. . . I believe that it must be the policy of the United States to sup-port free people who are resisting attempted subjugation by armed minorities or by outside pressures . . . We must take immediate and resolute action . . . The free peoples of the world look to us for support in maintaining their freedom . . .

. . . It is necessary only to glance at a map to realize that the sur-vival and integrity of the Greek nation are of grave importance in a much wider situation. If Greece should fall under the control of an armed minority, the effect upon its neighbor Turkey would be im-mediate and serious. Confusion and disorder might well spread through-out the entire Middle East . . . and . . . would have a profound effect upon those countries in Europe whose people are struggling against great difficulties to maintain their freedoms and their independence while they repair the damages of war. . . .

This presidential message revealed the determination of the United States Government to take over the task of containing Communist ex-pansion at all points where Soviet pressure might become too dangerous. In fact, the decision of the United States Government to assist Greece and Turkey involved much more than the Middle East region; it embraced the whole globe. It revealed that the United States Government was ready to accept world leadership in the struggle for freedom.

Political writers have occasionally criticized this decision as bearing the marks of genuine power politics. They overlook the fact that power politics, in one form or another, are as old as the division of this world into political entities called states. These critics, mostly fair-minded and objective, examine the chronological order of the steps taken by the two opposite camps and, thus, attempt to establish the guilt of the powers concerned in the fomenting of what has become commonly known as the Cold War. They search too close, however, to have a general perspective; because the plain fact remains that since the Presidential message of March 12, 1947, the United States has stepped decidedly into the arena of power politics. As to who started the Cold War that is another question.

The application of *Machtpolitik* methods by the Soviet Union and the United States, two world powers which had denounced such practices as a vicious characteristic of the imperialists, is one of the strange developments of the past two decades. The Russian disciples of Marx had fiercely condemned in the past both imperialism and power politics. They did so, as long as they were unprepared to enter the world arena; but when, after two five-year plans, the Soviet Union overcame the economic and social difficulties of the early post-revolutionary period, it adopted the classic principles of *Machtpolitik* with even more vigor and determination than other veterans of the game; power politics, thus, became a useful tool in the Communist master plan for world revolution. Chronologically, speaking, the Montreux Conference of 1936 gave the USSR an opportunity to join the other powers in the traditional game of power politics. Since that time the Soviet leaders have become real masters of those methods.

The United States on the other hand, as long as there was no visible threat against the homeland, thanks to the oceanic barriers, avoided any too active participation in world affairs. During World War I, the possibility of domination of the European Continent and the British Isles by a single power led the United States to intervene and avert such an eventuality. But soon as the danger was over, it retreated again to the homeland. Even shortly before the outbreak of the Second World War, the United States Government continued its efforts to keep out of international rivalries. When the Japanese attack on Pearl Harbor dragged the United States into the war, President Roosevelt's hope was that with the destruction of the Axis military machine international antagonism would come to an end and all the peace-loving nations would seek protection within the framework of a world organization. The dream was magnificent but failed to materialize; the end of World War II and the establishment of the United Nations did not eliminate international friction.

In spite of unmistakable evidence that the Soviet leaders intended to pursue the Communist objectives, the United States Government made constant efforts for almost two years after the end of the war to prove its willingness to cooperate sincerely with all nations in the preservation of peace. When Stalin was advocating on April 30, 1946 that:

    . . . it is necessary to remember the teaching of the Great Lenin to the effect that after switching to peaceful labor it is necessary to be constantly vigilant to protect as the apple of one's eye the armed forces and defensive power of our country ... and not forget a single minute the intrigues of international reaction, which is hatching plans of a new war. . . .

the Americans were racing to a speedy disarmament "(to bring about) as quickly as possible the reduction of (U.S.) armed forces to the size required for these tasks of occupation and disarmament."[1]

All the efforts to prove the determination of the United States Government to work for a united world failed to penetrate the Soviet complex of fear, fanaticism, and ambition. Finally, the American leaders reached the point where it became clear that there was no alternative but to fight the Soviet policies by similar tactics. The Presidential message of March 12, 1947, although prompted by the urgent need to avert the subjugation of Greece and Turkey, was in effect a declaration that unless renounced by all nations, the eradication of power politics is impossible.

In the modern version of the old game, there is, however, a significant difference; for centuries, the political and social structure of the various opponents was fairly similar, based on the same fundamental principles. This time, the political, social, and economic structure of the two camps are fundamentally different. Their strife may have all the characteristics of the traditional power politics, but there is something more than a struggle for strategic positions, markets, or areas with important raw materials. It is an all-out fight between two political and social systems, each being the denial of the other. The Soviet leaders—and this is the heart of the issue—have worked according to this fundamental notion for long time; long before March 12, 1947, when the United States finally accepted the challenge.

THE REPORT OF THE COMMISSION OF INVESTIGATION

On June 27, 1947 Urrutia, the Colombian representative who acted as the rapporteur of the Commission of Investigation, submitted to the Security Council the Commission's report which was indeed the product of extensive research. According to this report,[2] the evidence gathered by the Commission centered around the following basic issues:

(a) *Charges by Greece that Albania, Bulgaria and Yugoslavia, supported the guerrilla warfare in Greece.* Although the liaison representatives of these three Balkan countries repeatedly denied it and questioned the validity of the evidence presented by Greece in support of these charges, "little direct evidence was brought forward to disprove them. On the basis of the facts ascertained by the Commission, it is its conclusion that Yugoslavia and to a lesser extent Albania and Bulgaria have supported the guerrilla warfare in Greece." (Ch. I. Sec. A: 4.)

(b) *Charges by Greece that her northern neighbors interfere in her internal affairs and aim at detaching from Greece parts of her territory (Aegean Macedonia and Western Thrace)*. Evidence was introduced to the Commission, which indicated that "there was in Yugoslavia an organization known as NOF (National Liberation Front), one of whose objectives was to detach Greek Macedonia from Greece and to incorporate it into the Federation of Yugoslavia . . . Both, the Yugoslav and Bulgarian representatives denied, however, that NOF was engaged in activities of the type described in the Greek charge. Although certain witnesses testified to the Commission that they had not heard of this aspect of the functions of NOF, the references to NOF's relationship to the Macedonian movement were so numerous and so uniform as to leave little doubt on this point in the minds of the Commission." (Ch. I, Sec. B: 5.)

(c) *Charges by Greece in respect to provocation of border incidents by Albania, Bulgaria, and Yugoslavia and similar accusations made by these countries against Greece*. The Commission took cognizance of the mutual accusations and concluded that "the large number of incidents, the accusations and counter-accusations made by the governments against each other, and the willingness of the authorities on both sides to magnify minor incidents into important skirmishes, accompanied by shooting and bloodshed is evidence of the strained relations between the countries." (Ch. I., Sec. C: 9c.)

(d) *Albanian, Bulgarian, and Yugoslav contentions that the present regime in Greece is responsible for a state of civil war in the country*. The Greek Government refused to present any evidence in refutation of this contention on the grounds that an investigation of this charge would necessarily involve the domestic affairs of Greece, which were not within the Commission's competence. In consequence the evidence before the Commission was inevitably one-sided. Nevertheless, the Commission pointed out that its own experience showed that "there existed in Greece, especially in Athens and Salonika, a considerable degree of political freedom, freedom of speech, press, and assembly, despite disturbed conditions. Indeed, of the four countries visited by the Commission, only in Greece did it hear witnesses who criticized the policies of their government or receive delegations from free organizations which presented it with evidence against the government." At this point the report apparently referred to the evidence presented "by the three communist-controlled groups: the EAM, the Central Committee of the General Federation of Labour, and the EPON youth organization . . ." in addition to evidence presented by "representatives of the Left Liberal Party, as well as a number of individual witnesses" to the effect that opposition political groups had been subjected by the Greek Government to persecution and that the civil rights of the Macedonian and the Czamouriot minorities had been restricted. However, there was "a considerable body of evidence to show that EAM had itself violated the Varkiza Agreement by failing to carry out its obligation to surrender all its arms to the Greek government, and by urging its members to hide arms and to leave Greece or go underground." The commission also received sufficient evidence, to warrant the conclusion that immediately after the liberation of Greece, the small Slav-speaking and Czamouriot minorities in Greek Macedonia and Epirus had been the victims of retaliatory excesses. As a result, the members of the Czamouriot minorities who had not already left Greece with the Germans were forced to flee. (Ch. I, Sec. D: 101.)

(e) *Albanian, Yugoslav, and Bulgarian contentions that the Greek government conducts an expansionist foreign policy.* These accusations concerned the Greek national claims on northern Epirus and on the rectification of the Greek-Bulgarian border. Obviously the examination of the Greek foreign policy and of the Greek national claims fell outside the scope of the Commission's inquiry. However, it was admitted by the Commission that "the continued reiteration of Greece's claims against Bulgaria, and Bulgaria's claim to western Thrace, after they had been rejected at the Peace Conference, as well as Greece's claim against Albania, was a factor which tended to increase the tension between the countries." It is noteworthy that the Commission observed that EAM, the communist-led coalition, had supported the Greek claims and was "in the same position as the Greek government in this regard."(Ch. I, Sec. E.) It has been previously explained why EAM supported the Greek claims.

Although in the first instance the investigation and the findings of the Commission had established beyond any doubt the real causes of the situation in Greece, the Commission had failed in its basic task; that is, to prove that the United Nations and its organs were able to fulfill their primary purpose, the preservation of international peace and security. The aforementioned conclusions of the Commission were not accepted by the Soviet and Polish delegates who, instead, maintained their original convictions in spite of all evidence, and prepared their own conclusions which appeared in Part III, Chapter II, of the Commission's report. The Soviet conclusions set forth the view that the Greek government was solely responsible for the situation in Greece and that "the assertions of the Greek government regarding the alleged interference of Albania, Bulgaria, and Yugoslavia in the internal affairs of Greece are absolutely unfounded." (Ch. II, Sec. G: 18.)

In view of the Soviet attitude throughout the investigation, the delegates of Colombia and Belgium attempted to find some way of conciliation and expressed the view that it was not for the Commission "to give any decision as to the possible responsibility of the Albanian, Bulgarian, and Yugoslav Governments." They emphasized, however, that "the numerous presumptions which fit in with each other, tend to substantiate the charges brought by Greece against her northern neighbors." (Ch. III, Sec. A.) The French delegate also, on the grounds that "the French delegation is not without some doubt as to the necessity and some apprehension as to the advisability of including a chapter devoted to formal conclusions" refused to subscribe to the conclusions of the Commission as set forth in Part III.

It had been proved that the Commission was unable to operate as a "semi-juridical body." In fact the opposite would have been a paradox. It would be a farce of justice indeed—the juridical body in which the culprit participates as one of the judges; and it was beyond question that the USSR was the real source of the disturbances in Greece.

Although the Commission failed in its basic task, there was a positive result; the role of the Balkan People's Republics in fomenting public disorder in Greece was revealed to world opinion so that widespread misconceptions as to the sources of unrest in Greece were dissipated.

FIVE SOVIET VETOES

The discussion of the Greek question in the Security Council lasted practically throughout the summer of 1947 until the Council, after five Soviet vetoes, admitted its inability to deal effectively with the problem. The long, acrimonious debate during June, July, and August was merely a repetition of the familiar arguments which had harassed the members of the Security Council since January 21, 1946. With by now familiar uniformity, the Soviet-led delegations reiterated the over-repeated argument that "the fundamental reason for all the complications in the relations between Greece on the one hand and Yugoslavia, Bulgaria, and Albania on the other, may be found in the internal conditions in Greece . . . (and) in the persisting foreign interference in Greek internal affairs, which, however, is not ascribable to the neighboring countries." (U. N., S. C. Off. Rec. No. 55, p. 1253.) Moreover, the Soviet delegate repeatedly urged that "foreign troops and foreign military personnel be recalled from Greece" in order to improve the internal situation "by creating conditions for the formation of an independent democratic Greek state and bettering relations between Greece and the neighboring countries." In view of previous experiences, there was no doubt as to the real meaning of the Soviet suggestions.

The deterioration of the situation in Greece and the obvious inability of the Council to reach a constructive decision, prompted the Greek Foreign Minister to address a letter dated July 31, 1947, to the President of the Security Council. The Tsaldaris letter stressed that "the presently existing threat to world peace has become so serious that enforcement action under Chapter VII of the Charter is urgently required." Chapter VII has a much wider scope than chapter VI and provides for the application of such measures as "complete or partial interruption of economic relations . . . blockade, and other operations by air, sea, or land forces of members of the United Nations." (Art. 41, 42.) A Soviet veto, of course, would again prevent any positive action, but the purpose of the Greek appeal was to emphasize to the Security Council and world opinion the urgency of the situation.

It was only natural, of course, that the new Greek move met with the fierce opposition of the Soviet representative who once again insisted that conditions in Greece were the result of "the relentless conflict between the forces of democracy and the anti-democratic forces grouped around the present government . . . and (of) foreign intervention in Greece's internal affairs, (which) is not only continuing but is intensified. . . ." (U. N., S. C. Off. Rec. No. 76, p. 1968.) It became evident, however, that the whole issue had reached a point where the Security Council should either take positive action to settle the dispute or openly admit its inability to perform its duty.

With this in mind, the United States representative H. Johnson, in his speech, alluded to the possibility of transferring the Greek question to the General Assembly. He said, "in the case of the blocking of Security Council action by the veto, we are confident that the General Assembly will exercise it powers to the limit for the protection of Greece . . . (and) the United States Government (in that case) would be prepared to comply with any General Assembly recommendations for the solution of this problem." He also presented to the Council a draft resolution to the effect that:

> The Security Council . . . finds that Albania, Bulgaria, and Yugoslavia have given assistance and support to the guerrillas fighting against the Greek Government . . . determines that such assistance and support . . . constitute a threat to peace within the meaning of Chapter VII of the Charter. . . .
> calls upon Albania, Bulgaria and Yugoslavia to cease and desist from rendering any further assistance or support in any form to the guerrillas fighting against the Greek Government. . . . (U. N., S. C. Off. Rec., No. 74, pp. 1910-1911.)

Four other draft resolutions had been rejected, due to Soviet vetoes, before the United States draft resolution came to vote. Just before the voting on this draft, the President of the Council, Paris El Khouri of Syria, evidently disgusted, observed that "it would now seem that all the draft resolutions which have been submitted have been rejected for one reason or another. The Security Council appears to have failed to arrive at any solution of the problem . . . I think . . . that under the rule of unanimity, as outlined in Art. 27 of the Charter, the work of the Security Council may in some cases be paralyzed"; and he added, with bitter irony, "we have another draft resolution submitted by the United States, but I do not think its fate will be different from that of the previous draft resolutions of the same nature . . ." (U. N., S. C. Off. Rec., No. 79, p. 2094.) The American representative, however, insisted upon having his draft resolution voted on, regardless of the outcome. Thus, after a speech by the Bulgarian representative, Mevorah, who promised to repeat "the truth a thousand times if necessary," although he expressed his regret for asking the Council "to listen again to a phonographic record," the Council voted on the American draft resolution with the familiar result, nine votes in favor and two against. Again, as one of the two negative votes was that of the USSR, the resolution was rejected. The Security Council was at a dead end.

THE GREEK QUESTION IN THE GENERAL ASSEMBLY

On August 20, 1947, Johnson filed a motion with the Secretariat requesting that "the Greek question be placed on the provisional agenda of the next meeting of the Security Council in order that steps may be taken in accordance with Art. 12 of the Charter to enable the General Assembly to make recommendations with regard to that dispute. (U. N., S. C. Off. Rec., No. 89, p. 2367.) This step was a prerequisite, because as long as "the Security Council is exercising in respect of any dispute or situation the functions assigned to it . . . the General Assembly shall not make any recommendations . . . unless the Security Council so requests." (Art. 12 (1))

On September 15, 1947, the Security Council began the discussion of the American proposal. The debate followed the familiar pattern, with the addition of Soviet maneuvers to prevent by all means the transfer of the Greek question to the General Assembly, where the Soviet veto was ineffectual. Thus, when the United States draft resolution, whereby the Security Council was asked to request "the General Assembly to consider the Greek question and make any recommendations with regard to the dispute," was approved by a majority of 9 to 2, Gromyko, who was chairman of the Council at that time, ruled that the question of asking the General Assembly to place a dispute on its agenda was a matter of substance and therefore could not be adopted since one of the permanent members (USSR) had voted against it.

Heated debate ensued, but the American representative chose to solve the impasse by proposing that the Greek question be "taken off the list of

matters of which the Security Council is seized. . . ." He also proposed
that the Secretary General be instructed to place all records and documents in the case at the disposal of the General Assembly. Such a decision
would put automatically an end to the existence of the Subsidiary Group
of the Commission of Investigation, which had proved so valuable during
the summer of 1947;[3] unfortunately, there was no other way to take the
problem to the General Assembly where the rule of unanimity did not
prevail. The American proposal was voted on and received nine votes in
favor and two votes against (USSR and Poland). Since this was unques-
tionably a matter of procedure, the Soviet veto was ineffective and the
Greek question was taken off the agenda of the Security Council. The
way was now open for a more constructive action by the General
Assembly.

Two days later, on September 17, 1947, the second session of the General Assembly opened in New York. The United States Secretary of
State, Marshall, in his address to the Assembly, emphasized that:

> . . . A supreme effort is required from us all if we are to succeed in
> breaking through the vicious circles of deepening political and econ-
> omic crisis. That is why the United States has placed on the agenda of
> this Assembly the question of threats to the political independence and
> territorial integrity of Greece. . . . (*U. N. Official Records of the Sec-
> ond Session of the General Assembly; Plenary Meetings*, Vol. I, p. 20.)

The debate which followed lasted until October 21, 1947. It was char-
acterized by the efforts of the Americans to bring about positive action,
the Soviet opposition to any proposal short of putting all the blame on
Greece, and some attempts to pave the way for a compromise. Finally,
on October 21, the General Assembly, by a vote of 40 to 6 with 11 ab-
stentions, passed a resolution establishing a Special Committee on the
Balkans, with representatives of eleven nations including the Soviet Union
and Poland, and endowed it with powers of observation and conciliation,
in general accord with the recommendations of the original Commission
of Investigation. Albania, Bulgaria, and Yugoslavia were called forthwith
to cease giving assistance to the Greek guerrilla movement. These three
countries, together with Greece, were called upon to cooperate in the
settlement of their disputes by peaceful means. To that end, it was recommended that the four parties concerned should:

(1) Establish normal diplomatic and good neighborly relations
among themselves as soon as possible;

(2) Establish frontier conventions providing for effective machinery for the regulation and control of their common frontiers and the
pacific settlement of frontier incidents and disputes;

(3) Cooperate in the settlement of the problems arising out of the

presence of refugees in the four states concerned;

(4) Study the practicability for concluding agreements for the voluntary transfer of minorities.

The USSR and Poland refused to take part, and the Special Committee on the Balkans (UNSCOB), composed of the active representation of Australia, Brazil, China, France, Mexico, the Netherlands, Pakistan, the United Kingdom, and the United States, began its work in Greece in November 1947.

COMINFORM, TITO AND MACEDONIA

While the General Assembly was discussing the Greek question, the Communist Parties of the USSR, Yugoslavia, France, Italy, Poland, Bulgaria, Czechoslovakia, Hungary, and Rumania held a secret conference in Poland, and on October 5, 1947 they issued a manifesto full of caustic remarks against the "imperialist camp" and its "directing force," the United States of America. They also announced that they had established an Information Bureau in Belgrade "to organize and exchange experience and in case of necessity coordinate the activity of the Communist Parties on foundations of mutual agreement." The establishment of this Bureau, popularily known as the Cominform, was in fact a partial reincarnation of the late Comintern (European section), in a form to suit the new international conditions. Its apparent purpose was to counteract and undermine the American plan for a joint effort to speed economic recovery in the war-shattered countries. No question that economic conditions which bred bitterness and unrest were to the advantage of the world Communism; it is true indeed, that misery is the most fertile soil where Communism can flourish.

To undermine the recovery program was not, however, the only objective of the Cominform. Probably even more important was the task of keeping an eye on the Communist Parties in Europe, coordinate their policies and, if necessary, deal at an early stage with possible signs of insubordination and disobedience.

The attitudes of Yugoslavia's Tito were particularly annoying to the Soviet leaders. His objections to the complete economic penetration of his country by the Soviet Union through the device of joint stock companies had been regarded as anti-Soviet. But even more disturbing were Tito's plans for a federation of the Slavs of the South. He had discussed that project with Stalin in 1946 and with the Bulgarian Communist leaders on several occasions. Although the Bulgarians favored in principle such a federation, they disagreed as to the form of the proposed set-up. In their opinion, Bulgaria should be one member of the federation and Yugoslavia the other, while Tito took the position "that Bulgaria should join with the six Yugoslav republics to form a new federation based on mutual equality of the seven members. . . ."

In August 1947, Georgi Dimitrov, the Bulgarian Premier, visited Tito at the summer resort of Bled, and there they discussed again the question of a Balkan Federation. They finally agreed to take gradual steps, instead of an immediate proclamation of the federation. The published terms of the Bled agreement provided for the abolition of certain formalities on the Yugoslav-Bulgarian frontier and also for the preparation of a Customs Union at a later period.

In spite of the aforementioned agreement, serious issues still divided the two governments. It was not only the form of Bulgaria's participation in the proposed federation; just as important was the Macedonian question. It has been mentioned repeatedly that for the Bulgarians, both the Yugoslav (Pirin) and the Greek (Aegean) parts of Macedonia belong to Bulgaria and eventually must be "freed from the foreign yoke." Strangely, enough, the Bulgarian Communists were even more determined on this than their bourgeois predecessors. Tito's position was that Macedonia as a whole, including the Yugoslav, Greek, and Bulgarian parts should form an independent state to be incorporated in the proposed federation as an equal member. It was quite obvious that under Tito's scheme, Bulgaria would be deprived of Bulgarian Macedonia and her position within the federation would be similar to that of Serbia or Montenegro. In such a federation there was no question who the real boss would be.

Another of Tito's actions, taken by the Kremlin as an affront, was his triumphant trip through Bulgaria and Rumania in the fall of 1947. On September 24, 1947, Tito in a speech called for a more militant Communist international program and criticized the leadership of other Communist countries. The Kremlin was infuriated; Tito's assumption that he had an international role to play was an unforgivable sin in Stalin's eyes. The Soviet reaction to Tito's bold plans came in the form of an article in *Pravda*, on January 28, 1948. In this, the idea of "a Balkan or Danubian federation including Poland, Czechoslovakia, and Greece" was flatly rejected on the grounds that "these lands do not need a problematical or farfetched federation and customs union but the strengthening and the defense of their independence and sovereignty by way of mobilization and organization of internal popular democratic strength."

Dimitrov, who until that time was basically in favor of the federation, his objections on certain details notwithstanding, accepted the rebuke, and in a declaration published in the Sofia newspapers retracted and thanked *Pravda* for its "valuable and useful warning." The Kremlin, apparently, disliked the idea of having a strong federation in the Danubian-Balkan region, even under Communist leadership; above all the Soviet leaders opposed a Balkan federation under the leadership of Tito, whose independence and lack of servility was a thorn in Stalin's flesh.

These fermentations behind the Iron Curtain had an immediate impact upon guerrilla warfare in Greece. A strong element within the Greek Communist Party had an obvious orientation toward Tito and had always hoped to bring Greece into a federation of the east Communist states— precisely the sort of federation the Soviet leaders were determined never to tolerate lest it limit their own control over that area.

It is significant that at about the same time that Tito and Dimitrov were meeting at Bled, an announcement was broadcast by the Greek guerrilla radio, which operated from Yugoslav territory, declaring that a military government under General Markos Vafiades was about to be established. There were many indications that Marko was playing Tito's card, and signs that he was suspect in Moscow from then on are unmistakable. From statements made after the open break between the Greek Communists and Tito in July 1949, it appears that Tito's price for his support to Marko was the latter's consent to a fresh influx of military and political agitation among the Slavo-Macedonians. It is characteristic that the wartime Communist Slavo-Macedonian organization SNOF reappeared as early as 1947 under the slightly modified name of NOF. It was ostensibly operating under Marko's command, in fact preparing the detachment of Greek Macedonia, and its incorporation in the Yugoslav Federation of People's Republics.

On December 23, 1947, a Provisional Democratic Government, with Marko as its principal leader, was established somewhere in the Greek mountains. Immediately, a warning was issued by the Balkan Committee (UNSCOB) calling all governments to refrain from extending official recognition to the Marko government lest the situation grow worse. Marko's government was not accorded recognition by the Communist countries not only because of the UNSCOB warning; even more so, the conditions within the Greek Communist movement prevented such a recognition.

All this fermentation under the ostensibly monolithic structure of the Soviet empire, came to the surface only after Tito's rebellion ripped apart the Iron Curtain and permitted the world to take a glimpse through the fissure.

Tito's dramatic expulsion from the Cominform on June 28, 1948, presented the Soviet policy-makers with a hard choice in Greece. Tito's assistance to the Greek guerrilla movement had been extremely valuable.[4] According to Yugoslav sources, (*Borba*, Nov. 7, 1949) Yugoslavia had taken care of 6,317 Greek guerrillas wounded, and had sheltered some 11,000 Greek children kidnapped by the Greek Communists during the

warfare. Whatever the differences with Tito, the Greek guerrilla movement was, in a last analysis, a Communist movement, and its objectives
served the objectives of the Soviet Union as well. Greece's subjugation
would result in the advancement of the Soviet positions toward the eastern Mediterranean, upset the balance of power in that region, encircle
Turkey and in brief be a severe blow against American foreign policy.
The fact that a strong faction of the Greek Communists, led by Marko,
followed a pro-Titoist policy was immaterial; Marko could very easily be
replaced by pro-Soviet elements which existed within the party, headed
by the Moscow-trained N. Zahariades. As a result, the policy chosen by
the Kremlin was to continue the support of guerrilla warfare in Greece
and at the same time prepare for the liquidation of Marko. It is therefore
not surprising, that during the discussion of the Greek question by the
General Assembly of the United Nations in the fall of 1948, the Soviet
Union continued the familiar attacks against the Greek government and
"foreign intervention in Greece."

The crisis within the Greek Communist Party, precipitated chiefly by
the Macedonian issue and the Tito-Cominform rift, came to a head in
January 1949. During the preceding six months the pro-Cominform
faction of KKE had been working for the establishment of a new Slavo-
Macedonian organization to replace the Titoist NOF. In this, the impact
of the Bulgarian plan to use such an organization as a spearhead to wrest
the Macedonian People's Republic (Macedonia of Pirin) from Yugoslavia
and incorporate it together with the Greek part of Macedonia to Bulgaria
was unquestionable. One may also presume that such an organization
would further serve the Cominform objective to undermine Tito's regime
and agitate rebellion within Yugoslavia.

The struggle between the two factions of KKE came into the open at
the Fifth Plenary Session of its Central Committee held on January 30
and 31, 1949. By a decision of this Committee, Marko was relieved of "all
party work" allegedly on grounds of ill health. The story of ill health was
repeated in what purported to be an "open letter" from Marko, broadcast by "Free Greece" radio on February 8, in which he laid down the
premiership of the "Provisional Democratic Government" and the command of the "Democratic Army." Whatever the truth, the fact remained
that Tito had lost the game.

The man who was chosen to succeed Marko, was the same Yoannis
Joannides who had been willing to sacrifice Greek Macedonia in an agreement with the Bulgarian Communist Dushan Daskalov in 1943.[5] On
March 1, "Free Greece" radio broadcast a resolution passed by the Second Plenum of the NOF central Council on February 2, 1949. N. Zahariades and Karagiorges or Gyftodimos, the former editor of *Rizospastis*,

were present at the meeting. According to the NOF resolution, "NOF will mobilize all its available resources, social and human . . . (and) it will declare the Union of Macedonia into a complete, independent, and equal Macedonian nation within the Popular Democratic Federation of the Balkan Peoples." Obviously, behind the same name, a new organization was concealed since the proposed Union of Macedonia obviously entailed the detachment of Yugoslav Macedonia from Yugoslavia. Indeed, the new NOF was plainly anti-Titoist and aimed to create an "autonomous state under the auspices of the Cominform." The NOF declaration compared to the 1943 Agreement between Ioannides and Daskalov presents a surprising similarity. The Yugoslavs immediately attacked this declaration as being part of Bulgaria's drive for a Balkan federation under Soviet domination. The replacement of Bulgaria's Foreign Minister Kollarov by Vladimir Poptomov, a leading Macedonian, along with the appointment of two Slavo-Macedonians as members of the Greek "Provisional Democratic Government" were, of course, quite impressive indications that the plan of a Macedonian state under Soviet domination was receiving serious consideration. Moscow was in a dilemma over Macedonia; to promote an open campaign for an independent Macedonia might gravely weaken Tito, but would even more gravely weaken the Greek Communist Party's guerrilla movement, since it was beyond doubt that the Greek people would never approve detachment of Greek Macedonia. Moscow's indecisiveness at this crucial moment undermined the morale of the Slavo-Macedonian guerrillas who formed the backbone of the "Democratic Army" so that, when Tito, on July 10, 1949 disclosed in a speech in Pola that Yugoslavia had closed her frontiers with Greece and had suspended any assistance to the Greek guerrillas, the fate of the third round was evident.

THE THIRD ROUND FAILS

The General Assembly had considered the Greek question at its third session in Paris in the autumn of 1948. There was much speculation as to the attitude which was to be followed by the Yugoslav delegation, in view of the rift between Tito and the Cominform. During the discussions,[6] the Yugoslav representative, Bebler, to the surprise of many Western political observers, outdid the representatives of the other Communist countries, even the representative of the Soviet Union, in supporting the cause of the Greek guerrillas. It is not an exaggeration to say that he actually led the attack against the Greek government and particularly against the UNSCOB, which he denounced as illegal and as an imperialist organ in the hands of the United States. At times, he was left alone in supporting General Marko, and in some instances, the Soviet representative even disagreed with him. The exceptional zest of the Yugoslav representative in supporting the position of the Soviet bloc was interpreted by many observers as an effort on the part of Yugoslavia to prove to the Soviet leaders the willingness of the Tito government to bridge the gap and return to the Communist family. This interpretation, of course, was fully wrong. Tito, an old Communist, himself, knew that no apostate had ever been forgiven by the Soviet dictator; and he had no intention to be exterminated after "confessing" his sin. The real reasons behind the Yugoslav attitude in the General Assembly can be explained, however, if viewed in the light of the political realities, as outlined in the preceding pages.

After the usual debate, three draft resolutions were voted on by the General Assembly on November 27, 1948. The first draft resolution, which was adopted by 47 votes to 6, recommended that the northern neighbors of Greece should again be called upon to cease their efforts to aid the revolution against the Greek Government, and that the Special Committee (UNSCOB) should continue to observe the situation and try to act as conciliator between the parties, if an opportunity arose.

The second draft resolution, adopted by 53 votes, included three vital paragraphs taken from the Soviet draft resolution and called for the resumption of diplomatic relations between Greece, Yugoslavia, Bulgaria, and Albania and a renewal of frontier conventions.

The third was also adopted unanimously. It concerned the problem of the Greek children who had been kidnapped from Greece by the Communists and recommended "the return to Greece of Greek children . . . when the children, their father or mother or . . . their closest relative expresses a wish to that effect."[7]

These resolutions, however, as those before them, were all too academic to solve the problem and save Greece from the claws of Communism. True, the Commission of Investigation and the UNSCOB had played an important role in revealing the real causes of unrest in the Balkans; also the moral support given to Greece by the decisions of the United Nations was priceless. But if it were not for the Greek armed forces and American aid, there is little doubt that the Iron Curtain would have descended across the Aegean shores.

It is remarkable indeed, that the Greek people who had suffered since October 28, 1940 all misery that human nature can stand, who had seen their national dreams frustrated and who had reached the end of the war with more fighting and fresh disaster, were struggling with such faith and determination to preserve their freedom; and this, at a time when other peoples, living in far better conditions, were wavering in their policies and even deserting their ideals.

Today there is no doubt about the complicity of the three neighbors of Greece and of international Communism in fomenting the guerrilla warfare during the years of 1946-1949. Even without the innumerable proofs, only the fact that within one month after the closing of the Greek-Yugoslav frontiers, the Greek army was able to launch its final offensive and wipe out the guerrilla bands from the Greek soil, should be enough evidence.[8] On August 10, 1949, the Greek Armed Forces under the leadership of Marshal Papagos, the hero of the war with the Axis, launched a general offensive in Vitsi, and one week later in Grammos, the two citadels of the Communists on the Albanian border. Within two weeks, the third round was brought to its final end. The Communist leadership with the remnants of the "Democratic Army" sought refuge behind the Albanian border, and from there they announced that they had resolved to suspend the military operations temporarily in order "to bring peace to Greece." The third attempt of world Communism to subjugate Greece had failed.

FOOTNOTES

1. Annual message by President Truman on the State of the Union to Congress, January 14, 1946.

2. Report by the Commission of Investigation, Part III. *The United Nations and the Problem of Greece, op. cit.*, pp. 52-73.

3. The Subsidiary Group was established on April 18, 1947, by the Security Council over Soviet opposition. It was composed of the representatives of the member-states of the Security Council, with the exception of the USSR and Poland which refused to participate. The work of the Group, which practically continued the functions of the Commission of Investigation, was of great value, especially in view of the serious aggressive acts against Greece during the summer of 1947. For details see the Reports of the Group in *The United Nations and the Problem of Greece, op. cit.*, pp. 83-88.

4. "Soviet military equipment and arms went to the rebel bands over Yugoslav railways and Yugoslav food and uniforms nourished and clothed them. When the mountain fighters found themselves in a tight corner, the Yugoslav frontiers were always open to them, their wounded were cared for in Yugoslav hospitals, reinforcements were trained in Yugoslav camps and the Greek children whom they evacuated (or kidnapped) on their retreats found homes in Yugoslav institutions." H. Fish Armstrong, *Tito and Goliath*, New York: The Macmillan Company, 1951, p. 191.

5. "Yoannis Ioannides had agreed in July 1943 with a Bulgarian Communist named Dushan Daskalov to carve a Macedonian state out of Greek, Bulgarian, and Yugoslav territory after the war and incorporate it directly into the Soviet Union. The plan as reported was grandiose; apparently Turkey was to be deprived of Istanbul, which was to be included in the Macedonian SSR along with Salonika . . . When American Intelligence first got wind of the story it assumed that it had been plotted by Nazi propaganda; but it learned that Ioannides had visited Moscow just before this meeting with Daskalov, and other bits of corroborative evidence indicated the probability that the Soviets actually were setting up an alternative design for use in the event that Tito proved troublesome or Bulgaria in some manner escaped the Soviet net." Armstrong, *op. cit.*, p. 190.

6. *U. N. Official Records of the Third Session of the General Assembly*, Part I, Plennary meetings, pp. 622-662.

7. The Communist countries have abused this stipulation and still detain the Greek children. Out of 28,000 children who were kidnapped by the Communists, only a few hundred have been returned to Greece by Yugoslavia. Some of those children were forcibly enlisted in the guerrilla bands. Later, during the Vitsi and Grammos (1949) battles, many of them were captured and subsequently released by the Greek Army, as the author personally witnessed.

8. The author, serving with the Greek army at that time, saw among the captured weapons in the battle of Vitsi, rifles, mortars, and shrapnel of Soviet make. Some other weapons were manufactured in the Skoda plants (Czechoslovakia) in 1945.

CHAPTER FOURTEEN

SINCE . . .

As THE HOPES FOR world cooperation vanished in a stream of vilification, hatred, and strife, the Western Powers began to take more positive steps to cope with the Soviet policies. Early in 1948, the seizure of Czechoslovakia by the Communists and the blockade of Berlin, together with the Communist subversive activities in Greece and Indonesia, indicated that steps, such as the British-French pact of March 4, 1947, American aid to Greece and Turkey, or even the Marshal Plan were inadequate to discourage Soviet expansionism and aggressiveness. Responsible leaders in the United States and elsewhere, with the lessons of the past still fresh in their minds, emphasized that military weakness is a temptation to the prospective aggressor. These warnings presented a sharp contrast to the pre-war policies of neutrality and non-provocation.

GREECE JOINS NATO

On June 12, 1948, the United States Senate passed a resolution, prepared by Senator Vandenberg in close cooperation with Robert Lovett, then Under Secretary of State, declaring that the United States should join in "such regional and collective arrangements as are based on continuous and effective self help and mutual aid and as affect its national security." This resolution marked a fundamental shift in the United States foreign policy. For the first time in its history, the United States was prepared to participate in an alliance during peace time. This was one more step—and a major one—in the policy initiated by the Presidential message of March 12, 1947.

Less than one year later, on April 4, 1949, a treaty of mutual assistance was signed in Washington by France, Canada, Denmark, Portugal, Norway, Italy, Iceland, Belgium, the Netherlands, Luxemburg, the United Kingdom, and the United States. Article V of this treaty provided that:

an armed attack against one or more of them in Europe or N. Africa shall be considered an attack against them all; and consequently they agree that if such an armed attack occurs, each of them, in exercise of the right of individual or collective self-defense, recognized by Art. 51 of the Charter of the United Nations, will assist the party or parties so attacked, by taking forthwith, individually and in concert with other

183

parties such action as it deems necessary, including the use of armed force, to restore and maintain the security of the North Atlantic area.

Even though the new alliance lacked adequate military force, the fact that aggression against any one of the members would very likely precipitate a general conflagration, was enough protection. The tactics of the Soviet leaders indicated, thus far, that they were rather loathe to risk their war time gains in the uncertainties of another military adventure. Rather they preferred to expand through infiltration and creeping aggression carried on by their agents throughout the world. The conclusion of the North Atlantic Treaty, undoubtedly averted the repetition of events similar to those which dragged Czechoslovakia behind the Iron Curtain.

The North Atlantic Treaty "so far as the United States is concerned began in Greece and Turkey," as C. L. Sulzberger wrote in *The New York Times*, on March 9, 1952; yet, these two countries were not among the signatories of the treaty. Until late in July 1951, Great Britain remained one of the major opponents to the participation of Greece and Turkey in the North Atlantic Treaty Organization; in this attitude, she was joined by the majority of the European participants of NATO. The British opposition arose chiefly from a different conception of how the defense of the Middle East should be organized. In the opinion of the British Foreign Office and the military planners, Turkey should associate herself with a Middle East security organization and lead the Arab countries to form such an organization. They argued that there was a danger in extending the SHAPE command as far as the Caucasus, deep in continental Asia, and they preferred to link strategic planning for Greece and Turkey more directly to the Middle East than to Western Europe. Such an organization of the Middle East should be based, according to the British proposals, on the British Middle East Command which would take into account Commonwealth contributions and would practically place the proposed security arrangement under British leadership. The British, apparently, were very sensitive to the placing of their Mediterranean forces under American command.

The British objections were seconded by some of the European participants. They argued that Greece was already fighting Communist aggression, and no one could guarantee that the support to the Greek guerrillas would be forever limited to arms and supplies only. The Scandinavian and Benelux countries feared that an extension of the treaty might drag them into a war in the Mediterranean, an area in which they had little interest. They further argued that NATO forces were still inadequate to justify such extensive commitments. Some of the participants even argued that the addition of Greece and Turkey might reduce their share in arms and supplies from the United States, although both countries were already receiving considerable military economic aid.

The main concern of the United States was to secure the southern flank of the SHAPE command and to establish air bases in Turkey. American air experts were strongly in favor of the admission of Turkey to NATO, as the Turks refused to consider leasing air bases on their territory, unless the question of Turkey's participation in the Treaty organization was settled satisfactorily. It was argued that in the event of a Soviet attack against western Europe, American bombers would not be permitted to attack the Trans-Causasian oil fields, the industries of the Urals, or the Russian supply lines from Turkish bases, unless Turkey were a member of the Atlantic Alliance. In the opinion of American strategists, Greece and Turkey should take a leading part in the defense of the Elbe and the Rhine by lending new strength to the southern flank of the SHAPE command. Moreover they argued that the situation prevailing in the Middle East presented many obstacles to the realization of the British plan for a Middle Eastern security organization. Obviously such an organization which should necessarily include Great Britain and Egypt, the Arab countries and Israel, could not possibly come into existence until the issues dividing these countries had been settled.

Although the strategic arguments in favor of the inclusion of Greece and Turkey within the Atlantic defense system appeared to be virtually unanswerable, the opposition of Great Britain and of some European members prevented the admission of these two countries even after the termination of the guerrilla warfare in Greece in the autumn of 1949. Their policies were reoriented later, due to several important developments in the international field. The first atomic test by the USSR on September 9, 1949, and the invasion of South Korea by the armed forces of the North Korean People's Republic on June 25, 1950, undoubtedly were among those developments. Thus during the meeting of the NATO members in New York in September 1950, the delegates of the twelve nations discussed Turkey's application for admission. The majority still opposed the admission of the two countries as full-fledged members, but finally agreed to invite Greece and Turkey to participate in the defense planning related to the Mediterranean, and authorized Secretary Dean Acheson, as chairman of the Atlantic Treaty Council, to extend the invitations to them.

On October 4, 1950, the United States Department of State released an exchange of notes between Secretary of State Acheson, acting on behalf of the NATO Council, and the governments of Greece and Turkey. These two countries had accepted an invitation to associate themselves "with the appropriate phase of the planning work of NATO with regard to the defense of the Mediterranean" in the belief that such association "would contribute significantly to the defense of that area."

The participation of the two countries in the planning work of NATO, although an important step toward eventual admission, did not provide the political guarantees of mutual assistance enjoyed by the members of NATO. It was therefore only natural that Greece and Turkey continued their efforts toward full admission. In spite of American support, there was considerable opposition on the part of the majority of NATO members, led by Britain. As late as March 29, 1951, French Foreign Minister Shuman argued that "it would be almost impossible to obtain the approval of all the North Atlantic Treaty nations for the inclusion of Turkey and Greece in the Treaty organization." Nevertheless, the issue was gradually reaching the solution point.

At the beginning of 1951, the Turkish Ambassador to Washington had proposed that the United States should join the Turko-British-French defense alliance of 1939. This proposal was rejected by the United States as having too limited an application. It took no account of Greece and, furthermore, under the terms of the 1939 treaty (Protocol No. 2.), Turkey was explicitly excluded from taking part in a war with the Soviet Union.

On March 2, 1951, a United States Department of State spokesman said that the United States had been and was giving "serious consideration" to a question of "a security commitment to Turkey." He added that Turkish representatives had raised this question with the United States "on a number of occasions during the past several years," and he disclosed the Turkish proposal that the United States "adhere to the British-French-Turkish treaty of mutual assistance." United States policy had shifted by that time in favor of early admission of Greece and Turkey to NATO, and the State Department was determined to press more vigorously to that end. Reports concerning the increased arming of the Balkan satellites, together with the intensification of the Cominform threats against Tito, brought home the need to protect the southern flank of the European defense command. On May 15, 1951, the United States Department of State disclosed that:

the Governments of Greece and Turkey had discussed with the United States Government, as they have with other countries, the problem of security arrangements covering the two countries. The Government of the United States feels that there are valid reasons why further arrangements covering the security of Greece and Turkey should be considered. With this in mind and because the Governments of France and the United Kingdom already have such arrangements with Turkey, the

Government of the United States has taken the problem up with the Governments of the United Kingdom and France. Because membership in NATO would be one method of providing for the security arrangements we expect also to discuss the subject in the near future with the governments of all the countries of NATO.

In the meantime, British opposition had weakened due to the deterioration of the political situation in the Middle East during the early summer of 1951 and, in particular because of the alarm caused by the Iranian crisis. Only a few days after the American announcement, British Foreign Secretary, Morrison, stated to the House of Commons that the proposal for the admission of Greece and Turkey to the North Atlantic Treaty was examined by the British Government "with the greatest sympathy." Secretary Morrison's statement greatly encouraged the governments of the two countries concerned, since it was no secret that British opposition had been the principal cause for the failure of their previous efforts. Their confidence was strengthened after a second statement by Secretary Morrison on July 18, 1951, when he informed the House of Commons that the British Government was "ready to support the inclusion of Greece and Turkey in the North Atlantic Organization." A paragraph in his statement was an indirect explanation of the reasons behind British reluctance in the past to support the admission of Turkey to NATO. He said:

in regard to Turkey, the main difficulty has been to reconcile her desire to join NATO with her position in the general defense of the Middle East.

He added that after thorough examination, he had come to the conclusion that "the membership of Greece and Turkey in NATO is in fact the best solution."

The British Government, while pledging its support to Greece and Turkey, was still considering the possibility of a Middle East defense arrangement. On July 30, 1951, Secretary Morrison stated in the House of Commons that the Government was examining the possibility of creating in the Middle East an organization similar to NATO. What he really had in mind came into the open a few months later on October 13, 1951, when Britain, France, Turkey, and the United States presented to the Egyptian Government a plan for a Middle East Command. Point X of the draft provided that a relationship between the proposed Command and NATO should be worked out. This proposal came too late when the existing tension in the British-Egypt relations did not allow coolminded consideration; the plan was rejected by the Egyptians.

When the NATO Council met in Ottawa, Britain had shifted to a policy of unconditional support for the admission of the two countries. The

Egyptian demands for the evacuation of the British forces from the Suez
Canal and for full Egyptian sovereignty over the Anglo-Egyptian Sudan,
the Anglo-Iranian dispute over the nationalization of the oil fields, events
such as the assassination of the pro-British King Abdullah of Jordan, and
the still boiling Israel-Arab dispute, had finally convinced Britain that the
establishment of a Middle East organization was not attainable, at least in
the near future. Therefore, other steps should be taken in order to
strengthen the position of the Western Allies in the Eastern Mediterranean.

With British support secured, the objections of certain small countries
such as Denmark and Norway could not prevail. On October 22, 1951,
the North Atlantic Council signed in London a protocol which provided
for the admission of Greece and Turkey to NATO.

The Kremlin immediately reacted to the proposed participation of the
two countries in NATO. On November 3, 1951, the Soviet Ambassador
in Ankara delivered a note of protest to the Turkish Government, while
Tass, the Soviet news agency, announced that the Soviet Government had
drawn the attention of the Turkish Government "to the responsibility it
has assumed by joining the aggressive Atlantic block and allowing its
territory to be used for the establishment of foreign military bases on
Soviet frontiers. . . ." And it concluded that ". . . the Soviet Union as a
State neighboring on Turkey naturally cannot remain indifferent to such
affairs."

This Soviet attempt to intimidate Turkey failed to produce any result.
The Turkish reply, delivered on November 12, was firm and bold. A
second Soviet protest on November 30, with an open threat that "the
consequences (of Turkey's participation in NATO) would rest entirely
with the Turkish Government," also failed to discourage the Turkish
leaders. They realized that the consequences could possibly take the form
either of subversion in the interior of Turkey or of an open attack. The
first did not seem possible in view of the strong domestic front and the
insignificant strength of the Turkish Communists. As for the second, it
would in all probability mean the beginning of World War III, after
Turkey's participation in NATO.

On February 15, 1952, the United States Government, acting as the
depository government, announced that all parties to the North Atlantic
Treaty had given notice of their acceptance of the protocol which had
been signed in London the previous October, and that it had come into
force on that day in accordance with Art. 3 of the protocol. The United
States Government, on behalf of all parties to the North Atlantic Treaty
formally invited the two governments. Three days later, the Greek and
Turkish parliaments approved adherence to the treaty. Their instruments

of ratification were deposited in Washington, and the treaty became effective for the two new members on February 18, 1952.

YUGOSLAVIA, THE MISSING LINK

The admission of Greece and Turkey to NATO was a very important step toward the strengthening of European defense. These two countries indeed, possess between them the two largest land armies of NATO in Europe, more than thirty divisions of well-trained soldiers schooled in the use of modern equipment by British and American advisers. Yet without the cooperation of Yugoslavia, the problem of a defensible southern flank still remains unsolved. Tito's defensive plans, in case of an attack, are of vital importance to Greece, Italy, and Turkey, and indeed to the whole of Western Europe. For example, any hostile power in Bulgaria threatens both Greece and Turkey in Thrace, and the only natural counter to such menace is Yugoslavia's cooperation with the other two nations. If Tito withdraws his troops in the South towards Bosnia and Montenegro, he will expose to invasion Greece's most vulnerable gateway—the Vardar Valley which leads to Salonika, and the Monastir gap which leads into north and central Greece. If Tito's army, in case of attack from Hungarian or Austrian soil, withdraws to the mountains abandoning the key city of Ljubljana in Slovenia, the Soviet armies will find the gates to Trieste and the valley of the Po wide open. A mere glance at the map reveals Yugoslavia's key position in an integrated European defense system.

Tito's rapprochement with the non-Communist world since his break with the Cominform, reached an advanced stage on February 26, 1953. On that day a political agreement was signed in Ankara by the governments of Turkey, Yugoslavia, and Greece. Although it is not a military alliance, it marks an important step toward Tito's cooperation in European defense. This three-power agreement, a new version of the pre-war Balkan Entente, was obviously chosen as the best preliminary step in preparing Yugoslavia's eventual adherence to NATO. In the opinion of many western leaders, Yugoslavia's immediate adherence to the Atlantic Treaty, even if Tito was willing to join NATO, would not necessarily be to the advantage of the West. They argue, that Tito's position as an independent Communist leader is a most disturbing example for the satellite countries, and that it is advantageous for the West to help Tito preserve his independence. In any event, the outright adherence of Yugoslavia was considered by many as a premature action. On the contrary, a "Balkan Entente," while linking Yugoslavia with the European defense system through Greece and Turkey's participation in NATO, would be less provocative abroad and less disturbing to the political situation in the interior of Yugoslavia.

During the negotiations of the Ankara agreement, Italy displayed great interest, and the Italian Premier Alcide de Gasperi visited Athens in January 1953. Although the interdependence of Italo-Yugoslav defense is beyond question, the three Balkan countries were very sensitive to Italy's participation in a "Balkan Entente." Such an arrangement would be inconsistent indeed with the Balkan character of the proposed agreement. Therefore, it was decided that participation in the new Balkan Entente should be limited to the Balkan countries alone.

As long as the Trieste question remains unsettled, Italo-Yugoslav cooperation is practically impossible. It must be the next objective of Western diplomacy to find a solution of that problem, because once the Trieste dispute is settled, an arrangement for Italo-Yugoslav military cooperation can be worked out easily.

The Ankara agreement is not a military alliance. It offers the opportunity for a closer contact of the three General Staffs, and to this end the three Balkan countries must channel their efforts.

The agreement provides for political cooperation, as the foreign ministers of the contracting parties "will meet in conference once a year, and more often if deemed necessary, to examine the international political situation and adopt such decisions as may be required in conformity with the aims of the present pact." (Art. 1.)

More important, it provides for joint efforts to preserve peace, and cooperation in studying "all matters relating to their security, including the matter of such measures of collective defense as may be necessitated in the event of unprovoked aggression against them." (Art. 2.) It is worth noting that in contrast to the pre-war Balkan Entente this pact refers to any unprovoked aggression, not only to one by a Balkan Power.

A practical step toward military cooperation is the provision of Art. 3, concerning the cooperation of the general staffs of the three contracting parties. Interesting also is the provision of Art. 6, whereby the contracting parties committed themselves "to abstain from concluding any alliances, and from participating in any action that may be directed against any of them, or be of a character prejudicial to their interests." It is quite obvious that under this provision Greece and Turkey shall not support the Italian claims on Trieste or conclude any separate agreements which may be "of prejudicial character" to the Yugoslav interests. On the other hand any Yugoslav action concerning Albania is excluded insofar as it may be "prejudicial" to the Greek claims on northern Epirus. The wording of the pact is rather vague and reveals the intention of the parties to avoid any too extensive commitment, at least for the time being. Even the five-year validity of the treaty is an indication of the desire of the contracting parties to limit their respective obligations to a short period only; a possible extension obviously will depend on the international situation at the time of expiration. It is beyond doubt that the wording of an international agreement has little, if any, bearing upon its fate. Specific or vague, its fulfillment depends upon the willingness of the parties to abide with its provisions; and this, in the last analysis follows the respective interests of the parties. Therefore, the Ankara agreement, however vague, may very easily become the stepping stone for a strong southern flank of the European defense plan, provided that the leaders of the three countries concerned continue to see that the interest of their respective countries lies in their cooperation.

Art. 9 of the treaty provides that "it may be acceded to, under identical conditions and rights . . . by every state whose participation is regarded by all of the contracting parties as being beneficial from the viewpoint of attaining the objective of the treaty." This offers a valuable opportunity to countries such as Albania or Bulgaria to escape the Soviet grip. Recently, some political observers expressed hopes that these two countries may take advantage of this offer. This is not probable for at least as long as one can foresee. In Bulgaria, the fact that the Soviet objectives coincide with the deep-rooted nationalistic aspirations of the Bulgarian people in Yugoslav and Greek territories, greatly facilitates the task of the Soviet agents in keeping that country behind the Iron Curtain. Furthermore, the presence of Soviet troops in Rumania, like the presence of Nazi troops there in 1941, overshadows Bulgarian policies and excludes the possibility of a deviation such as Tito's on the part of the present Bulgarian regime.

The case of Albania is entirely different. This small country, separated from the main body of the Soviet empire, would have thrown off the Soviet yoke long ago, if it were not, unlikely as it may be, for the differences of opinion among the governments of Italy, Yugoslavia, and Greece as to the future of Albania. The overthrow of the present regime would immediately bring home the question of what the next government should be. There is in Rome a "Committee for a free Albania," exerting considerable influence among those who in 1939 were in favor of an Italian protectorate over Albania. These people have very little, if any, possibility of inspiring and leading a national uprising against the Hodja regime. In Yugoslavia, there is another organization under the name Mitrovitsa, definitely pro-Titoist, which enjoys extensive influence over the dissatisfied masses of the Albanian peasants, particularly in the northern and central regions of the country. The Greek population of northern Epirus is a third factor, and the concern of the Greek Government for the future of the Epirotans has been expressed on many occasions. The Greek Government is also very much interested in the future of the rest of Albania, since the fate of that country directly affects the security and the interests of Greece. Of course, in view of the Soviet menace these issues should not be magnified to a serious dispute. Unfortunately this is not the case; under the present conditions, the collapse of the Hodja regime, before a solution of the problem concerning Albania's future has been worked out by the three interested parties, would very likely result in a serious controversy which obviously would undermine the efforts for a closer cooperation among them. Therefore, a settlement of this question must be achieved before any other step is taken.

With regard to the Middle East, the recent improvement in the British-Egyptian relations may become a prelude to a new effort toward the formation of a Middle Eastern defense organization. Turkey can play a leading part in this and, because of her relations with the European countries through NATO, and also of the Ankara agreement of February 26, 1953, she may become the connecting link between Europe and the countries of the Middle East.

There are many important problems to be solved before this may be accomplished but the determination of the free world to merge its potentialities in a gigantic coalition is the most encouraging factor in the present international tension.

IN LIEU OF AN EPILOGUE

Within a period of ten years, Greece has faced the aggressiveness of all types of totalitarianism. Nazism, Fascism, and Communism all found Greece an obstacle to their drive toward world domination, and attempted to subjugate the Greek people. Today Greece stands free among the nations. This has been the dream and the work of thousands of unknown people who sacrificed their lives on the altar of freedom; whether Greeks, British, Australians or Americans, all were united in a common belief in human decency.

The story which has been unfolded in these pages is not merely the story of Greece; far beyond that, it is the story of international antagonism focused around one of the trouble spots of the world. As such, the moral of the story is of interest not only to the Greek people but to all those who seek guidance in order to meet the present world complexities.

The reader has seen in the previous pages that a false conception of neutrality in 1940-1941, only sped up the disintegration and the subjugation of the neutrals "one by one"; it is beyond doubt that a similar course today will lead to the same catastrophe.

The tactics of the Greek Communists offer a valuable example of Communist strategy; whenever their militant force was weakened, they were ready to compromise—only in order to find time to reorganize their forces. In this, they were following the Lenin formula of strategy in dealing with the "capitalist" world. Today it is known that the foreign policy of the Soviet Union follows exactly the same formula. In this respect, the Communist intrigues in Greece offer priceless guidance to those who are entrusted with the defense of the free world against Communist subversion.

Located in a strategic key point, where the trails of international forces cross each other, Greece is bound to play a far more important role in the present struggle than ever before. The Greek people, therefore, must set up concrete national aims, and adjust themselves to the new world realities; because only peoples with integrated and solid objectives will be able to survive as national entities.

It has been said that strength is the only thing the Soviet leaders understand and respect. This is true, as it has been true for all those who pursue their objectives by sheer force. It is, therefore, beyond question that a strong and united free world is the only answer to Soviet aggressiveness. Consequently, signs of disunity, as those occasionally displayed by certain European nations, are pitiful indications that their leaders have not yet grasped the full meaning of our time. The memories of a dead past still permeate their policies. Voices calling for neutrality are heard again, as though the Communist gospel has set aside a peaceful resort for the neutralists.

The Greek people have displayed international responsibility and political realism in many instances. They have peacefully cleared up accounts with their age-old enemies, the Turks, and now they are ready to cooperate with Tito even though he still holds most of the kidnapped Greek children. They are also ready to cooperate with the Italians as though nothing had happened a few years ago. They do so because they realize that their survival depends on their solidarity and close cooperation with all those who are determined to withstand aggression.

For many years to come, the life of the Greek nation will not be easy. The protective barrier of the Danubian-Balkan states, which in the past separated Greece from the gigantic masses of the north has now disappeared, and Greece has common frontiers with the Soviet empire. Living virtually on the top of a volcano, the Greeks must stand ready for any eventuality. They must promote cooperation with the neighboring countries and with the major powers which lead the defense of the free world. Above all, they must be united around the fundamental national objectives, never losing the sense of proportion. The duty of the Greek leaders to foster unity and increase national self-confidence is unquestionable. To accomplish this they must work constantly for the improvement of the social and the economic standards of the people, always keeping in mind that a sound morale is the prerequisite of a successful defense. In this, they must be assisted by the United States not by handouts but by a constructive development of the Greek resources.

It is an open question whether the present rivalry will ever become a hot war. In any event, only unity among the free nations and a sound appraisal of the communist threat may provide effective protection. Only strength can convince the Soviet leadership that world domination is practically impossible. On the contrary, wavering and indetermination may tempt the Soviet leaders to "speed up the collapse of capitalism" and attempt to establish the Soviet millenium, as the fathers of Communism have prophesied. If they decide to do so, no matter who the victor may be, he will be master over a world for vultures. Unity and solidarity can and will avert such a catastrophe. The price of freedom is never too high.

APPENDICES

Note A. The Ottoman Empire was organized in the 14th century by Orkhan. Under Amurath I (1359-89) the Balkan Peninsula became a Turkish possession with the exception of the territory immediately surrounding Constantinople. Amurath II (1421-51) extended Ottoman rule over Macedonia and conquered the Hungarians. Amurath's son Mohammed II, the Conqueror, entered Constantinople on May 29, 1453, and the Byzantine Empire collapsed.

Note B. Constantine Palaiologos, the last Byzantine emperor, fell on the Walls of Constantinople while fighting the enemy. When Sultan Mohamed II, shortly before the last attack, demanded surrender of the City, Palaiologos gave an answer of immortal grandeur, "I cannot abandon the City, neither can any one of us. Because we all decided to die willingly for our salvation." A fierce battle followed this message, and the fall of Constantinople marked the end of the Byzantine Empire, which for more than a thousand years guarded Europe against the Asiatics.

Note C. The Greek-Orthodox church of Aghia Sophia was built in Constantinople during the reign of Justinian I (483-565). One of the most impressive churches in the world, it became after 1453 a national symbol for the enslaved Greek nation. At the present time it has been turned into a museum of Byzantine art by the Turkish government.

Note D. The Greek insurrection began on March 25, 1821. In spite of insufficient armaments, the Greeks were able to inflict heavy losses upon the Sultan's armies. Heroic actions such as the Exodus of Messolongi and the sacrifices of the Massacre of Chios aroused great sympathy in Europe and the United States. Finally, after the destruction of the Ottoman fleet in Navarino by the combined fleets of Great Britain, France, and Imperial Russia, warfare was brought to an end. The first Greek state which was established the following year (1828) consisted of a small area including Pelloponesus, Sterea Ellas, Eboea, and a few minor islands. Millions of Greeks were left under Ottoman rule.

mains libres pour donner son concours dans certaines éventualités à la France et à l'Angleterre.

Une lettre du Gouvernement fasciste redigée dans les mêmes termes que celle du Gouvernement hellénique serait publiee simultanément.

Ill n'existe en tous cas aucun accord secret, comme on l'a prétendu, entre l'Italie et la Grèce, et l'échange des lettres annonce ne doit pas être interprète comme une modification dans l'orientation politique de ce dernier pays. . . .

Pol Lahalle

Documents 110, 111, 119 are taken from the *Official Documents on the Conflict with Yugoslavia and Greece, op. cit.*

APPENDIX III

Note A. The conditions in Greece during the occupation. (Excerpts from letters written by the Democratic leaders Sofoulis and Gonatas, and brought to Cairo, together with other documents, by Colonel Fradelos on March 6, 1944.)
Letter by Themistokles Sofoulis to the Greek Minister of the Army, dated January 18, 1944.

Now I come to the examination of the question concerning the guerrilla organizations, whose civil conflicts cause distress to all. Unfortunately, it is not upon you to cure this plague, because it depends entirely upon the attitude of the Allies towards the EAM. Only a severe warning followed by the threat that all contact with EAM will cease and that EAM will be denounced can bring about the conciliation of the antagonizing factions. No one can guarantee, however, that such conciliation will last because the basic purpose of the EAM is the monopolization of the resistance movement and the subjugation of the country so that EAM will be able to impose by force its own objectives. . . .

The movement must be organized under a unified command with a regular officer of high rank, trusted by all, as the Commander-in-Chief. But first of all, the great evil which dwells in the heart of EAM-ELAS, that is, the socalled political instructors (commissars), who diverted EAM from the national objectives and led it in directions which are dangerous and undesirable to the people, must be eradicated. . . .

At this point, I feel that I must tell you, dear friend, the naked truth, even though I may displease certain quarters. In the opinion of the people and particularly in the opinion of the villagers, EAM is a great plague for the present and a source of terrible danger for the future. . . .

The Greek people, ready to offer any sacrifice, welcomed with sincere enthusiasm the creation of the guerrilla resistance. Unfortunately, because of ignorance or misinterpretation of persons and conditions in

Greece, the guerrilla resistance was entrusted to irresponsible, unqualified, and dangerous persons. The net result is that the fight for liberation had been actually transformed into a movement for the destruction of the Greek people. . . .

The present situation can be summarized in a few words: Greece suffers today under the pressure of a double occupation. On the one hand is the enemy and on the other the domestic Conqueror who in the name of Freedom prepares in blood and fire the enslavement of Greece. Because of their (EAM) terroristic pressure, the economic blackmail and the numerous murders, the people have lost any feeling of security. . . .

The Greek people have never refused to suffer the heaviest sacrifices in order to serve the Allied cause. But today, they suffer terrible losses and inconceivable disaster with no advantage to the Allied cause at all. I would like to beg the Allies to order EAM to stop the savage, inhuman slaughter of isolated German prisoners captured, not on the battlefield but in ambush or casual encounter. The murder of fifty or hundred German prisoners killed so far by EAM obviously does not harm the fighting force of the enemy seriously, but these murders have caused the eradication of many townships and villages, and the execution of many thousands of hostages by the Germans, in retaliation. Because of their (EAM) practices, the Greek people have mourned thus far more victims than during the entire Italo-Greek war. But above all the honor of the Greek people is insulted by the slaughter of isolated prisoners. . . .

Letter by E. Gonatas to the Greek Government in Cairo, dated February 1944.

First appeared the EAM, a communist organization under camouflage, with purely patriotic disguise. The people extended all possible help, and so they formed the first guerrilla groups and, thanks to British supplies and moral support, they proceeded to the organization of the ELAS Army. But soon it became evident that this organization did not fight for liberation but it had political objectives and was preparing the ground for the eventual subjugation of the country by force. Suppression of any other resistance organization, that is monopolization of the armed force; disarmament of any individual not subordinated to the EAM; communistic organization of the countryside with political instructors (commissars), committees, courts, taxation etc.

The various nationalistic organizations, without weapons and supplies, were and still are unable to resist the Communist danger, which has been organized and armed by the British. The intimidated citizens, under the open threat of the EAM, offer their money contributions; in the towns and the villages, everyone who does not comply with their demands is murdered. The victims are numerous, especially among the former officers of the Army. But, in order to show that they fight for the liberation, they kill isolated Germans with the result that villages in whole districts are burnt down and thousands of innocent hostages have been executed. All these calamities, not only failed to shock the EAM, but they even found that misery served their objectives. Meanwhile, the London Radio acclaims the heroic fight of the guerrillas in Greece, and thus arouses the spirits and strengthens the EAM morale.

Most of the people in Greece, in view of the coming Allied victory, do not see any German danger for Greece in the future; they see, however, a terrible danger for the country in case of even a temporary Communist domination after the liberation. . . .

Attached is the latest report concerning EAM activities in Macedonia. This report shows that EAM cooperates with the Serb and Bulgarian Communists. Similar reports reveal that EAM cooperates in Northern Epirus with the Albanian EAM. It is strange, however, that only the Greek Communists are Internationalists, while all others are Nationalists. From Macedonia we have admonitions concerning the looming danger. . . ." (Both letters quoted by E. I. Tsouderos, *Ellinikes Anomalies sti Messi Anatoli, op. cit.,* pp. 103-114.)

APPENDIX IV

Note A. The Greek National Claims.

Memorandum submitted by E. I. Tsouderos, the Greek Premier to King George II of Greece, dated July 4, 1941.

It is too early to define the National Claims as a whole in view of our position as a Balkan and Mediterranean country. From one moment to another, new developments in the war or in diplomacy may enable us to pursue much broader claims which, if materialized, will assure to our country the position of an important factor within the International or the Allied policy in the Eastern Mediterranean.

I proceed, therefore, to outline the minimum of our national claims under the present conditions. These claims are: 1. Northern Epirus. 2. Dodecanese. 3. Cyprus. 4. The readjustment of our frontiers with Bulgaria, and 5. The strengthening of our frontiers at Gevgeli (Yugoslavia). . . . From an economic viewpoint, Greece must claim the right of free immigration and settlement in the enemy colonies in Africa. (E. I. Tsouderos, *Diplomatic Paraskinia, op. cit.,* p. 86.)

Memorandum handed to President Roosevelt by King George II, dated June 12, 1942.

3. The national claims of Greece are based on the experiences and the lessons of the recent past. Greece's desire is, above all, to be assured that she will not become again the victim of aggression from the north in case of another international upheaval. Four times within thirty years, Greece has been attacked without any provocation: in 1913, 1916, 1940, and 1941. . . .

5. The readjustment of the northeast Greek frontiers on the Rodopi mountains, and the northwest on the Adriatic and also the re-adjustment of the Greek-Yugoslav frontiers (on Gevgeli) will strengthen essentially both Greece and Yugoslavia against any assault through the Balkans. . . .

6. Fortunately, the territories involved have been only recently annexed by their present occupants . . . The ethnologic composition of the inhabitants of these mountains . . . is no obstacle at all to the proposed re-adjustment which will contribute to peace in the Balkans. In any event, the size of the territories involved is insignificant. . . .

8. In addition to the aforesaid re-adjustment, the question which must become the subject of our concern and of your favor, are: a) northern Epirus, b) Dodecanese, c) Cyprus and d) financial support, so that Greece will not face an economic crisis immediately after the war because of over-population or the lack of sufficient production. . . .

9. Detailed information concerning northern Epirus and the Dodecanese has been included in the Preface of the *Greek White Book* (Diplomatic Documents relating to Italy's aggression against Greece.) . . . The analysis of the facts proves beyond doubt that northern Epirus and the Dodecanese are Greek provinces, occupied for about twenty years by our common enemies (the Italians) without any right at all. . . .

10. The question of Cyprus is different. This island is occupied by a friendly country (Great Britain). In 1914, Great Britain proposed the cession of Cyprus to Greece on the condition of the latter's participation in the war on the side of the Allies. Greece did not accept the offer at that time, but she has entered the war twice since and has fought with all means in her power on the side of the Allies for the same objectives and against the same enemies. After the end of World War I, at the time of the signing of the Peace Treaties, a separate protocol was signed by Italy and Greece, which provided for the simultaneous cession of Cyprus and Rhodes to Greece.

The island of Cyprus is populated by Greeks in a proportion of five to six. The fact that one sixth of the population is of Turkish descent, is not enough reason to deprive the other five sixths of the Cypriot people of their right to self-determination which is assured to all peoples on Earth. . . . (*ibid.*, pp. 113-114).

BIBLIOGRAPHY

BOOKS

Armstrong, Hamilton F., *Tito and Goliath*, New York: Macmillan, 1951.

Balkanicus, *The Aspirations of Bulgaria*, London: Marshal and Kent, 1915.

Barker, Elisabeth, *Macedonia, its place in Balkan Power Politics*, New York: Royal Institute of International Affairs, 1950.

Belloff, Max, *Foreign Policy of Soviet Russia, 1929-41*, 2d imp., New York: Oxford University Press, 1949.

Byford-Jones, W., *The Greek Trilogy*, New York: Hutchinson and Co., 1946.

Byrnes, James F., *Speaking Frankly*, New York: Harper and Bros., 1947.

Ciano, Galeazzo, *The Ciano Diaries*, ed. Hugh Gibson, 2 vols., New York: Doubleday, 1946.

Churchill, Winston S., *The Second World War*, 5 vols., Boston: Houghton Mifflin, 1948-1950.

Dallin, David J., *Soviet Russia's Foreign Policy, 1939-42*, Transl., Leon Dennen, New Haven: Yale University Press, 1942.

Eddy, B., *Greece and the Greek Refugees*, London: G. Allen and Unwin, 1931.

Eisenhower, Dwight D., *Crusade in Europe*, New York: Doubleday, 1948.

Fischer, Louis, *The Soviets in World Affairs*, 2d. ed., Princeton: Princeton University Press, 1951.

Gould Lee, Arthur, *The Royal House of Greece*, London: Ward Lock, 1948.

Guerin Songeon, P. P., *Histoire de la Bulgarie, 485-1913*, Paris: Nouvelle Librairie Nationale, 1913.

Hull, Cordell, *Memoirs*, New York: Macmillan, 1948.

Kleist, Peter, *Zwishen Hitler und Stalin*, Bonn: Athenaüm-Verlag, 1950.

Kyrou, Achiles A., *I nea Epithesis kata tis Ellados*, Athens: Aetos A. E., 1949.

Leahy, W. D., *I Was There*, New York: Whittlesey House, McGraw-Hill, 1950.

Lebanov-Rostovsky, A., *Russia and Asia*, New York: Macmillan, 1933.

Ludwig, Emil, *The Mediterranean*, New York: McGraw-Hill, 1942.

Mackenzie, Compton, *Wind of Freedom*, London: Chatto and Windus, 1944.

McInnis, Edgar, *The War; Second Year*, London: Oxford University Press, 1941.

McNeil, William H., *Greek Dilemma; War and Aftermath*, New York: Lippincott, 1947.

———, *Report on the Greeks*, New York: The Twentieth Century Fund, 1948.

Miller, William, *The Balkans*, 3d. ed. London: T. Fisher Unwin, 1923.

Mishew, D., *The Bulgarians in the Past*, Lausanne: Librairie Central des Nationalités, 1919.

Noel-Baker, Francis, *Greece; The Whole Story*, London: Hutchinson and Co., 1946.

Orr, C. W. J., *Cyprus under British Rule*, London: Robert Scott Roxburghe House, 1918.

Papagos, Alexander, *O Polemos tis Ellados, 1940-41*, New York: New World Publishers, 1946.

Papandreou, George, *I Apeleftherosis tis Ellados*, Athens: Elliniki Ekdotiki Eteria A. E., 1945.

Pipinellis, Panagiotis N., *Istoria tis exoterikis Politikis tis Ellados, 1923-41*, Athens: Skaziki, A. E., 1948.

Schuman, Frederick L., *International Politics*, 4th ed., New York: McGraw-Hill, 1948.

Sereni, A. P., *The Italian Conception of International Law*, New York: Columbia University Press, 1934.

Sherwood, R. E., *Roosevelt and Hopkins; An Intimate History*, New York: Harper and Bros., 1948.

Stettinius, Edward R. Jr., *Roosevelt and the Russians; the Yalta Conference*, New York: Doubleday and Co., 1949.

Stickney, Pierpont E., *Southern Albania or Northern Epirus in European International Affairs, 1912-23*, Stanford: Stanford University Press, 1926.

Sumner, B. H., *Russia and the Balkans, 1870-80*, Oxford: The Clarendon Press, 1937.

Swine, J., *Bulgarian Conspiracy*, London: Robert Hale, 1939.

Temperley, Harold W. V., *The Second Year of the League*, London: Hutchinson and Co., 1922.

Tsouderos, E. I., *Diplomatic Paraskinia, 1941-44*, Athens: Aetos A. E., 1950.

———, *Ellinikes Anomalies sti Messi Anatoli*, Athens: Aetos A. E., 1945.

Ward, B., *Turkey*, London: Oxford University Press, 1942.

Wilmot, Chester, *The Struggle for Europe*, New York: Harper and Bros., 1952.

DOCUMENTS

British Speeches of the Day, New York: British Information Services, 1944.

Ciano, Galeazzo, *Diplomatic Papers*, ed. Malkolm Muggeridge, transl. Stuart Hood. London: Odhams Press, 1948.

Die Diplomatischen Akten des Auswärtiges Amtes, 1871-1914, Berlin: Deutsche Verlagsgeselschaft für Politik und Geschichte, 1922.

Diplomatic Documents; Italy's Aggression against Greece, Athens: Royal Ministry for Foreign Affairs, 1940.

Documentary Background of World War II, 1931-41, ed. James W. Cantenbein, New York: 1948.

Documents on American Foreign Relations, ed. Leland M. Goodrich, Boston: World Peace Foundation, 1942.

Documents on American Foreign Relations, ed. Raymond Dennett, Princeton: World Peace Foundation, 1948. vol. III.

Documents of International Affairs, London: Oxford University Press, 1936.

Forrestal (The) Diaries, ed. Walter Millis, New York: Viking Press, 1951.

Nazi-Soviet Relations, 1939-41, U. S. Department of State, 1948.

Official Documents on the Conflict with Yugoslavia and Greece, Berlin: Auswärtiges Amt/No. 7, 1941.

Paris Peace Conference, Selected Documents, U. S. Department of State Publication 2868, 1947.

Report on Cyprus for the Year 1949, London: British Colonial Office, 1950.

Report of the International Commission to inquire into the Causes and Conduct of the Balkan Wars, Washington, D. C.: Carnegie Endowment for International Peace, 1914.

Soviet Documents on Foreign Policy, ed. Jane Decras, London: Royal Institute of International Affairs, 1951.

Treaty Series, Lausanne: League of Nations.

Trial of the Major War Criminals before the International Military Tribunal, Nuremberg: International Military Tribunal, 1947.

U. N. Official Records of the Second Session of the General Assembly, U. N. Publications, 1947.

U. N. Official Records of the Third Session of the General Assembly, U. N. Publications, 1948.

U. N. Security Council Official Records, U. N. Publications, 1946-1947.

PERIODICALS AND OTHER PUBLICATIONS

Barghoorn, Frederick C., "The Soviet Union between War and Cold War," *The Annals of the American Academy of Political and Social Science*, Vol. 263.

Bulletin, The Department of State, 1949-51.

Congressional Record, Vols. 59 and 92.

Current Developments, The Brookings Institution: 1949-51.

Foreign Policy Reports, 1945-1949.

Islands of the Northern and Eastern Aegean, London: British Foreign Office, Historical Section—No. 64, 1920.

Knezevich, Zivan L., *General Mihailovich and USSR*, Washington: 1945.

Official Journal, Lausanne: League of Nations, 1921, 2nd Year, No. 12.

South Eastern Europe, London: The Royal Institute of International Affairs, Oxford University Press, 1940.

Soviet (The) Yugoslav Dispute, New York: The Royal Institute of International Affairs, 1948.

10 Eventful Years, Chicago: Encyclopedia Brittanica, 1950.

Yearbook of the United Nations, 1946-47, New York: Department of Public Information of the United Nations, 1947.

The United Nations and the Problem of Greece, Department of State Publication 2909, 1947.

The United States in World Affairs, 1945-47, New York: Council on Foreign Relations, Harpers, 1947.

United Nations Journal of the Security Council, U. N. Publications, 1946-49.

INDEX